James Clarence Mangan

The poets and poetry of Munster

a selection of Irish songs by the poets of the last century. Third Edition

James Clarence Mangan

The poets and poetry of Munster
a selection of Irish songs by the poets of the last century. Third Edition

ISBN/EAN: 9783744738057

Printed in Europe, USA, Canada, Australia, Japan

Cover: Foto ©Thomas Meinert / pixelio.de

More available books at **www.hansebooks.com**

THE

POETS AND POETRY

OF

MUNSTER:

A SELECTION OF IRISH SONGS

BY THE POETS OF THE LAST CENTURY.

WITH POETICAL TRANSLATIONS

BY THE LATE

JAMES CLARENCE MANGAN

NOW FOR THE FIRST TIME PUBLISHED,

With the Original Music,

AND

BIOGRAPHICAL SKETCHES OF THE AUTHORS.

BY JOHN O'DALY.

THIRD EDITION.

DUBLIN:
JOHN O'DALY, 9, ANGLESEA-STREET.
MDCCCLI.

TO

THE FAIR DAUGHTERS OF MUNSTER

WHOSE MANY VIRTUES

HAVE ENDEARED THEM TO ALL,

This Volume

IS RESPECTFULLY DEDICATED

BY

THEIR ADMIRING AND HUMBLE SERVANT,

Seághan Ua Dálaigh.

CONTENTS.

PAGE.

John O'Cunningham—Maurice Griffin—William Cotter (the Red)—George Roberts—James O'Daly—Thomas Cotter—Edward Nagle 37
Eoghan (Owen or Eugene) O'Keeffe . . . 38
John Murphy (of Ráṫaoinneaċ) 39

POETRY.

As I was Walking one Evening fair, &c. . . . 5
Bean na Cleiċe Caoile — Dame of the Slender Wattle 13
Gile na Gile . . . . . — The Brightest of the Bright 24
Bean na n-Or-Ḟholt Donn — Maid of the Raven Locks 41
Bán-Chnoic Eireann O! . — The Fair Hills of Eire, O! . . . 45
Uaill-ċúṁaiḋ na Féinne — A Lament for the Fenians 51
Móirín Ní Chuillionnáin — Moirin Ni Chuillionnain 57
Cuisle na h-Eigse . . . — Spirit of Song . . 61
Ol-dán Sheáġain Uí Thuama . . . . — John O'Tuomy's Drinking Song 65
Freagraḋ Aindriais ṁeic Craiṫ air Sheáġan Ua Thuama — Andrew Magrath's Reply to John O'Tuomy . 67
An Bhéiṫ . . . . . . — The Maiden . . . 73
Freagraḋ air an m-Béiṫ — A Reply to the Maiden 75
Léir-ruaṫar Whiggiona . — A Whack at the Whigs 77
An Bhláṫ-Bhruinġioll . — The Flower of all Maidens 83

AIRS IN THIS VOLUME.

PREFACE TO THE SECOND EDITION.

THE publication of this little volume was undertaken with the desire of presenting to the public, in a cheap and attractive form, the songs and music which were popular among the peasantry of Munster during the last century, and which are still preserved among the natives, in the more remote districts of the South. The songs themselves afford favorable specimens of the intellectual capacity of that humble and persecuted class who contrived, under the most adverse circumstances, to acquire that education and learning which the English laws interdicted under the heaviest penalties. They also possess a high value, as illustrative of that dreary portion of our history which intervened between the violation of the Treaty of Limerick and the relaxation of the Popery Laws: a period characterized by the ruthless tyranny of the dominant Anglo-Irish faction, which drove the oppressed peasantry into rash and violent acts of aggression, and called into life a spirit of lawless resistance (not yet extinct) which has sent thousands of misguided, but injured men, to the gibbet and the penal settlements.

The deep-seated hatred to the English government and settlers everywhere pervading the songs of this period, furnishes us with the best index to the political feelings of the people; and clearly demonstrate that the old natives were ripe for revolution, and desired but a leader in whom they might confide, and a shadowy hope of success, to induce them to rise in arms against their cruel oppressors. Their designs, however, were frustrated by the partial relaxation of the penal code in 1745, and the strict surveillance which the government maintained in Munster, where the revolutionary spirit was most prevalent.

Religious oppression being now banished from this country for ever, one great source of discontent has been annihilated, and the two races have been so commingled, that the sentiments of these songs are daily becoming more obsolete, and valuable only to the lover of our national music, or to the philosophic historian, who desires to study the character of a people and a period through the truest medium—the popular literature of the time.

The first attempt to form a collection of Irish popular poetry was made by James Hardiman, Esq., whose "Irish Minstrelsy," published in 1831, and which, we must confess, stimulated us to the slight exertions we have made in the cause, has maintained the high position to which it was entitled, from the well-merited literary reputation of its learned editor; but the high price at which it was published placed it beyond the reach of the majority of those to whom works of such a nature are most interesting.

After the publication of Mr. Hardiman's work, the Irish songs were allowed to lie in obscurity, until the editor of the present volume published, in 1843, a small collection of Irish Jacobite Songs, with metrical versions of very high merit by Edward Walsh; and in 1847, the spirited publisher, Mr. James M'Glashan, brought out a very beautiful volume of "Irish Popular Poetry," also edited by the same gifted writer.

In the present volume, the original music has been prefixed to the songs, and is the first attempt of the kind ever made in this country: many beautiful airs are thus rescued from inevitable oblivion. The English versions, by the ill-fated but lamented Clarence Mangan, are all in the same metre with the originals.

The first edition of this book having been exhausted in a very short period, the entire work has been carefully revised, many inaccuracies corrected, and five pieces of new music, with nineteen additional pages of new matter, inserted.

The poem on Sarsfield, at p. 271, is curious, as the production of one who evidently witnessed the scenes he commemorates; and was probably in connexion with that intrepid body of men, known in history as the Irish Rapparees, whose services against the rebels during the revolutionary war were of the highest importance to the Royal cause.

For the memoir and notes accompanying that poem, we are indebted to J. C. O'Callaghan, Esq., whose talents and research, as displayed in his edition of the "*Macariæ Excidium,*" just published by the *Irish Archæological Society,* entitle him to a high position as an historian, even in the age which has produced a Lingard, an Alison, and a Thierry.

JAMES CLARENCE MANGAN.

JAMES CLARENCE MANGAN was the son of James Mangan, a native of Shanagolden, in the county of Limerick, who married, early in 1801, Miss Catherine Smith, of Fishamble-street, Dublin. The subject of our brief notice, the first offspring of this union, was born in the spring of 1803.

His father carried on the grocery business for some time at No. 3, Fishamble-street, but being of a restless disposition, he removed to another locality, having consigned the establishment and his son to the care of his brother-in-law, whom he induced to come from London for that purpose.

By his uncle, young Mangan was placed at the academy of Mr. Courtney, Derby-square, Dublin, where he continued as day pupil until he had attained his fifteenth year; a short time after which he entered a solicitor's office, and by his earnings supported himself and his parents. How long he continued in this situation we have been unable to ascertain; but we next find him engaged in the library of the University, where, it is supposed, he acquired that profound knowledge of various languages displayed in his translations of "The Lays of Many Lands," and "Literæ Orientales," which appeared in *The Dublin University Magazine*. A selection of his translations from the German, from this periodical, were collected and printed in two small volumes, under the title of "Anthologia Germanica" (Dublin: 1845), the expense of which, we are informed, was borne by C. G. Duffy, Esq. Some of his best productions will be found under the signatures of "Clarence," "J. C. M.," and "M.," in the *Dublin University Magazine*, *Dublin* and *Irish Penny Journals*, *Duffy's Catholic Magazine*, and *The Nation* newspaper. To the latter he was a constant contributor of poetry; and we have been informed, that many of his early pieces were printed in the *Comet* and *Satirist* newspapers. He wrote many articles, both in prose and verse, for *The Irishman;* and also contributed to *The United Irishman* and *Irish Examiner*, during their short career.

The "res angusta domi" opposed an insuperable barrier to Mangan's advancement. All his earnings were devoted to the support of his indigent parents and family. His spirit at length became broken from over exertion, and he was obliged to have recourse to stimulants, which he occasionally abandoned, but finally they produced the usual fatal results. A short time before his death his constitution was greatly weakened by an attack of cholera. On his recovery, we found him in an obscure house in Bride-street, and, at his own request, procured admission for him to the Meath Hospital on the 13th of June, 1849, where he lingered for seven days, having died on the 20th,* the day on which we placed the first sheet of our book in the printer's hands.

For two years before Mangan's death, we were in constant intercourse with him, and induced him to undertake the versification of some of the native poetry of Ireland, of which the songs here printed form part. The remainder of his translations from the Irish, including the satires of Angus O'Daly (known to Irish scholars as "Aonġus na n-Aor," "Angus the Satirist;" or "Bárd Ruaḋ," "Red Bard"), a poem of the seventeenth century, we hope soon to present to the public; and in giving this an English dress, we beg to assure our readers that the original lost none of its beauty in poor Mangan's hands, as may be seen by the following specimen:—

* The fate of Mangan closely resembled that of Camoens. The following is M. Chaufepiè's account of the death of the great poet of Portugal:—"Le chagrin que lui causérent les mauvais traitemens qu'il essuya, augmenta ses autres infirmités; en sorte que le trouvant enfin destitué de tout secours, il fut obligé de se retirer dans l'hôpital."

Clann n-Dálaiġ.

Dá n-Aorainn clann n-Dálaiġ,
  Níor ḋíon ḋam síol sean-Aḋaiṁ;
  Clann n-Dálaiġ ba ḋíon ḋam,
  Agus síol Aḋaiṁ do Aoraḋ.

THE CLAN DALY.

By me the Clan Daly shall never be snubbed:
    I say nothing about them.
    For, were I to flout them,
The world wouldn't save me from getting well drubbed;
    While with *them* at my beck (or my back) I
Might drub the world well without fear of one black eye!

Muintir Ara.

Muintir Ara, bualta beaga,
  Finne iad nár ċosain clú ;
  Is é is ceól ḋóiḃ, ceól na cuile,
  Ampall a m-bcól gaċ duine ḋiu !

THE GOOD PEOPLE (NOT THE FAIRIES) OF ARA.

The good people of Ara are four feet in height;
They are soldiers, and really stand stoutly in fight;
But they don't sacrifice overmuch to the graces,
And hunger stares forth from their fly-bitten faces.

Tiġ fada fairsing air lár bealaiḋ,
  'S gan sáiṫ seangáin ann do ḃiaḋ ;
  Cúraḋ a ċroiḋe air an g-ceaṫarnaċ gortaċ,
  Naċ dearnaḋ tiġ crom-ṡlaite air ṡliaḃ !

There is one waste, wide, void, bleak, blank, black, cold odd pile
On the highway: its length is one-third of a mile:
Whose it is I don't know, but you hear the rats gnawing
Its timbers inside, while its owner keeps sawing.

Mangan's acquaintance with the modern tongues was very extensive, as may be seen by his translations from almost every language in the world. His powers of versification were extraordinary. Many of his most beautiful poems were written in an incredibly short period, and with such accuracy, that they never required revision.

As a translator he stood unrivalled. His original compositions, though small in number, possess very high merit. We may here observe, that all his versions of Gaelic poetry were made from literal translations furnished him by Irish scholars, as he was totally unacquainted with the original language.

In person, Mangan was below the middle size, and of slender proportions; the ashy paleness of his face was lighted up by eyes of extraordinary brilliancy. His usual costume was a light brown coat: he wore his hat closely pressed over his eyebrows, and used to carry a large umbrella under his arm. Of his manners and conversation it would be impossible to give a correct idea; they may be best described by an extract from his favourite Schiller:—

> " His dreams were of great objects,
> He walked amidst us of a silent spirit,
> Communing with himself: yet I have known him
> Transported on a sudden into utterance
> Of strange conceptions; kindling into splendour,
> His soul revealed itself, and he spake so
> That we looked round perplexed upon each other,
> Not knowing whether it were craziness,
> Or whether it were a god that spake in him!"

Mangan's remains lie in the cemetery of Glasnevin, and a subscription is about being raised to erect a monument to his memory—an act of posthumous generosity which adds another name to the sad catalogue of the many men of exalted genius who asked for bread and received a stone.

The humble hearse that bore all that was earthly of him had but few followers. Amongst these, however, who strove to console him in his hours of bitterest affliction and most poignant despondency, was the Rev. C. P. Meehan, who discharged the last obsequies to the soul of this son of song.

Mangan was never married: his brother still survives in destitute circumstances.

THE

POETS AND POETRY OF MUNSTER.

DONNCHADH MHEIC CON-MHARA.

Donogh Mac Con-Mara, or Mac na Mara, as the name is vulgarly spelled, was surnamed, from the red colour of his hair, Donnċaḋ Ruaḋ;* for, as many of our readers may be aware, the Irish peasantry have been long accustomed to designate individuals from certain personal marks or peculiarities — not unfrequently ludicrous; a man with crooked legs being, for instance, called "Cam-ċosaċ," and one with a nose turned awry, "Cam-ṡronaċ," while a corpulent person is styled "Bolg-ṁór."

Donnċaḋ was a native of Cratloe, in the county of Clare, and connected by blood with the Mac Con Maras of that locality. He made his appearance in the county of Waterford about the year 1738, while on his way homeward from a foreign college, whither he had been sent in early youth to pursue his theological studies— the penal laws at that period, as we need scarcely remark, rendering it imperative on a candidate for the Catholic priesthood to forsake his own country, and seek that instruction abroad which he was not suffered to

* The use of *soubriquets* to denote personal peculiarities is of very remote antiquity in Ireland, and still exists to a great extent among the peasantry.

obtain at home. His wild and freak-loving propensities had procured his expulsion from college, after he had spent four years within its walls; and thus he was compelled to return to his native soil, and locate himself in Waterford.

He had not long sojourned in this county before he became acquainted with one William Moran, a kindred spirit, celebrated in bardic lore among the peasantry of his native county. Moran kept a classical hedge-academy at Knockbee, in the parish of Sliaḃ Cua,* a village within an hour's walk of the birth-place of the writer of this sketch; and here, he and his friend laboured conjointly for the enlightenment and edification of the young students who attended their school, and taught them the various languages which Donnċaḋ Ruaḋ learned abroad, and Moran acquired at home.

How long the alliance lasted between the erudite pair we have no certain means of ascertaining; but, according to the tradition of the peasantry, it held good until the bards, "in an evil-starred hour," as the Orientals phrase it, or, as we would say, in a moment of luckless frolic, happened, in one of their poetical effusions, to "damn to immortal fame" a certain fair and frail young damsel of the neighbourhood, who, enraged at being thus publicly satirised, set the hedge "academy" in flames; so that a dissolution of partnership between

* *Sliabh Cua* (now called *Sliabh g-Cua*), a large mountain district lying midway between the towns of Clonmel and Dungarvan, in the county of Waterford. In an ancient MS. life of St. Mochuda, which we perused some years ago, much light is thrown on the ancient topography of this locality; for it appears that St. Mochuda and his community made a short stay here, with the view of founding a monastery, but afterwards proceeded to Lismore. One of the five prerogatives of the King of Cashel was "to pass over Sliabh Cua with [a band of] fifty men, after pacifying the South of Eire."—See *Leabhar na g-Ceart* (Book of Rights), p. 5, published by the Celtic Society. The name is still preserved, but applied to the parish of Seskinan, which is the most fertile in the district.

the "fratres fraterrimi" was the immediate and melancholy result.

The next locality chosen by Mac Con-Mara appears to have been the barony of Imokilly,* an extensive district in the immediate vicinity of Youghal, in the county of Cork, where he commenced business "on his own account;" but his stay here must have been very brief, for we find him shortly afterwards located in the barony of Middlethird, in the county of Waterford. The hedge-school occupation not prospering here, he soon departed for Newfoundland.

Accordingly, being well equipped, by the munificence of his neighbours, with food and raiment for the voyage, he set out for Waterford, and thence repairing to Passage, a small seaport town on the Suir, below Waterford, he embarked for his new destination on the 24th of May, 1745, or, as some accounts have it, 1748, or 1755. But, alas! the winds and waves proved adverse to his wishes. He had been but a few days at sea when a storm arose, which drove the vessel on the coast of France, where the crew fell in with a French frigate, which forced them to hoist sail and steer their course homeward to the Emerald Isle; and consequently, poor Mac Con-Mara was obliged to resume his former avocation in the very place which he had so recently left. A Mr. Power, one of his patrons, who died but a short time ago, humorously insisted upon having a narrative of the voyage from him, and our hero accordingly produced a mock Æneid of about eighty stanzas on the subject, which he entitled, "Eaċtra Ghiolla an Abraoin," "The April Fool's Tale." Of this poem Edward O'Reilly, in his "Irish Writers," remarks: "There are some lines in it by no means inferior to any of Virgil's;" and

* That portion of this extensive district which immediately adjoins the town of Youghal is known among the natives as "The Barony."

he quotes the shout of Charon, as described by the Irish bard, thus :—

"Do léig sé gáir ós-árd 's béiceaċ,
Le fuaim a ġuṫaḋ do ċrioṫaḋ na spéarṫaḋ,
Do ċualaḋ an ċruinne é, 's ċuir Ifrionn géim as !"

"He lifted up his voice ; he raised a howl and yell
That shook the firmament, as from some vast bell ;
Awakened one grand peal, that roused the depths of hell !"

Among other eloquent passages in it, we find the following allusions to his partnership with Moran, his location at the Barony, and his removal to Middle-third :—

"A n-deirim, do ṫaḃarfainn mar ṁalairt le buiḋeaċas,
Air a ḃeiṫ san m-baile, nó a g-calaṫ-ṗort éigin ;
Nó san m-Barúṁain am neartsgaḋ 'dir Ghaeḋiliḃ,
Ag reic mo ċeaṫraṁann 's ag smaċtúġaḋ mo ṫréadta
No san g-Creatalaiḋ a g-cleaċtaḋ mo ġaoḋaltaḋ,
Nó a Luimneaċ for Sionainn na g-caol m-barc,
Nó air Shliaḃ geal Cua rug buaḋ féile,
Ag riar luċt duan, draġa, 's cléiric,
Nó a b-foċair Uilliam Ui Mhóráin, fonn árd-léiġionta,
Dhéanfaċ sean-dán ós cionn clár m'éagaḋ !"

"All I have penned I would joyously give away,
To be at home, or in some snug seaport town ;
Or in the Barony, with the Gaels to-day,
Following my trade, and keeping my pupils down ;
Or in Cratloe, where my ancestors dwelt of old,
Or in Limerick, on the tall-barked Shannon agen,
Or in Sliabh Cua, the hospitable and bold,
There feasting bards, and sages, and learned men ;
Or with William Moran, the Prince of Poets, who reigns,
Who would chant a death-song over my cold remains !"

A series of unpropitious circumstances, however, once again drove him from home, and sent him anew to tempt the ocean in search of Newfoundland. Here, on this occasion, he arrived safely, and spent some time at St. John's, where his old freakish propensities broke out afresh, though they do not appear to have involved him in any unpleasant affair with the natives or others.

Having one evening met at a public-house a party of English sailors, whom he well knew how to "fool to the top of their bent," he sang the following song, extempore, to the great amusement of the Irish present, and indeed to that of the English, though the latter understood but one part of it, while the former chuckled in comprehending the entire:—

As I was walking one evening fair,
  Agus mé go déanaċ a m-Baile Sheáġain;
I met a gang of English blades,
  Agus iad dá d-traoċaḋ ag neart a námaid:
I boozed and drank both late and early,
  With these courageous "Men-of-War;"
'S gsr binne liom Sagsanaiġ ag riṫ ar éigin,
  'S gan do Ghaoiḋeil ann aċt fíor beagán.

I spent my fortune by being freakish,
  Drinking, raking, and playing cards;
Giḋ ná raiḃ airgiod agam, 'ná gréiṫre,
  Ná rad san t-saogal, aċd niḋ gan áird!
Then I turned a jolly tradesman,
  By work and labour I lived abroad;
'S bioċ ar m'ḟallaing-ṅ gur mór an bréag sin,
  Is beag de'n t-saoṫar do ṫuit le m' láiṁ.

Newfoundland is a fine plantation,
  It shall be my station until I die,
Mo ċráḋ! go m'ḟearr liom a beiṫ a n-Eire,
  Ag díol gáirtéiriġe, 'ná ag dul fá'n g-coill:

Here you may find a virtuous lady,
  A smiling fair one to please your eye,
An faca staigionnaḋ is measa tréiṫe,
  Go m-beireaḋ mé ar a ḃeiṫ ar raḋarc!

I'll join in fellowship with "Jack-of-all-Trades,"
  The last of August could I but see;
Atá ḟios ag Coirḋealḃaḋ 's as maġaisdir báid é,
  Gur b'olc an Láiṁ mé ar muir 'ná air tír;
If fortune smiles then, I'll be her darling,
  But, if she scorns my company,
Déanfad "Bainistíḋe an Toill anáirde,"
  'S as fada ón áit-si do ḃeiḋeaḋ mé 'rís.

Come, drink a health, boys, to Royal George,
  Our chief commander, nár órdaiġ Críosd;
'S bíoċ·ḃ'ḟr n-aṫċrṅngíḋe ċrm Ṁṅre Ṁháṫair,
  É féin 's a ġárdaiġe do leagaḋ síos:
We'll fear no Cannon, nor "War's Alarms,"
  While noble George will be our guide,
A Chríost go b-feiceaḋ mé an ḃrúid dá ċárnaḋ.
  Ag an Mac* so ar fán uainn ṫall san b-Frainc.

Mac Con-Mara made three voyages across the Atlantic; and it was in the city of Hamburgh, where he conducted a school, that he wrote the "Bán-ċnoic Eireann O!" "The Fair Hills of Eire O!" a song we have introduced into this volume. It is the genuine production of an Irishman, far from his native home—full of tenderness and enthusiastic affection for the land of his birth.

As evidence that our poet was skilled in the Latin tongue, we need only call the attention of our readers to the following elegy, which he composed in the year 1800, at the advanced age of ninety, on the death of a brother bard named Taḋg (Gaoḋlaċ) Ua Súilleaḃáin.

* Prince Charles Edward Stuart.

"Thaddeus hic situs est; oculos huc flecte viator:
  Illustrem vatem parvula terra tegit.
Heu! jacet exanimis, fatum irrevocabile vicit!
  Spiritus e terrâ sidera summa petit.
Quis canet Erinidum laudes? quis facta virorum?
  Gadelico extincto, Scotica musa tacet.
Processit numeris doctis pia carmina cantans,
  Evadens victor munera certa tulit.
Laudando Dominum, præclara poemata fecit,—
  Et suaves hymnos fervidus ille canit.
Plangite Pierides; vester decessit alumnus;
  Eochades* non est, cunctaque rura silent.
Pacem optavit, pace igitur versatur in alto;
  Ad superi tendit regna beata patris."

In person Ꝺoɲɲċaꝺ was tall and athletic; but becoming blind towards the close of a life considerably extended beyond the average term allotted to man, and being rather straitened in pecuniary circumstances, he was compelled to appeal to the beneficence of the schoolmasters of his neighbourhood, who imposed a "Rate-in-Aid" for him on the scholars. We saw him ourselves in 1810, and paid our mite of the impost. He died about the year 1814, and his remains lie interred in Newtown churchyard, within half a mile of the town of Kilmacthomas, on the Waterford road, where no stone has yet been placed to commemorate his name, or indicate his last resting-spot to the passer-by: indeed, but for the interference of the worthy priest of the parish, the Rev. Mr. Veale (and to his honor be it spoken), a drain would, some few years back, have been passed through the place of his interment by some Goths, who were at the time turning off a stream of water from a distant corner of the churchyard.

* Eoghan (Ruadh) O'Suilliobhain, of Sliabh Luachradh, in Kerry; a near relative of Tadhg (Gaodlach) O'Suilliobhain, and a celebrated poet, who died A.D., 1784. For a sketch of his life see page 42 of our "Reliques of Irish Jacobite Poetry."

II.

SEAGHAN NA TUAMA.

John O'Tuomy was born at Croome, in the county of Limerick, in 1706. Through his own diligence, and by means of the scanty educational facilities which the country afforded, he made considerable proficiency in Latin and Greek, and was tolerably well versed in the literature of his time. The brief sketch which we propose to give of the life of this poet, interesting as we trust it will prove in itself, will be attended with this advantage, that it may serve to elucidate the meaning of much that might otherwise have appeared obscure in his poetry; and the nature of his compositions will be the better understood from a previous view of his character, and a short narrative of the vicissitudes that marked his career. His poverty, and the restrictions then imposed on education, interrupted his studies too soon, and involved him prematurely in worldly cares. He married young, and embarked in the vintnery business, first at Croome, but subsequently at Limerick, where the site of his residence in Mungret-street is still pointed out with veneration, as having once been the abode of a philanthropist and a true-hearted Irishman. His success in the line he had chosen, as may be anticipated, was but indifferent; for, besides that poets are rarely frugal or fortunate in the management of their temporal concerns, the malediction which invariably pursues the man who trades upon the intemperance of others, marred the best-directed efforts of his industry. His liberality, moreover, far exceeded his means, and must have inevitably led to bankruptcy. The most generous are usually content with relieving those who crave assistance from them ; but the house of O'Tuomy was open to all ; his hospitality was unbounded; and, in order that this might be made known to all, the following general invitation was written in broad letters on a large board over his door:—

"Ní'l fánaċ ná sáir-ḟear ar uaisle Gaoiḋeal,
Bráṫair de'n dáiṁ-ġlic, ná suairc-ḟear groiḋe,
A g-cás go m-beiḋeaḋ láiṫreaċ gan luaḋ na diġe,
Ná go m-beiḋeaḋ míle fáilte ag Seáġan Ua
Tuama roiṁe!"

"Should one of the stock of the noble Gael,
A brother bard who is fond of good cheer,
Be short of the price of a tankard of ale,
He is welcome to O'Tuomy a thousand times here!"

After this, it is unnecessary to mention that his house was much frequented. Himself, too, the soul and centre of his company (whence his appellation of "Seáġan Ua Tuama an Ġrinn," "John O'Tuomy, the Gay,") was not more courted for his hospitality than for his gaiety and good humour. His house was a general rendezvous for the bards and tourists of Munster, who came thither on occasional visits, and sometimes met there in a body, so as to form a sort of poetical club. These bardic sessions,* as they may be called, exercised a healthful influence in the country, and aided powerfully towards reviving the national spirit, bowed and almost broken, as it was, beneath the yoke of penal enactments: they were also a source of unalloyed pleasure to all, Mrs. O'Tuomy alone excepted, to whom patriotism and poetry were of less moment than the interests of her establishment, to which it was impossible that such meetings could contribute any advantage. She often warned her husband that his extravagance was disproportioned to his circumstances; she told him that their means of subsistence must not be consumed by "strollers," and that, unless he disconnected himself from

* For a history of those bardic schools, see Haliday's edition of "Keating's History of Ireland," p. vi., note ‡.

such society, he would soon be as penniless as any of his associates. Literary pursuits, she insisted, were barren and useless accomplishments, not unbecoming in persons of large fortune, but altogether unfitted for any one who had no resource but his own exertions for the maintenance of a wife and family. From prudential motives like these, she cherished a general dislike of all O'Tuomy's brother rhymers, and at length succeeded, by her continual remonstrances and objurgations, in breaking up for a season the bardic musters altogether.

We will here introduce an anecdote illustrative of the friendship which existed between O'Tuomy and a brother poet, Andrew Magrath, of whom we shall have more to say presently. One day, our friend, according to the custom of country publicans, had erected a tent on the race-course of Newcastle (or, as some assert, at the fair of Adare), which was surmounted by a green bough,* as a distinctive mark of his occupation, and also as an emblem of the love he bore his own "green isle." He was eyed at some distance by Magrath, who approached and accosted him, and the following short but pithy dialogue took place between the brother wits :—

* This ancient custom gave rise to the old adage, that "Good wine needs no bush."

In 1565, the mayor of Dublin ordered that no person should sell wine or ale in the city without a sign at the door of the house.—*Harris's Dublin.*

An "Act" of Charles II., "for the improvement of His Majesty's revenues upon the granting of licenses for the selling of ale and beer, provided—"**That every one so to be licenced "shall have some Sign, Stake, or Bush at his "Door, to give notice unto Strangers and Tra- "vellers where they may receive Entertainment of "Meat, Drink, and Lodging for their reasonable "money.**" Hence the custom of using the green bush at fairs and patterns.

Magrath.*

"Is baċallaċ glas an ċleaċ-sa a d-tóin do ṫiġe,
Ag tarraing na b-fear a steaċ ag ól na diġe."

"How clustering and green is this pole which marks your house!
Enticing men in to drink your ale, and carouse."

O'Tuomy.

"Airgiod geal go fras a réiġfioċ sliġe,
'Tá'n ċaraid ag teaċd, an braiṫ 's an hóp gan díol."

"Bright silver will pave your way, to quaff your fill,
But the hops and malt, alas! are unpaid for still."

It is to be regretted that O'Tuomy's many excellent qualities were not accompanied by greater economy in the management of his domestic affairs. But his improvidence was unfortunately incorrigible, for vain were all his wife's impassioned remonstrances and expostulations. At length his little capital began to melt away in the sunshine of convivial enjoyment; business first languished, and then entirely ceased, and with a young and helpless family he was cast once more an adventurer on the world. After undergoing many reverses he was compelled to accept the situation of servant at Adare, to Mr. Quade, a caretaker or steward on the farm of a gentleman residing in Limerick. Here he seems to have borne his change of fortune somewhat impatiently, for we find him engaged in frequent contests with his mistress, whose ill-treatment evoked his bitterest invectives. This old woman frequently transferred the duties of her office, as poultry-keeper, to the poet, who, however, did not feel at all honoured by the trust; and his most pointed satires against her indicate this to be the chief cause of his hostility. Poets are seldom to be offended

* We should here observe that Magrath was somewhat deep in the books of O'Tuomy for certain old scores.

with impunity. Having the means of reprisal so near at hand, they are not slow to use them with effect against the aggressor. In justice, however, to O'Tuomy, it should be observed that his was not a vindictive disposition; and this, perhaps, was the only instance in which his talents were made subservient to the indulgence of private resentment. From a cane which the old woman carried, both as a support in walking, and to keep the hens in order, O'Tuomy contemptuously designated her in rhyme as "Bean na Cleiċe Caoile," "The Dame of the Slender Wattle," and the poem so entitled we beg to introduce here:—

BEAN NA CLEIĊE CAOILE.

Níor ṫagair liom ceart, beart 'ná briaṫar aoib'nis
Leaḃar ná ceaċt, ná rann a ḋeilḃ díreaċ;
Níor cáṫag mé ar fad go teaċt am ḟeirḃíreaċ,
'S am reaċtaire ceart ag Bean na Cleiċe Caoile!

Do ċaiṫiosaḋ seal fá raiṫ air leirg laoiṫe,
A g-cairdrioṁ fear, 's flaiṫ, 's creidioṁ Íosa;
Airgiod geal am ġlaic gan doirb níḋ ar biṫ,
Cia dealḃ mo ṁeas ag Bean na Cleiċe Caoile!

Is é lagaiḋ mo ṁeas, do ṁeaṫ, do ṁeirḃ m'inntinn,
Naċ mairion na flaiṫ do lean an creidioṁ díreaċ;
Do ċannaḋ na rannaḋ a scannaḋ treiḃ a sinnsear,
'S do ḃainfeaḋ an ḟail de Ḃhean na Cleiċe Caoile!

'Is fearaċ nár ċleaċtas teaċt a n-deire coiṁeas-
gair,
Ag ceasaċt 's ag caismirt cailliḋe ceisniḋe cinte;
Ná'n aċaran aṁ, a b-fad o ḃreiṫ an ḟír-ċirt,
Go n-deaċaḋ fá smaċt ag Bean na Cleiċe Caoile!

Cia fada mé taisdiol treaḃ, 's tiġthe taoiseaċ,
'S go b-feacaḋ gaċ Reaċt 's Aċt ar fead na ríog-
aċta;
Níor b-feasaċ mé ar ċleasaḋ frasaḋ feill-ġníoṁaċ,
Go "Preabaire an Ghaid"* atá ag Bean na Cleiċe
Caoile!

Aitċim an Mac do ċeap na ċeiṫre ṡoillse,
Flaṫas, Fearn, Feart, 's Dealḃ daoine;
Go ngaḃaḋ m'anam feasda 'na ṡeilḃ dílis,
'S me sgaraḋ fá ḃlas le Bean na Cleiċe Caoile!

THE DAME OF THE SLENDER WATTLE.

Ochone! I never in all my dealings met with a man to snub me,
Books I have studied, however muddied a person *you* may dub me,
I never was tossed or knocked about—I never was forced to battle
With the storms of life, till I herded your hens, O, Dame of the
Slender Wattle!

I spent a season a chanting poems, and free from toil and troubles,
The faith of Christ I ever upheld, though I mixed with the proudest
nobles,
And gay was my heart, and open my hand, and I lacked not cash
or cattle,
Though low my esteem to-day with you, O, Dame of the Slender
Wattle!

My spirits are gone, my face is wan, my cheeks are yellow and
hollowed,
Because the nobles are dead by whom the true old Faith was followed,
Who sang the glory of those that died for Eire's rights in battle,
And would soon bring down your paltry pride, my Dame of the
Slender Wattle!

'Tis very well known I always shunned contention, clamour, and
jawing,
And never much liked the chance of getting a barbarous clapper-
clawing;
I always passed on the other side when I heard a hag's tongue rattle,
Till I happened, *mo vrone!* to stumble on you, O, Dame of the
Slender Wattle!

* An appropriate name for a flail among the Kerry peasantry.

Though used to the ways of tribes and chiefs, and reading the deeds that appear in
The chronicles and the ancient books that embody the lore of Erin,
I scarce ever knew what cruelty was, except through rumour or prattle,
Till the dismal day that I felt your flail, O, Dame of the Slender Wattle!

O! I pray the Lord, whose powerful Word set the elements first in motion,
And formed from nought the race of Man, with Heaven, and Earth, and Ocean,
To lift my spirit above this world, and all its clangor and brattle
And give me a speedy release from you, O, Dame of the Slender Wattle!

The history of this woman and her husband, and of their subsequent elevation to rank and fortune, is very extraordinary. Tradition represents them as living at Adare in distressed circumstances, when a stranger one day presented himself before them in search of a treasure, which he had dreamed was buried in the neighbourhood. Though he seemed unacquainted with the locality, his accurate description of a ruined mansion in the vicinity, as the place of its concealment, made a deep impression on the old woman, who cunningly resolved to turn the information to her own account. She accordingly advised him to relinquish his foolish search, which, originating from a dream, did not deserve to be prosecuted; and the stranger, according to her advice, left the place. He had no sooner departed, however, than she and her husband visited the spot indicated, and digging, discovered a "crock of gold," covered with a flag-stone inscribed with some half-effaced characters, which they did not take much trouble to decipher, supposing them merely to refer to the treasure they were already in possession of. Filled with joy, they conveyed home the money with secrecy and caution. But it happened that a certain itinerant literary character, who lodged with them, seeing the inscription on the flag-stone, or pot-lid—for into such an utensil had it been converted—fell to deciphering it, and at length succeeded in discovering the words—

"Atá an oiread céadna ar an d-taoḃ eile,"

"*There is as much more on the other side.*" This, though mysterious enough to the poor scholar, was quite intelligible to the initiated pair, who, at once acting on the suggestion, proceeded to the well-known spot, and secured the remainder of the booty. This treasure was shortly afterwards the purchase-money of a large estate in their native county; and it is said that at this day the blood of the Quades commingles with that of Limerick's proudest nobility.

O'Tuomy's poems are mostly illustrative of his own condition and habits of life. His songs, especially, sparkle with the glow shed over the festive scenes in which he was accustomed to spend so many gay hours with his brother bards. Their inspiration and eloquence would seem to favour the once popular, but now (thanks to Father Mathew) exploded doctrine of Cratinus:—

> "Nulla placere diu, nec vivere carmina possunt,
> Quæ scribuntur aquæ potoribus."

All the poets of this period, it should be remarked, combined in denouncing the persecuting policy of their rulers, and exposed with indignant patriotism the cupidity and bigotry which brought into action the worst passions of the heart, and perpetrated in the name of religion those atrocities which will for ever sully the fame of Britain. But as the sufferer was not permitted to complain openly, the voice of discontent was often veiled in the language of allegory. Ireland was usually designated by some endearing name, such as—"Siġile Ni Ghaḋaraḋ," "Caitilin Ni Uallaċáin," "Móirín Ni Chuillionáin;" and introduced under the form of a female of heavenly beauty, but woe-stricken, and dishonoured by the stranger. O'Tuomy's compositions on these subjects are replete with Irish sentiment and melody, especially his songs to the airs of "Móirín Ní Chuillionáin," and "Cnotaḋ Bán," "White Cockade," which will be found in this collection (p. 50).

This lamented bard expired, at the age of sixty-nine, in Limerick city, on Thursday, 31st August, 1775, and his remains were borne to his ancestral burial-place — the graveyard of Croome — by a numerous assemblage of the bards of Munster, and others of his friends. James O'Daly, a contemporary bard, who chanted his elegy, gives the precise period of his death in the following stanzas :—

Ar fada faon gan fearantas,
  Gan bailte-puirt, gan réimeas ríġ;
Meic Móġana n-éaċt do ċleaċtaċ cion,
  Calmaċt, 's cáin, 's cios :—
Slioċt Lúġaiḋ, 's Chéin, 's Chairbre,
  Faoi eaċtrannaiḋ mar ṫárlaiḋ tim ;
D'ḟuig drong na n-éaċt gan ṁarḃna,
  Ar sgaraḋ leat, Ui Thuama an Ghrinn !

Is dóḃaċ, 's as léan, 's as dainid liom,
  Ar d-tagraḋ, ár d-teann, ár n-dion ;
A g-Cromaḋ, faon faoi ġairḃ-lic,
  'S glasfarnaċ na n-Gall re d' ṫaoiḃ !
Seaċt g-céad déag gan dearmaḋ,
  Seaċt-moġatt 's cúig, gan ċlaoin ;
Aois ṁic Dé do ċeannaig sinn,
  Ar sgaraḋ leat, Ui Thuama an Ghrinn !

Stricken and feeble, without land, or name,
  Mansions, or princely sway,
Are Mogha's ancient race of ancient fame,
  And might, and wealth, to-day!
The noble sons of Cairbre, Conn, and Lughaidh,
  Alas! are foreigner's prey,
But bitterest grief is ours for losing you,
  O'Tuomy, once the Gay!

O, woe! O, sorrow! waking heart-wrung sighs,
    Our guide, our prop, our stay,
In Croome, beneath an unhewn flag-stone, lies
    While the stranger treads his clay.
'Tis seventeen hundred years—the account is true—
    And seventy-five this day,
Since Christ, His death, that we by death lost you,
    O'Tuomy, once the Gay!

III.

ANDREW MAGRATH

(Surnamed "Mangaire Súgaċ").

PERHAPS there is nothing more melancholy and deplorable than the sight, too often, unfortunately, witnessed in this world of contradictions — the union of lofty genius with grovelling propensities. To see talent of the highest order debased by an association with vulgar and low-lived habits—the understanding pointing one way, while the bodily requirements and appetites drag their degraded victim in an opposite direction—is indeed a spectacle calculated to excite to thoughtfulness and sorrow every generous mind. The world is familiar with examples of this lamentable and ill-assorted union; and we need only mention the names of Savage, Burns, Byron, and Maginn, as a few of those who have made the most mournful and conspicuous exhibitions of its effects. The subject of our present sketch unfortunately adds another to the muster-roll of those ill-starred children of genius; but we should be unfaithful to the requirements of the task we have undertaken, if we did not allot a place here to the biography of the gay, the eccentric, the jovial, but withal, the witty, learned, and intellectual Andrew Magrath.

This distinguished poet, who, from his convivial

habits, was usually called the "Mangaire Súgach" (*i. e.*, "Jovial," or "Merry Dealer"), was a native of the county of Limerick, and born on the banks of the Maig, a river which he has frequently made the theme of eulogy in his poems. Of his earlier years there are scarcely even any traditional accounts; but we find him, as he grew to manhood, engaged in the occupation of a country schoolmaster. Magrath was the contemporary of John O'Tuomy, and a host of others who at this period acquired a high reputation among the admirers of wit and lovers of song; but, unhappily for himself and those connected with him, his life, and even many of his productions, were at variance with, and unworthy of, his great intellectual powers. Habitual indulgence in intoxicating drinks—that foe to all aspiring thoughts and noble impulses—was his peculiar besetting sin; and, as a consequence, a great number of his songs are so replete with licentious ideas and images, as to be totally unfit for publication. Many of these, however, but particularly some others, in which his better muse predominates, are sung to this day by the Munster peasantry, and, doubtless, will remain unforgotten as long as the Irish spirit shall remain unbroken by the tyranny under which it has groaned and struggled through ages of misrule and unparalleled oppression.

The habits of Magrath were migratory and wandering; he seldom tarried long in any one spot, though usually long enough to leave behind him some rather marked *souvenirs* of his drollery, and reckless love of mischief and merriment. The caustic severity of his sarcasms rendered him an object of dread to such as were conscious of deserving exposure for their misdeeds. He delighted, like Burns, in mixing with low company, over whom, of course, he reigned supreme as a triton among the minnows. We may well believe this, however, when we recollect that one of the brightest wits and orators of his day, Philpot Curran, is said to have on one occasion disguised himself in the garb of a tinker, and taken up his quarters for a month with a fraternity of "jolly brothers" who sojourned on the Coombe, in this city, until one of them raffled his tools to enable "the tinker" to go on a "tramp." So has it been related by Moore of Byron, or rather by Byron of himself, in his "Journal," that frequently at night, when ennuyé to death by the ice-cold manners of the aristocratic society in which he mingled, he was accustomed to rush into the streets, and take refuge in——a cider cellar!

Many of the productions of our poet were penned amid these bacchanalian revels, and are, indeed, redolent of the Uırᵹe Beaṫa* bottle.

Magrath tried his master-hand upon several species of literary compositions, and succeeded in all. He is said to have been the author of those beautiful and soul-stirring words adapted to the air called "An Sean-duıne" (literally "The Old Man"), which is known in Scotland under the name of "The Campbells are Coming." The incident which gave birth to this exercise of the poetical powers of the Maᵹaıre Súᵹaċ, has been preserved by tradition, and is highly interesting. In the course of his wanderings through the country, our poet chanced to meet with a young woman by the roadside who was weeping bitterly, and appeared to be abandoned to inconsolable grief. Upon inquiring the cause of her affliction, he found that she had been induced, at the urgent request of her parish priest, to wed, for the sake of his great wealth and worldly possessions, an old man, the coldness of whose nature presented but an imperfect requital to her youthful warmth of affection. Magrath, who, with all his failings, possessed a heart ever sensitively alive to the wrongs of injured youth and innocence, was moved by the affecting narrative, and immediately produced an

* *Uisge Beatha*, water of life, equivalent to the Latin *aqua vitæ*, and French *eau de vie*.

extempore song on the occasion. The first stanza of which runs thus :—

"Cóṁairle do fuaras amuiċ ar an n-bóṫar,
O ṙóġuiṫe sagairt an seanduine a ṗósaḋ:
Ba ċumaḋ leis é, aċd go ṁéadóġuiġin a ṗócaḋ,
'S a ḃeiṫ fad do ṁairsin ag braiṫ ar na cóṁarsain!"

"A priest bade me marry 'for better or worse,'
An old wretch who had nought but his money and years—
Ah! 'twas little he cared, but to fill his own purse;
And I now look for help to the neighbours with tears!"

The additional notoriety acquired by Magrath from the circulation of this song was not of a very enviable kind. A general outcry was raised against him by all the old men of the whole surrounding country, and he was compelled, like Reynard, to betake himself to "new quarters." Repairing to Cnoc Fírinn, he there resumed his former occupation of school-teaching, and varied his leisure hours by the composition of political and amatory ballads. Here he wrote his popular song to the air of "Craoiḃín aoiḃinn áluinn óg," and declares in the opening stanza that he had been invited to Cnoc Fírinn by Donn Fírinneaċ,* chief of the Mun-

* DONN. One of the sons of Milesius, who, being separated from the rest of his brethren by a magic storm raised by the *Tuatha de Danans*, when effecting a landing on the coast of West Munster, was, with his ship's company, drowned at a place called "*Dumhachaibh*," "Vaults." In recording his death, *Eochaidh O'Flainn*, a poet of the tenth century, writes thus:—

"Donn, 's Bile, 's Buan, a bhean,
Dil, 's Aireach mac Mileadh,
Buas, 's Breas, 's Buaidhne go m-bloidh,
Do bhathadh ag Damhachaibh."

"Donn, and Bile, and Buan, his wife,
Dil, and Aireach, son of Milesius;
Buas, and Breas, and Buana, found,
Were at the Vaults drowned."

It is traditionally believed that *Donn* is chief of the Munster Fairies, and holds his court at *Cnoc Firinn* (hence the appellation *Donn Firinneach*), a romantic hill in the county of Limerick. See Haliday's Keating, p. 294. Dub. 1811.

ster Fairies; and here also he produced another song, in derision of those old women who "lay themselves out" to entrap young men into the snares of matrimony, a production, in our opinion, quite as clever and sarcastic in its way as the "Seanduine," though, on account of its perhaps unjustifiable attacks upon the softer sex, who, whether juvenile or ancient, are entitled to our respect, we forbear quoting any portion of it here.

Andrew Magrath was, perhaps, the most melodious Gaelic poet of his day; and we believe that few who peruse his song to the air of "Cailín Deas Crúiḋte na m-Bó," "Pretty Girl Milking the Cows," given in this volume, will dispute the correctness of our opinion. To his biography we have nothing more to add. He reached, notwithstanding all his irregularities and excesses, an advanced age; but the precise period of his death we are unable to ascertain, though we have been informed that he was living in 1790. His remains repose in the churchyard of Kilmallock, in the county of Limerick; and we have learned, upon good authority, that shortly before his death he bequeathed his manuscripts, which, as may be supposed, were exceedingly voluminous, to a farmer named O'Donnell, residing at Ballinanma, near Kilmallock, at whose house this eccentric genius, but true poet, breathed his last. Peace to his erring spirit! Let us remember his faults but to compassionate and avoid them, while we honour his talents, which were, undoubtedly, of a high and striking order.

IV.

AODHAGAN UA RAIGHEALLAIGH.

Egan O'Reilly, the subject of our present notice, was, according to Edward O'Reilly's "Irish Writers," the son of John Mor O'Reilly, a gentleman farmer, who resided in the village of Crossarlough, on the borders of Lough Sheelan, in the county of Cavan, about the commencement of the eighteenth century. John had been intended by his father, Eoghan, for the priesthood, and was sent to receive his education in Kerry, a county celebrated at that period for the facilities it afforded of communicating a knowledge of the classics, by means of its hedge-schoolmasters, who frequently made the very cowherds Greek and Latin scholars. Our young aspirant, during his stay here, made considerable proficiency in his studies; but Fate had willed that he should never reach the goal which his father had pointed out as the object of his ambition. Happening, on his journey homeward, during vacation, to give offence to some person whose name we have been unable to discover, he was waylaid, and attacked by six men armed with bludgeons, one of whom he killed with a single blow. Apprehended and tried for murder, he was acquitted; but having taken away the life of another, he was, by the canon law, disqualified for the priesthood, and obliged to relinquish the hope of ever attaining to it. He returned to Kerry, where he married a young woman of the name of Egan; and the subject of our memoir, called also Egan, in compliment to his mother's name, was the eldest son of this marriage. John Mor, we may observe, was the author of several poems, with which the peasantry of his native county are stated to have been familiar but a few years since; and it is also said that copies of many of them are extant in Kerry at the present day.

Egan was left by his father in comfortable circumstances; indeed in the possession of what, at the present day, would be considered almost opulence. His residence was at Sliaḃ Luaċraḋ, in the county of Kerry. He was the author of a great variety of admirable songs, copies of which are in our possession, as other copies are also scattered through Munster, and abound particularly in his native district. His "Vision," or "Reverie," which we give here, is, perhaps, as beautiful a piece of modern poetry as can be found in the Gaelic language, and is, in fact, a perfect gem amid the jewels of song.

Gile na Gile do ċonarc ar slíġe an uaignios,
Criostal an Chriostail a gorm-rosg, rín, uaiṫne ;
Binnios an ḃinnis a friotal, nár ċríon-ġruamaḋ,
Deirge 's finne a fionnaḋ 'na gríos-ġruaḋ'naḋ.

Caise na Caise ann gaċ ruibe dá buiḋe-ċuaċaiḃ,
Bhaineas an ċruinne dá ruiṫne le rín-sguabaiḋ ;
Iorraḋ ba ġlaine ná glaine air a bruinn ḃuacaiḋ,
Do geineaḋ ar ġeineaṁain d'isi san tír uaċtraiḋ.

Fios fiosaċ dam d'inis 's isi go fíor-uaignioċ,
Fios filleaḋ do'n duine do'n ionad ba ríġ-ḋualgas ;
Fios milleaḋ na droinge ċuir eision ar rín-ruagaḋ,
'S fios eile ná cuirfiod am luiḋṫiḃ le fíor-uaṁan.

Leiṁe na leiṁe dam druidim 'na ċruinn-ṫuairim,
'S mé am ċuinge ag an ċaime do ṡnaiḋmeaḋ go fíor-ċruaiḋ mé ;
Ar ġoirm ṁic Muire dam ḟurtaċt do ḃiog uaimsi,
'S lingios an ḃruinngioll na luisne go Bruiġin Luaċraḋ.

Ruiṫim le mire am ruiṫiḃ go croiḋe-luaimneaċ,
Tre iomallaiḃ currais, tré ṁongṫaiḃ, tré ṡlim-ruaiḋṫiḃ ;
Do'n ḟinne-ḃrog tigim, ní ṫuigim cia 'n t-slíġe fuaras,
Go h-ionad na n-ionad, do cumaḋ le draoiġeaċt Druagaiḃ.

Brisiḋ fá sgiġe go sgiġeaṁail, buiḋin Ghruaġaċ,
'S fuireann do ḃruingiollaiḃ siosgaiḋṫe, dlaoi-
ċuaċaċ;
A n-geiṁeallaiḃ geiṁeal mé cuiriḋ gan puinn
suaiṁnis,
'S mo ḃruingioll ar bruinniḃ ag bruinnire bruinn-
stuacaċ.

D'innisios d'isi san ḃ-friotal ba ḟíor uaim-si,
Nár ċuiḃe ḋi snaiḋme le slibire slím-ḃuarṫa;
'S an duine ba ġile air ċine Scuit trí h-uaire,
Ag feiṫioṁ ar isi-ḃeiṫ aige mar ċaoin-nuaḋċar.

Ar ċluisdin mo ġuṫaḋ ḋi, guilion go fíor-uaiḃreaċ,
Ruiṫean an ḟliċe go life as a gríos-ġruaḋnaiḃ;
Cuirean liom giollaḋ mar ċoimirc ó'n m-Bruiġin
uaiṫe.
'S í Gile na Gile, do ċonarc ar sliġe an uaignios!

An Ceangal.

Mo ṫréigiḋ, mo ṫubairt, mo ṫurrainn, mo ḃron,
mo ḋiṫ!
Mo ṡoillseaċ ṁuirneaċ, ṁioċair-ġeal, ḃeól-tais,
ċaoin,
Air aḋairc ag fuireannuiḃ, miosgaiseaċ, crón-duḃ,
buiḋe;
'S gan léigios na goire go ḃ-filliḋ na leóġain tar
toinn!

The Brightest of the Bright met me on my path so lonely;
The Crystal of all Crystals was her flashing dark-blue eye;
Melodious more than music was her spoken language only;
And glories were her cheeks, of a brilliant crimson dye.

With ringlets above ringlets her hair in many a cluster
Descended to the earth, and swept the dewy flowers;
Her bosom shone as bright as a mirror in its lustre;
She seemed like some fair daughter of the Celestial Powers.

She chanted me a chant, a beautiful and grand hymn,
Of him who should be shortly Eire's reigning King—
She prophesied the fall of the wretches who had banned him;
And somewhat else she told me which I dare not sing.

Trembling with many fears I called on Holy Mary,
As I drew nigh this Fair, to shield me from all harm,
When, wonderful to tell! she fled far to the Fairy
Green mansion of Sliabh Luachra in terror and alarm.

O'er mountain, moor, and marsh, by greenwood, lough, and hollow,
I tracked her distant footsteps with a throbbing heart;
Through many an hour and day did I follow on and follow,
Till I reached the magic palace reared of old by Druid art.

There a wild and wizard band with mocking fiendish laughter
Pointed out me her I sought, who sat low beside a clown;
And I felt as though I never could dream of Pleasure after
When I saw the maid so fallen whose charms deserved a crown.

Then with burning speech and soul, I looked at her and told her
That to wed a churl like that was for her the shame of shames,
When a bridegroom such as I was longing to enfold her
To a bosom that her beauty had kindled into flames.

But answer made she none; she wept with bitter weeping,
Her tears ran down in rivers, but nothing could she say;
She gave me then a guide for my safe and better keeping,—
The Brightest of the Bright, whom I met upon my way.

SUMMING UP.

Oh, my misery, my woe, my sorrow and my anguish,
My bitter source of dolor is evermore that she
The loveliest of the Lovely should thus be left to languish
Amid a ruffian horde till the Heroes cross the sea.

To an intimate acquaintance with his mother tongue, Egan O'Reilly united a thorough knowledge of the classics, and had, perhaps, been designed, like his father, John Mor, for the sacerdotal profession. To the kindness of Mr. Patten, librarian to the Royal Dublin Society, we are indebted for the following extract from a MS. copy of Keating's Ireland, made by him in 1772, and now deposited in the Society's valuable library. It will serve to prove that our bard was living at that period, being the year in which it was written by him.

It runs thus:—"A na sgrıoḃ le h-Aoḋagán Ua Raġallaiġ do Ruiġri ṁic Seáin oig, ṁic Siṫe, a n-Drom

Coluċuin san m-bliaġain d'aois Chriosd; mile, seaċt gc7, agus an 2ra bliaġain fiṫċ7. July an seaċtṁaḋ lá." "Written by Egan O'Reilly, for Rughri, son of John Og Mac Sheehy, of Dromcullaghar, on the 7th day of July, 1722." The book is written in a plain, legible, and bold character, and establishes the writer's power and skill as a perfect philologist in the structure and idiomatic peculiarities of his native tongue. We have one rather curious remark, however, to make with respect to it—that he writes his name in two forms. At the commencement of the work he subscribes himself Ua Raġallaiġ (O'Reilly); whereas, at the close of the second volume, he thus writes :—

Finis Libri Secundi, 7br the 9th, 1722.

AODHAGAN UA RATHAILLE, -

by which name, indeed, he is best known throughout Munster at the present day.

There are two songs of our author's in the present collection. One of these, called "The Star of Kilkenny," was composed on occasion of the celebration of a marriage, in the year 1720, between Valentine, third Viscount Kenmare, and Honoria Butler, of Kilcash, great grand-niece of James, Duke of Ormond. The other was written as a tribute of praise to a poetess, a lady named Fitzgerald,* who resided at Ballykenely, in the county of Cork, and who, from her extraordinary beauty, was a perpetual theme of eulogy among the bards of Munster.

* This lady had a brother named Pierse, a poet of no mean celebrity; his productions, and many amusing anecdotes relating to him, are still remembered throughout the province. He flourished about the middle of the last century; but the only fragment of his poetry in our possession is an elegy on the death of John Power, Esq., of Clashmore, in the county of Waterford, who died in the summer of 1754.

We have only to add, that notwithstanding all our inquiries and researches, we have been unable to discover either at what precise period or locality the death of Aoḋaġán Ua Raṫaille occurred.

V.

AN T-ATHAIR UILLIAM INGLIS.

THE Rev. William English* was an Augustinian friar, and stationed in the convent of that community in Brunswick-street, Cork. It is said that he was born in Newcastle, in the county of Limerick, and that he passed a considerable portion of his early life as schoolmaster in Castletownroche, in the county of Cork, and Charleville, in the county of Limerick. Previous to his assumption of the Augustinian habit, he had produced many striking and beautiful songs in his native tongue, among which we may reckon the celebrated "Caisiol Múṁan," "Cashel of Munster," and "Cois na Brí-ġide,"† "By the Bride's Silvery Waters," both well known to our Munster readers. His admission into the ranks of the regular clergy is said to have been on the condition of abandoning song-writing for the rest of his life—an obligation which he faithfully kept until the occurrence of an incident which tempted him to call once more his rhyming powers into action, and, at all hazards, to violate his anti-poetical resolve; as indeed he did,

* We have seen this name in an old Irish MS. Hibernicised *Gall-Oglaoich.*

† The river Bride, which has its source in the barony of Barrymore, county of Cork, near a place called *Gleann an Phriachain* (Glinville), and falls into the Blackwater at Strangcally Castle, county of Waterford.

though not without having obtained permission from his ecclesiastical superior.

A brother friar, who had been despatched from the convent, according to the custom of the order in Munster, at a particular period of the year, for the purpose of collecting provisions, obtained a quantity of butter among the benevolent farmers' wives of his district, which he packed in a firkin, and sent to Cork market for sale. Upon inspection, however, by the merchant to whom it was offered, it was found to exhibit, owing to the various sources from which it had been procured, such a strange combination of colours, that the poor friar was, perforce, compelled to return home, and use it himself. Such an opportunity for displaying his satirical genius, even at the expense of a brother of the order, was too tempting to be forfeited by our poet; and he immediately commenced and produced the well-known sarcastic poem, beginning—

"Cré na Cill nár ḟagaiḋ an Bráṫair,
Chuir spéis na suim an im na a m-bláṫaig!"

"May that friar never know peace in the dust,
Who in butter or buttermilk places his trust!"

Several of the Rev. William English's poems are, we are happy to state, in our possession. The song by him which we present our readers in this volume, is adapted to a very pleasing air called the "Seanduine" (The Old Man), of the merits of which we have already spoken in our biographical sketch of Andrew Magrath. We regret that our limited acquaintance with the minuter details of our poet's life, precludes us from doing him that justice which his high moral character unquestionably deserved, but which would be better understood by the reader, were we in a position to illustrate it by anecdote and narrative.

The Rev. William English closed his life on the 13th of January, 1778, in Cork, and his remains repose in St. John's churchyard, Douglas-street, in that city.

VI.

TADHG (GAODHALACH) UA SUILLIOBHAIN.

TIMOTHY O'SULLIVAN, a poet, who, either from his simplicity of manner, or from the fact of his being an humble peasant,* altogether ignorant of the language of Bacon and Shakspeare, usually went by the surname of "Gaeḋlaċ," or "The Simple," was a native of Kerry, and, unfortunately, was not in his earlier years a model of the strictest rectitude in point of conduct. To his honour, however, be it stated, that he subsequently reformed, abandoned his irregularities, and succeeded in acquiring the esteem and friendship of all who knew him.

Born a poet—as every true poet, according to Horace, must be†—he early "lisped in numbers," and ere the heyday of his youth was over, had composed a considerable number of amatory songs, rather too remarkable, it must be confessed, for warmth of sentiment and expression. In after-life, however, he atoned for the sins of his youthful muse by a collection of sacred poems, which he left behind, and which are published under the title of "The Pious Miscellany," a work at the present day in the hands of almost every peasant in Munster, and, although not comparable in point of style to some pieces of a similar character in our volume, yet characterized by much depth of feeling and energy of language. The book, moreover, possesses this distinguishing merit, that every page, every verse, we might almost say every line, reflects back, as from a mirror, the leading traits in the character of the amiable author.

* "The ancient natives were universally prejudiced against the dialect of the colonists; insomuch, that any of them known to speak the rude jargon of the foreigners seldom escaped a reproachful nickname." —*Hardiman. Note on the Statute of Kilkenny.*

† "*Poeta nascitur non fit.*"—HOR.

O'Sullivan was accustomed to make periodical excursions to a district in the county of Waterford, celebrated for its hospitality, and known by the name of "Paoraċa," which comprises the barony of Middlethird. In all probability, it was owing to his repeated visits to this territory, that an eminent writer has fallen into the error of supposing him to have been a native of Waterford. There he passed the latter years of his life, and frequently sojourned at the house, and sat at the table of the father of the writer of this sketch. The precise period of his death is unknown—to us at least—but that it probably occurred towards the close of the last century may be conjectured by the following quotation from one of his sacred poems, entitled "Duain an Doṁain," or "The Lay of the World."

"Dúbail seaċt ain ċeaċt do ċéadaib,
'S trí ċéad na g-cómar de'n g-cóimirioṁ
ċéadna;
Dias dá ḟiċċid bliaḋan, bliaġain 's aoin-deiċ,
Sin an bliaġain d'aois Chríost an laoiḋe-si
ḋéanaṁ."

"Since born was GOD'S Eternal Son,
Came fourteen hundred years to an end;
Three hundred, four score, ten, and one,
Before this lay of mine was penned."

According to popular report, his remains were interred in Ballybricken churchyard, Waterford, but we cannot vouch for the correctness of the tradition. There is much beauty and pathos in the epitaph written on his death by Donnċaḋ Mheic Con-Mara, but it is extremely doubtful whether it was ever engraved on his tomb.

VII.

PEADAIR UA DOIRNIN.

Were we not sincerely desirous of rescuing from the wrecks of the Past the names and memories of the truly-gifted children of genius who have flourished, though in comparative obscurity, in our island, we might pass over in silence the claims of Peter O'Dornin. But we cannot so far forget the duty we owe to our country and our readers. Although the bones of this poet lie in a remote part of Ireland, the remembrance of what he achieved and essayed shall not die with him; and, as far as lies in our power, we shall endeavour to wreath with a garland of verdure his distinguished, though humble, name.

Peter O'Dornin was born in the year 1682, in the county of Tipperary, near the renowned Rock of Cashel. At an early age he displayed the most astonishing evidences of an intellect far advanced in knowledge; and his parents accordingly resolved on educating him for the priesthood. But the laws of that dark and dreary period—the statutes against education, domestic or foreign—the operation, in short, of the Penal code—interposed a veto on their wishes, and prevented them from carrying their purpose into effect.*

* The following extracts from the Irish Statutes will at once exhibit the state of the Popish schoolmasters and students in Ireland during the penal times:—

I.

"No person of the Popish religion shall publicly teach school or instruct youth in learning, or in private houses teach or instruct youth in learning, within this realm (except only the children or others under the guardianship of the master or mistress of such private house), under the penalty of £20, and three months' imprisonment."—7th William III., ch. 4, s. 9. 1694.

II.

"In case any of his Majesty's subjects of Ireland shall go or send any person to any public or private Popish school, in parts beyond the

Menaced in his early youth by political dangers and hostilities, O'Dornin became a fugitive from the home of his childhood. Directing his course towards the north, which he regarded as the safest retreat from the storms of persecution, he arrived at Drumcree, near Portadown, in the county of Armagh. A Catholic clergyman, an ardent lover of his country's language and literature, who has kindly furnished us with materials for this brief biographical notice, states that the following quatrain, in O'Dornin's handwriting, is in the possession of Mr. Arthur Bennett, of Forkhill; and, as will be seen, it completely precludes any controversy on the subject of our poet's birthplace.

"Do ḃiḋ árus mo ċáirde ag Caisiol na ríoġ,
Is é dásaċt na Gallaċt do sgar mise ḋioḃ;
Thug mé rása fó'n tráṫ sin go mullaiċ Dhruim
Críoċ,
Mar a ḃ-fsair mé fáilte gan táiṁleas 's mea-
ḋair gan ċios."

"The lands of my fathers were at Cashel of the Kings,
But the black English tyrant-laws they drove me out from thence;
So I bounded to Drumcree, as an eagle flies on wings,
And I found a welcome there, without grudging or expense."

seas, in order to be educated in the Popish religion, and there be trained in the Popish religion, or shall send money or other thing towards the maintenance of such person gone or sent, and trained as aforesaid, or as a charity for relief of a religious house, every person so going, sending, or sent, shall, on conviction, be disabled to sue, in law or in equity, or to be guardian, executor, or administrator, or take a legacy or deed of gift, or bear any office, and shall forfeit goods and chattels for ever, and lands for life."—7th William III., ch. 4, s. 1. 1694.

III.

"If any person, after 1st September, 1709, shall discover any Popish schoolmaster, or any Papist teaching or instructing youth in private houses, as tutor, or as usher, under-master, or assistant to any Protestant schoolmaster, so as the said Popish schoolmaster, tutor, or usher, under-master, or assistant to any Protestant schoolmaster, be apprehended and legally convicted, every person making such dis-

While sojourning in this locality, he produced an elaborate poem, entitled "The Ancient Divisions of Ireland, and an Account of the different Septs that from time to time have colonised it." The peculiarly powerful style of this poem attracted the attention of the Hon. Arthur Brownlow, ancestor of the present Lord Lurgan, who requested an interview with O'Dornin; and finding, upon a close acquaintance with him, that he possessed high talents, had received a liberal education, and was withal, a man of polished manners and profound penetration into human character, he took him into his own house to instruct his family, revise his Irish records, enrich his library with Gaelic poetry, and, above all, to infuse into his own mind a deep and lasting love for the literature of his native country. The friendship, thus happily commenced, continued unabated for several years, until, unfortunately, the electioneering contest of the Brownlows of Lurgan, the Copes of Loughgall, and the Richardsons of Richhill, supervened, and the independent conduct of O'Dornin on that occasion aroused the wrath of Brownlow: the result, after some angry altercation, was a final separation between the poet and his patron.

The thoughts of O'Dornin now once more reverted towards home: he desired to spend the evening of his days among the friends and companions of his youth, and was anxious that his remains might mingle with the dust of his ancestors. Fate, however, ordained otherwise. A handsome young woman, named Rose Toner, laid siege in due form to our poet's heart; and he bowed his scholarly head beneath the yoke of Hymen. He spent the "honey-moon" in the parish of

covery shall receive as a reward for the same £10, to be levied on the Popish inhabitants of the country where such Popish schoolmaster, tutor, usher, under-master, or assistant, taught or instructed youth, or did most commonly reside, and shall be convicted thereof."—8 Anne, c. 3, ss. 20, 21. 1701.

Loughgilly, at Ballymoyre, and subsequently established himself in the neighbourhood of Forkhill, where he opened a school as a competitor with one Maurice O'Gorman,* who bore a high character for ability in teaching. The insinuating address and extensive learning of O'Dornin, however, soon drew over a majority of the scholars to his side; and O'Gorman, fancying himself deeply injured by his rival, but having no means of redress or retaliation at his command, was forced to leave the neighbourhood, and retire to Dublin. In and about the vicinity of Forkhill, O'Dornin passed a considerable time. Here he wrote a humorous poem, in which he unmercifully satirized the luckless O'Gorman; and here also he penned the song (to the air which we give in our present collection) of "Sliaḃ Féiḋlim," with many other minor poetical compositions, some of which we shall have the gratification of introducing at a future day to the notice of our readers.

In his latter years, O'Dornin was honoured with the friendship, and enjoyed the esteem, of many of the most eminent men in Ireland. He lived to a green old age, and closed a life which he had consecrated to the vindication of his country's literary renown, and the advancement of the happiness of his numerous friends and acquaintances, on the 5th of April, 1768, in his eighty-sixth year. His death occurred in the townland of Shean, at a place called Friarstown (Shean, we may observe, is now divided into quarters), adjacent to the village of Forkhill, in Armagh; and his remains were interred near the north-east wall of Urney churchyard, in the county of Louth, somewhat more than three miles northward of Dundalk. The parish priest of Forkhill, the Rev. Mr. Healy, when on his death-bed, requested

* We possess a copy of the 4to. edition of O'Brien's Irish-English Dictionary, with numerous marginal notes and additional words, collected from ancient Irish MSS., in the autograph of Maurice O'Gorman, written at Dublin, in the year 1781.

to be laid beside O'Dornin; and the poet and the clergyman now repose beneath one stone.

Our readers will understand that the poets at whose lives and labours we have thus cursorily glanced, form but a few of the great band of native Irish writers whose genius illumed the political gloom and dreariness of the eighteenth century. Among their contemporaries, and not less distinguished for their poetical talent, we may mention—

I.—Eóġan Ruaḋ O'Súilliobáin, a native of Sliaḃ Luaċraḋ, in the county of Kerry, who flourished towards the close of the last century, and was justly celebrated for his judgment and skill in the production of compound epithets. He wrote many songs both in Irish and English, though he always entertained an undisguised contempt and dislike for the latter language. As a specimen of his English versification, we give here the opening stanza of one of those—a song called "Molly Casey's Charms," which he penned for a village beauty of his acquaintance:—

"One evening late, it was my fate
 To meet a charming creature,
Whose airy gait and nice portrait
 Excel both art and nature:
Her curling hair, in ringlets fair,
 Down to her waist doth dangle;
The white and rose—united foes—
 Her beauteous cheeks bespangle.
Her rolling, glancing, sparkling eyes,
Each gazer's heart at once surprise,
And bind a train of love-sick swains
In Cupid's close enthralling chains.
Whoever views her lovely face,
That is bedecked with youth and grace,
Must every hour, proclaim the power
 Of Molly Casey's charms."

II.—John Mac Donnell, a poet of almost unrivalled power and sweetness, surnamed "Cláraċ," from the broad cast of his features, or from the fact of having been born at the foot of *Clarach* mountain, near Mill-street, in the county of Cork.

III.—William Heffernan, surnamed "Ɗall," or the Blind, a native of Shronehill, in Tipperary, and one of the most delightful of versifiers. Our limited space will not permit us to enlarge upon the writings and characters of these poets; but we refer the reader to our "Reliques of Irish Jacobite Poetry," in which will be found detailed biographical notices of them.

At this period there flourished a host of other gifted men, of whom but "Random Records" remain—men whose powers of denunciation and satire were unsparingly exercised against the abuses of authority, and the oppressions which their unhappy country was compelled to suffer at the hands of her mis-rulers. Among those men, who, although less famous than the O'Tuomys and Magraths of their time, yet scarcely inferior to them in poetical ability, we may record the names of—

I.—Hugh and Andrew Mac Curtin, both natives of Clare, who flourished in the early part of the eighteenth century.*

II.—Conor and Donogh O'Sullivan, both of Cillín, or, as they style it, "Cillín cam-rannaċ an Chrónáin," in the parish of Whitechurch, near Blarney. Some of their songs, printed from the original manuscripts, will be found in this volume.

III.—Bryan O'Flaherty, a mason, who lived at Bruff.

IV.—James Considine, of Aṫ na ȝ-Caoraċ, in the county of Clare.

* A copy of Dr. Keating's "*Tri Bir-Ghaotha an Bhais*," "Three Pointed Shafts of Death," in the handwriting of Andrew M'Curtin, bearing date 1703, is in the hands of a young man in this city. Hugh Mac Curtin wrote an Irish Grammar, an English-Irish Dictionary, and a Brief Discourse in Vindication of the Antiquity of Ireland, which were published early in the last century. Both were celebrated poets, and some of their compositions will be found in this volume.

V.—John Cunningham, who lived near Castletownroche, and flourished in the year 1737. We have seen some of his MSS. bearing that date.

VI.—Maurice Griffin, who followed the profession of schoolmaster at Ballingaddy, in the county of Limerick, about 1778.

VII.—William Cotter (the *Red*), a native of Castlelyons, some of whose manuscripts, dated 1737, we have in our possession.

VIII.—George Roberts, one of whose poetical pieces, a fairy-song of remarkable beauty, appears in this volume.

IX.—James O'Daly,* a native of the parish of Inagh, county of Clare, and contemporary with John O'Tuomy, whose elegy he chanted.

X.—Thomas Cotter, of the Cove of Cork.

XI.—Edward Nagle, also of Cork, a contemporary of the Rev. William English.

We might append to these the names of a number of others; but as we do not present the reader with any of their songs, and as we purpose, according to our promise, devoting a volume exclusively to their "Lives and Times," it is unnecessary for us to particularise them here. There are, however, two of the number who cannot be passed over in silence. We allude to

* Since the time of Donogh Mor O'Daly, abbot of Boyle, A.D. 1244, styled the Ovid of Ireland, from his beautiful verses, the tribe of O'Daly has produced a vast number of eminent poets.

Edward O'Reilly gives a catalogue of twenty-eight writers of the name; and they were so numerous in the sixteenth century, that an English chronicler of that period uses O'Dalie as synonymous with poet or rhymer.

We may here also mention Fa. Dominick O'Daly, O.S.D., founder of the College of "Corpo Santo," and the Convent of "Bom Successo" at Lisbon, and ambassador, in 1655, from Portugal to the court of Louis XIV., on which occasion he gave a series of magnificent fêtes to the citizens of Paris. He died in 1662, having been elected Bishop of Coimbra, and was buried in his own college at Lisbon. His "History of the Geraldines" is known to most of our readers, through the excellent translation of the Rev. C. P. Meehan. 12mo. Dublin, 1847.

Eóġan O'Caoiṁ (Owen O'Keeffe), and John Murphy. O'Keeffe, who, like his namesake, the dramatist, possessed the most varied and versatile powers, was born at Glenville, in the county of Cork, in 1656. He married early, and had a son, whom he reared for the priesthood, but who died in 1709, at Rochelle, in the flower of his youth, while engaged in the prosecution of his theological studies. Eoġan, the father, entered Holy Orders after the decease of his wife, in 1707, and closed his life on the 5th day of April, 1726, as parish priest of Doneraile. His remains are interred in the grave-yard of Sean-Chúirt (Old-Court), about half a mile west of Doneraile. The following inscription was graven on his tomb by a sculptor named Donnċaḋ O'Dálaiġ:—

"Ag seo ionad ioḋlaicṫe Eóġain Ui Chaoiṁ, ṫug tréiṁisi dá aimsir pósda, agus tar éis éaga a ṁná do ġlac Gráḋ Coisreagṫa; oir ba ḋuine gaosṁar, geanamnaiḋe, greannṁar; agus do ba ḟile fóġlamṫa, fír-eólaċ, agus cléireaċ cliste, caoin, a b-prioṁ-ṫeangaḋ a ḋúiṫċe agus a ṡinnsear é. Gur ab uime sin do cuireaḋ an sgríḃinn neaṁ-ċoitċeann so ós a ċionn.

"Do éag an cúigṁaḋ lá de'n Abrán, A.D. 1726; agus ar doilg d'ógaiḃ na Múṁan é, agus fós dá cléir; óir is ioṁḋa leaḃar lán-ḟoġlamṫa, léir-sgrioḃṫa, dá ḟaoṫar re na ḟaicsin a n-Eire aniuġ."

The Rev. John O'Brien, afterwards Bishop of Cloyne, wrote the following epitaph, or Feart Laoiḋe, which is also engraven on the same stone:—

"Sin agad a lic, mo ḋiṫ! fá d' ṫaoḃ go lag!
Sagart ba ċaoin, 's a n-dlíġe ṁic Dé ba ḃeaċt;
Farraire groiḋe d'ḟuil Chaoiṁ ba ṫréine a d-treas,
Fear seanċaḋ a sgrioḃ go fíor an Ghaoiḋeilib seal."

"A grave-stone lies above thee laid this night,
Thou mildest priest, in GOD's great laws well versed—
O'Keeffe, of heroes mightiest in the fight,
Whose lore illumed the Gaelic learning erst."

John Murphy (Seáġan O'Ṁurċúġaḋ), born at Raṫaoinneaċ, county of Cork, in March, 1700, was distinguished for the beauty and pathos of his elegiac compositions. In the year 1726, he had transcribed, with his own hand, many native historical tracts of high value. He was the chief patron of a bardic sessions, or academy, held periodically at Charleville, and in the parish of Whitechurch, near Blarney; and we have seen a poem of four stanzas composed by him on the fate of four brothers named Armstrong, who were killed at the battle of Aughrim, for which composition it has been asserted that their sister presented him with four bullocks. Murphy continued his labours as an Irish scribe of high repute to the year 1758. We have in our hands some MSS. beautifully written by him at that period, for a gentleman named Wallace, of Cork. We cannot tell how long he lived, as we have no records bearing on that subject.

About this period the introduction into female dress of that singularly ridiculous and unsightly article of head-gear known as the "High Cauled Cap," called forth the unsparing satire of the poets of Munster. Numerous and bitter were the rhyming diatribes which they levelled against it. The offensive specimen of bad taste in apparel, however, maintained its elevated position for at least forty years, from 1760 to 1800, and some old dames kept up the custom till 1810, when it entirely ceased to disfigure the flowing ringlets of our fair countrywomen. Even poetry and satire, it will thus be seen, are not omnipotent. But if Horace, Young, and even Swift, failed in their attempts to correct the manners of their times by ridicule and sarcasm, it can hardly be deemed surprising that such weapons should prove powerless against a cause which influences of so potent a character as vanity and fashion had enlisted under their special protection.

Upon the "High Cauled Cap," several songs were composed to the air which we here present to our readers, but unfortunately we have not been able to procure the original words.

THE HIGH CAULED CAP.

A species of rhythmical composition, similar to the following, was extensively in vogue among the Irish peasantry, about the middle of the last century. In giving it a place here, however, we willingly confess that we are less actuated by its poetical merit, than by a desire to display the extreme facility with which our native rhymers were able to bring into juxta-position with the Irish lines that Anglo-Irish phraseology, for a knowledge of which few of them have ever obtained credit :—

BEAN NA N'OR-FHOLT DONN.

As í ḃean na n-ór-ḟolt donn, mo ġrádh-sa gan dóḃat,
Is suiġte deas a com 's a ċnáṁa ;
Likewise her features round, excel the Lady Browne's ;
Her equal can't be found ann san áit-si :
If I had a thousand pounds, I'd pay the money down,
D'ḟonn tú ḃeiṫ agam a b-Port-láirge ;
Ghlacfamaois ann long, 's do raċfamaois a rún
Tar fairge, 's níor ḃ'eagal dúinn ḃeiṫ báiḋte.

Ní ġéillim-si dod' ġlór, mar is mór do ḋúil sa n-ól,
'S tar fairge ní raċad-sa go bráṫ leat ;
I believe you're for sport, I beg you'll let me alone,
'S gur le bladaireaċt do ṁeallann tú na mná leat,
If I bade my friends adieu, and to go along with you,
Geallaim duit gur fada do ḃeiṫ tráċt orruinn,
I believe I'll stay at home, and never go to roam,
Seaċain me ? do radaireaċt ní áil liom.

Tréigfiod feasda an t-ól, 's ní leanfaḋ mé an spórt,
'S beiḋ airgiod go fairsing ann mo ṗócaiḋe,
Gur milse liom do ṗóg ná siuicre beaċ ar bórd,
'S go m'aite liom am aice tú ná ceól síṫ ;
What I do to you propose, you may take as a joke,
'S a naċaṁann, ní magaḋ leat ḃim a óg-ṁnaoi,
If I had you in my bower, do ṡinfinn sios le d' ċom,
'S ḃeiḋeaċ m'aigne-si ceangailte ann do ṁór-ċroiḋe !

Is buaḋarṫa 'tá mo ċroiḋe le taiṫnioṁ mór dod' ġnaoi,
Agus adaḃuim ó m'aigne gur león me !

When I go to bed at night, no comfort can I find,
  But lying on my side in sore grief!
By this and that indeed, and the Bible we do read,
  Ní sgaraim leat air airgiod, ná air ór buidhe,
My treasure, wealth, and store, you shall be evermore,
  Tair a bhaile liom 's bhéarfad m'acfainn duit a stóirín!

Your civil silver tongue I think is moving on,
  Your chattering or flattering won't coax me;
Dá ngéillinn-si do d' shlighe 's an cam do bheith ad chroidhe,
  Nár bh'é an peacadh duit me mheallad le d' chuid gnodhtuidhe,
Can't you come and try—my kindness you shall find,
  'S thabharfainn m'acfainn duit go rabhairneach le mór-chroidhe,
I'll buy you decent clothes, silk and satin shoes,
  'S annsa n-Gaillimh do ghlacach sinn ár lóistín.

My mind would give consent to go with you, I think,
  Acht le h-eaglad gur cleasa clis do ghnóthaighe;
If I thought you were true, do rachainn leat a rún,
  Tar fairge, gan eachrad, gan cóistighe,
Ní'l agam le rádh acht, "go mad buan do bheidh na mná,"
  'S gur thaithniomhach liom gasarad 'ca ag ól dighe,
To you I give my oath (and what could I do more?)
  Ná sgarfainn leat go g-casfad sruith a g-clódh dighe.

One word in reference to our translator,* and we are

* The earliest known translation of an Irish poem into English verse is Michael Kearney's version of John O'Dugan's chronological poem on the Kings of the race of Eibhear, translated, A.D. 1635, "to preserue that antient Rhyme from theoverwhelmeing floods of oblivion which already devoured most part of our Nationall Memoraryes." 8vo. J. Daly, Dublin. 1847.

done. His reputation as a linguist has been long established, and his peculiar skill in versification is generally acknowledged. It will be seen, that he has executed the task allotted to him with equal fidelity and success. We have only to add, that we have awarded him this tribute of praise altogether against his will; but all who are acquainted with his poetical powers will acknowledge that we have not transgressed the strict limits of truth.

In conclusion, may we be allowed to hazard the hope that our volume may prove influential in the further advancement of our native literature? Ulster for the last century has been totally disregardful of the glory to be acquired from this source: it is time for her at length to awake and exert herself to retrieve and redeem the past. Leinster has produced an O'Donovan; Connaught, a Hardiman; but the great and crowning praise is due to Munster for her continuous literary efforts. Surely, the literary achievements of that province, even under the most discouraging circumstances, ought, when contrasted with the inactivity of the other three, rouse them to emulate her services in the cause of Irish literature.

JOHN O'DALY.

Dublin, July, 1850.

BÁN-CHNOIC EIREANN O!

Donnċaḋ (Ruaḋ) Mheic Con-Mara, cct.

Fonn—Uileacán Duḃ O!

Beir beannaċt ó m' ċroiḋe go tír na h-Eireann,
Bán-ċnoic Eireann O!
'S ċum a maireann de ṡíolraċ IR 's EIBHEAR,
Ar ḃán-ċnoic Eireann O!
An áit úd 'nar b'aoiḃinn binn-ġuiṫ éan,
Mar ṡáṁ-ċruit ċaoin ag caoine Gaoḋal,
Is é mo ċás a ḃeiṫ míle míle i g-céin,
O ḃán-ċnoic Eireann O!

THE FAIR HILLS OF EIRE O!

BY DONOGH (THE RED) MAC CON-MARA.

AIR:—"*Uileacan Dubh O!*"

We have no means of tracing the antiquity of the air to which these beautiful words are written; but it may with probability be ascribed to the early part of the seventeenth century. "*Uileacan Dubh O!*" literally means *a black-haired head of a round shape, or form;* and we have frequently heard it so applied by the Munster peasantry, with whom it is a favourite phrase, when speaking of the head, particularly that of a female. Some writers are of opinion that "*Uileacan Dubh O!*" allegorically means Ireland; but we cannot concur in this opinion, for it is evidently a love expression. The song entitled "*Plur na m-ban donn og,*" of which we give the first stanza, can be sung to this air. It must be played rather mournfully, but not too slow:—

"Da d-tiocfadh liomsa go Conntae Liath-druim,
A phluirin na m-ban donn og!
Do bhearfainn siuicre ar liun mar bhiadh dhuit,
A phluirin na m-ban donn og!
Do bhearfainn aor long duit 's bathad faoi sheol,
Ar bharr na d-tonn ag filleadh chum tragha,
'S ni leigfinn aon bhron ort choidhche na go brath,
A phluirin na m-ban donn og!"

"Would you only come with me to Leitrim county fair,
O, flower of all maidens young!
On sugar and brown ale I'd sweetly feast you there,
O, flower, &c.
I'd shew you barks and ships you never saw before,
So stately and so gay, approaching to the shore,
And never should you sigh or sorrow any more,
O flower, &c."

Take a blessing from my heart to the land of my birth,
And the fair Hills of Eire, O!
And to all that yet survive of Eibhear's tribe on earth,
On the fair Hills of Eire, O!
In that land so delightful the wild thrush's lay
Seems to pour a lament forth for Eire's decay—
Alas! alas! why pine I a thousand miles away
From the fair Hills of Eire, O!

Bíḋeann bárr bog slím ar ċaoin-ċnoic Éireann,
Bán-ċnoic Éireann O!
'S as fearr 'ná 'n tír-si ḋíṫ gaċ sléiḃe ann,
Bán-ċnoic Éireann O!
Do b' árd a coillte 's ba ḋíreaċ, réig,
'S a m-bláṫ mar aol ar ṁaoilinn géig,
Atá gráḋ ag mo ċroiḋe a m'inntinn féin,
Do ḃán-ċnoic Éireann O!

Atá gasraḋ líonṁar a d-tír na h-Éireann,
Bán-ċnoic Éireann O!
'S fear-ċoin ġroiḋe ná claoiḋfeaċ céadta,
Ar ḃán-ċnoic Éireann O!
M'ḟáṫ-tuirse croiḋe! 's mo ċuiṁne sgéal,
Iad ag Gall-ṗoic síos fá ġreiḋim, mo léan!
'S a m-bailte dá roinn fá ċíos go daor,
Bán-ċnoic Éireann O!

Is fairsing 's as mór iad Cruaċaiḃ* na h-Éireann.
Bán-ċnoic Éireann O!
A g-cuid meala 'gus uaċtair ag gluaiseaċt na slaoda,
Ar ḃán-ċnoic Éireann O!
Raċad-sa ar cuairt, no is luaċ mo ṡaoġal,
Do'n talaṁ mín suairc is dual do Ġaeḋal,
'S go m'ḟearr liom 'ná duais, dá uaisleaċt é, beiṫ,
Ar ḃán-ċnoic Éireann O!

* *Cruachaibh na h-Eireann.* There are various hills in Ireland bearing this name: *Cruach Phadruig*, in Mayo; *Cruachan Bri Eile*, in the King's County; but the Cruachan the poet alludes to is a large hill in the parish of Kilgobnet, county of Waterford, within four miles of the town of Dungarvan; on the summit of which there is a conical pile of stones, known among the natives as *Suidhe Finn*, or the resting place of *Fionn Mac Cumhail*, of which we find the following account in a MS. of the seventeenth century, now in our possession:—

"And for the monuments from them (the Fenians) in this country anciently named, and still yet contynued, wee have from ffion O'Baoisgne, *Suidhe Finn*, that is the sitting seate of ffion, vpon the mountaine called *Sliabh na m-ban.* Gleann Garraidh, in the

The soil is rich and soft—the air is mild and bland,
Of the fair Hills of Eire, O!
Her barest rock is greener to Me than this rude land—
O! the fair Hills of Eire, O!
Her woods are tall and straight, grove rising over grove;
Trees flourish in her glens below, and on her heights above,
O, in heart and in soul, I shall ever, ever love
The fair Hills of Eire, O!

A noble tribe, moreover, are the now hapless Gael,
On the fair Hills of Eire, O!
A tribe in Battle's hour unused to shrink or fail
On the fair Hills of Eire, O!
For this is my lament in bitterness outpoured,
To see them slain or scattered by the Saxon sword.
Oh, woe of woes, to see a foreign spoiler horde
On the fair Hills of Eire, O!

Broad and tall rise the *Cruachs* in the golden morning's glow
On the fair Hills of Eire, O!
O'er her smooth grass for ever sweet cream and honey flow
On the fair Hills of Eire, O!
O, I long, I am pining, again to behold
The land that belongs to the brave Gael of old;
Far dearer to my heart than a gift of gems or gold
Are the fair Hills of Eire, O!

barony of Iffahy, so called from Garrae mac Mornae, and *leabba Dhiermoda Vi Duiffne* and *Grayne*, ymplying their bedding there together, at *Polltyleabayne*, in the country of *Vi ffiachragh Aidhne*, now called the O'Sheaghnussy his country, which are but a few of many other monuments from them named in divers other places of this k.dome."

In the next line the poet alludes to the fertile district of Cumeragh (properly *Com-Rathach*, from *Com*, nook, declivity, or opening between two hills which meet at one extremity; and *Rathach*, forts, which abound in the locality), in the parish of Kilrosenty, and barony of Middlethird, where the cuckoo is heard earlier in spring than in any other part of Ireland.

Sgaipeann an drúċt ar ġeaṁar 's ḟéar ann,
        Ar bán-ċnoic Eireann O!
'S fásaid ablaḋ cúbarṫa ar ġéagaḋ ann,
        Ar bán-ċnoic Eireann O!
Biḋeann biolar 's saṁaḋ ann a n-gleanntaiḃ
    ceóḋaiġ,
'S na sroṫaiḃ san t-saiṁraḋ ag labairt uim neóin,
Uisge na Siuire* ag brúċt na ṡlóġaiḋ,
        Cois bán-ċnoic Eireann O!

As osguilteaċ, fáilteaċ, an áit sin Eire,
        Bán-ċnoic Eireann O!
Biḋeann "Toraḋ na Sláinte" a m-bárr na déise,
        A m-bán-ċnoic Eireann O!
Ba ḃinne liom ná méaraiḃ ar ṫéada ḃ ceoil,
Seinnim 's géimreaḋ a laoġ, 's a m-bó,
Taiṫnioṁ na gréine orra aosda 's óg,
        Ar bán-ċnoic Eireann O!

* *Siuir.* This river has its source in *Sliabh Ailduin* (the Devil's Bit Mountain, better known as *Greidhim an Diabhail*), in the county of Tipperary. It takes a circuitous route by Thurles, Holycross, Caher, Ard-Finan, Clonmel, Carrick-on-Suir, and Waterford; and, being joined by the rivers Nore and Barrow (hence the appellation "Sister Rivers") at Cheek Point, six miles below Waterford, falls into the British Channel. *Donnchadh Ruadh* describes its waters in the following line :—

"*Uisge na Siuire ag brucht na Shloghaidh.*"
"The waters of the Suir swelling into whirlpools."

The scenery of these rivers (with which we happen to be well acquainted) recalls to our mind the lines of the poet Spenser, in his "Faërie Queene," Book IV., Canto XI., Verse XLIII. :—

The dew-drops lie bright 'mid the grass and yellow corn
On the fair Hills of Eire, O!
The sweet-scented apples blush redly in the morn
On the fair Hills of Eire, O!
The water-cress and sorrel fill the vales below;
The streamlets are hushed, till the evening breezes blow;
While the waves of the Suir, noble river! ever flow
Near the fair Hills of Eire, O!

A fruitful clime is Eire's, through valley, meadow, plain,
And the fair land of Eire, O!
The very "Bread of Life" is in the yellow grain
On the fair Hills of Eire, O!
Far dearer unto me than the tones music yields,
Is the lowing of the kine and the calves in her fields,
And the sunlight that shone long ago on the shields
Of the Gaels, on the fair Hills of Eire, O!

"The first, the gentle Shure, that making way
By sweet Clonmell, adornes rich Waterforde;
The next, the stubborne Newre, whose waters gray,
By fair Kilkenny and Rosseponte boord;
The third, the goodly Barow, which doth hoord
Great heapes of Salmons in his deepe bosome:
All which long sundred, doe at last accord
To ioine in one, ere to the sea they come,
So flowing all from one, all one at last become."

Although the *Suir* and *Nore* flow from the same source, *Sliabh Ailduin*, the *Barrow* rises in *Sliabh Bladhma*, in the Queen's County, which Spenser makes as the parent of the three; but we must presume that he took Giraldus Cambrensis as authority, he being the only writer on Irish history who fell into this sad mistake.—See *Haliday's Keating*, p. 29. Dub. 1809. *Cambrensis Eversus*, vol. i., p. 123, edited for the Celtic Society by the Rev. Matthew Kelly. Dublin. 1848.

UAILL-CHUMHAIDH NA FEINNE.

Seáġan Ua Tuama, cct.

Fonn—An Cnotaḋ Bán.

Mo ṁíle truaġ! mo ḃuairt! mo ḃrón!
An sgéiṁle ruaig ár n-uaisle ar feóḋ!
Gan sliġe, gan suaġa, gan suaircios sóġaċ,
Gan laoiḋe, gan duain, gan cnuas, gan ceól!
As é do léig mo ṁilleaḋ a g-ceas,
As é do ṫraoċ mo ċuisle ar fad,
Uaisle Gaoḋal—fá ċruaḋ-smaċt ġéar,
Ag cuaine an ḃéarlaḋ ḋuiḃ a n-glas!

A LAMENT FOR THE FENIANS.

BY JOHN O'TUOMY.

AIR:—" *The White Cockade.*"

THE air to which this song is written is very much misunderstood, as many persons suppose the White Cockade to mean a military cockade, and with that view, doggrel rhymers have polluted the good taste of the public by such low ribaldry as the following:—

> " A Shaighdinir! a Shaighdinir! a b-posfadh bean,
> Le Heigh! no le Ho! no le bualadh an drum!"

> " O soldier! O soldier! would you take a wife,
> With a heigh! or a ho! or a beat of the drum."

The *Cnotadh Ban* (White Cockade) literally means a *bouquet*, or plume of white ribbons, with which the young women of Munster adorn their hair and head-dress on wedding, and other festive occasions. The custom prevailed early in the seventeenth century, for we find a poet of that period, *Muiris Mac Daibhi Duibh Mac Gearailt*, addressing a young woman in these beautiful words:—

> " A chailin donn deas an chnotadh bhain,
> Do bhuar is mheall me le h-iomad gradh;
> Tar si liom 's na dein me chradh,
> Mar do thug me greann duit 's dod' chnotadh ban!"

> " O brown-haired maiden of the plume so white,
> I am sick and dying for thy love;
> Come then with me, and ease my pain,
> For I dearly love you, and your White Cockade."

The Munster poets, who adhered with devoted loyalty to the cause of the Stuarts, wrote many beautiful Jacobite songs to this air; of which two different versions will be found at pp. 26, 34, of our "Reliques of Irish Jacobite Poetry;" and probably it is on this account that the Scotch claim the air as their own.

It makes my grief, my bitter woe,
To think how lie our nobles low,
Without sweet music, bards, or lays,
Without esteem, regard, or praise.
O, my peace of soul is fled,
I lie outstretched like one half dead,
To see our chieftains, old and young,
Thus trod by the churls of the dismal tongue!

'Bé ċiḋfeaċ uaiḋ gaċ ruaḋtar bróin,
Gaċ daoirse ċruaiġ, gaċ cruaḋtan fós;
Gaċ sgéiṁile fuair ár n-uaisle reóṁainn,
Ba líontaḋ a ġruaḋ le duartan deór!
As é do léig, 7c.

Mar a m-biḋeaċ na sluaiġte, mór-ṡlioċt Eoġain,*
D'ár ċuibe, 's d'ár ḋual an uaisle ar d-tóis†
Ba buiḋeanṁar, buanaċ, buacaċ, beóḋa,
Soillseaċ, suaġaċ, snuaḋ-ġlan, sóġaċ.
As é do léig, 7c.

Mar a m-biḋeaċ Mac Cúṁail na b-fionn-ḟolt óir,‡
'S an buiḋin nár ḋiúlta cúinse a n-gleó;
Coillte lúṫṁar, lúinneaċ, leóġaċ,
Mac Dhuibne, 's Dúḃlaing, ṫúrnaċ treoin.
As é do léig, 7c.

An garṫaċ Goll, gniḋeaċ foġail ar ṫóir,
'S Osgur oll, do lann-ḃris slóiġ;
Conall cabarṫaċ, ionnċaiḃ, óg,
Níor ċlos Gall ba ḋeallraċ leó.
As é do léig, 7c.

Mar a m-biḋeaċ slioċt IR 's Eiḃear ṁóir,
Ba líonṁar, daon-ṁar, craoḃaċ, cóir;
'S fír-ṫreiḃ aoibinn Eireaṁóin,
An Ríġ fá'r ḟiolraḋ tréine treóin.
As é do léig, 7c.

* *Eoghan Mor*, King of Munster, and ancestor to the Ui Fidhgheinte, who possessed that portion of the county of Limerick lying west of the river Maig, besides the barony of Coshma in the same county, and were exempt from tribute, as being the seniors of the Eugenian line, having descended from Daire Cearba, the grandfather of the great monarch, Criomhthan Mor Mac Fidhaigh.—*See O'Flaherty's Ogygia*, pp. 380, 381; *Book of Rights* (*published by the Celtic Society*) p. 63, 66, *n*, 67, *n*.

† Other copies read "*ar bord.*"

‡ *Mac Cumhail na bh-fionn-fholt oir*, Mac Cumhal of the golden locks of hair. Fionn Mac Cumhail, commander-in-chief of the Irish militia, of whom it is traditionally related, that his hair was of the

Oh! who can well refrain from tears,
Who sees the hosts of a thousand years
Expelled from this their own green isle,
And bondsmen to the Base and Vile?
O, my peace, &c.

Here dwelt the race of Eoghan of old,
The great, the proud, the strong, the bold,
The pure in speech, the bright in face,
The noblest House of the Fenian race!
O, my peace, &c.

Here dwelt Mac Cumhal of the Flaxen Locks,
And his bands, the first in Battle's shocks;
Dubhlaing, Mac Duinn, of the Smiting swords,
And Coillte, first of heroic lords.
O, my peace, &c.

The Goll, who forced all foes to yield,
And Osgur, mighty on battle-field,
And Conall, too, who ne'er knew fear,
They, not the Stranger, then dwelt here.
O, my peace, &c.

Here dwelt the race of Eibhear and Ir,
The heroes of the dark blue spear,
The royal tribe of Heremon, too,
That King who fostered champions true.
O, my peace, &c.

colour of the finest gold, and in graceful curls covered his shoulders. We ourselves know many of the Irish peasantry who take pride in these "golden locks." Many extravagant stories are told of Fionn, as to his enormous size and strength; but Dr. Keating states, on the authority of the ancient records of the kingdom, that "Fionn did not exceed the common proportion of the men of his time; and that there were many soldiers in the Irish militia that had a more robust constitution of body." See his History of Ireland, vol. i. p. 412, Dublin, 1809. For an account of all the other Fenian heroes whose names are introduced in the song, I would also refer the reader to Keating's History, which seemed to be a text-book with the Munster poets, to furnish them with historical incidents for their poetic effusions.

Mar a m-biḋeaċ Niall na n-daor-ḃrat sróill,
San ríġeaċt fuair géille tréiṁire a g-c'róinn;
Fir Craoiḃe* ṫraoċaċ tréiṫ, gaċ treóin,
Le cloiḋeaṁ gaċ caoiṁ-ḟear céad de'n tóir.
Ar é do léig, 7c.

An caiṫ-ṁíleaḋ Brian† do'n ḟiann-ḟuil ṁór,
Ba ṫaṫaṁail, diaḋa, a ṁian 's a ċlóḋ;
Le feartaiḃ o Dhia ṫug riaġ'laḋ 's nós,
Chuir Danair fá ċiaċ ar iaṫaiḃ Eoġain.
Ar é do léig, 7c.

Ar é do líon mo ċroiḋe le brón,
Gur aontaiḋ Críosd a d-tiġeaċt a g-c'róinn;
Na Béir ċuir Bíobla Iosa ar cóir,
'S nár ġéill dá naoiṁ, dá ḋlíġe, 'ná d'órd!
Ar é do léig, 7c.

* The Red Branch Knights were the chief military force of Ulster, and resided at *Eamhain* (Emania), the palace of the Kings of Ulster. They were highly celebrated during the first century for their victories under their champions, *Cuchullainn* and *Conall Cearnach*. See *Annals of the Four Masters*, translated by Owen Connellan, p. 267, note. *Book of Rights*, published by the Celtic Society 1847, p. 249.

† *Brian*, surnamed *Boroimhe*, assumed the sovereignty of Ireland A.D. 1002; and was killed at the Battle of *Cluain Tairbh* (Clontarf) on the 23rd April, 1014. An account of the various tributes exacted by Brian may be seen in the *Leabhar na g-Ceart* (Book of Rights).

And Niall* the great, of the Silken gear,
For a season bore the sceptre here,
With the Red Branch Knights, who felled the foe
As the lightning lays the oak-tree low!
O, my peace, &c.

The warrior Brian, of the Fenian race,
In soul and shape all truth and grace,
Whose laws the Princes yet revere,
Who banished the Danes—he too dwelt here.
O, my peace, &c.

Alas! it has pierced mine inmost heart,
That Christ allowed our Crown to depart
To men who defile His Holy Word,
And scorn the Cross, the Church, the Lord!
O, my peace, &c.

* Nial, surnamed "*Naoi n-Giallaidh*" (Of the Nine Hostages) monarch of Ireland at the close of the fourth century, was one of the most gallant of all the princes of the Ultonian race. He made several descents on Britain, and it was against his incursions that some of those successes were achieved by the Romans which "threw such lustre round the military administration of Stilecho, and inspired the muse of Claudian in his praise."

Nial was killed, anno 406, during one of his invasions of Gaul.—*O'Flaherty's Ogygia. Moore's Ireland.*

MOIRIN NI CHUILLIONNAIN.

Seáġan Ua Tuama, cct.

Fonn:—Móirín ní Chuillionáin.

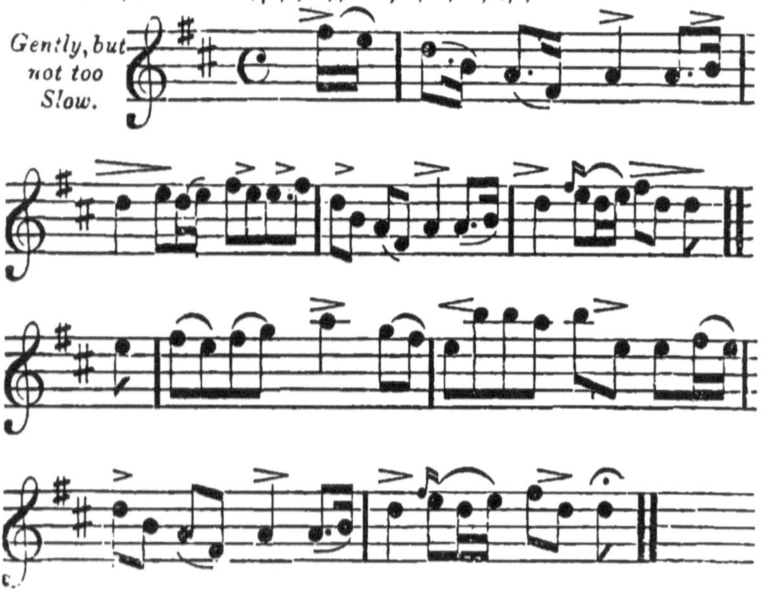

Am aonar seal ag róduiġeaċt,
  Cia ṡeólfuiḋe am ċuinne lá?
Aċd an spéirbean ṁaiseaċ ṁóir-ṁín,
  As í Móirín Ní Chuillionnáin!
Ba réiġ, ba raṫṁar, ró-ġroiḋe,
  Ba ċóir, ciorṫa, clisde, cáiġ;
A craob-ḟoilt cas mar ór buiḋe,
  Na d-tóirsiġib go troiġṫe ag fás.

MOIRIN NI CHUILLIONAIN.

BY JOHN O'TUOMY.

AIR:—"*Moirin Ni Chuillionain.*"

MOIRIN NI CHUILLIONAIN (Little Mary Cullenan) is one of those allegorical names by which Ireland is known in Irish song, and which became a favourite theme with our Munster poets. We have no less than sixteen different versions bearing this name in our collection, three of which we select for our present volume. The Irish reader will readily perceive that it is of that Jacobite class peculiar to the middle of the last century; for at that period the poets, excited to the highest degree, gave vent to their deepest passions in order to rouse the fallen spirit of the nation in behalf of the Stuart family.

This beautiful air approaches that of the "*Beinsin Luachra*" (Little Bench of Rushes) in plaintive tenderness of expression and melody, and is known in various districts of the south by different names. In Waterford, for instance, the peasantry call it "*Moirin Ni Ghiobarlain*" (Little Mary Giblin). In Tipperary, it is called "*The Rose-tree of Paddy's Land.*" In all the other southern counties the original name is still preserved—as, indeed, it ought to be, for there is nothing so hateful as calling our airs by strange names and after stranger incidents.

It must be played in moderate time—neither too slow nor too quick, but rather mournfully, like most of the Jacobite airs.

One evening roaming lonely,
  As pale twilight just began,
I met the fair, the only,
  The bright Moirin Ni Chuillionain!
The maid whom Eire blesses,
  The dignified, the gay, the neat,
Whose brilliant golden tresses
  Wave down o'er her waxen feet.

Ba ġlé, ba ġeal, ba ġleoiḋte í,
B'óg í, 's b'oilte árd;
Ba ṡéiṁ, ba ṡlaċtṁar, seólta í,
Ba ṡnóġ-ṁín, ba ṡnuiġte sáiṁ;
Ba ḃéasaċ, blasda, beóḋ' í,
Ba ḃeol-ḃinn dar linn an ḃáb,
Ba ṁaorḋa, maiseaċ, mórḋa í,
Ba ṁodaṁail, mionlaḋ, mioċair, mná'úil.

Ag teaċt re m'ais do'n óġ ṁín,
'Nois móidiġim gur ḃinne an ḃáḃ;
'Ná éanlaiṫ ag cantainn nótaiḋe,
A mór-ċoill cois imioll tráġa;—
'S ná'n té do spreagaċ ceól-síṫ,*
Chuir ceó draoiḋeaċt' ar Uisniġ† lá,
'S as péarlaḋ ó neaṁ an t-seoid ġrinn,
Do ṡeóil Críosd am ċoinne an t-sráid.

Do ṡléaċdas seal do'n óg-ṁnaoi,
'S ba ḋóiṫ linn nár ṁisde a ṫráċt;
D'ḟéaċain créad do ṡeóil í,
Gan mór-ḃuiḋin dá coimirc slán,
An aon tar sleasaiḃ bóċna í,
Do ḃreóḋaiġ sinn le h-iomad gráḋ;
No cread an treiḃ 'na g-coṁnuiġea
A mór ċríoċaiḃ Inis Fáil?

Is mé do ṡearc a g-cóṁnuiḋe,
Cia iul-ḃaois anois do ṫráċt;
Om' ṫaoiḃ 's ó laċt mo núaḋ-ċíoċ,
Thig Eóġan groiḋe 's gaċ cineaḋ is fearr:—
Slioċt Néill, 's Airt, 's ṁór-Chuinn,
'S pór Mhileaḋ uile d'ḟás;
Le h-éad do ṁarḃaiḋ beó sinn,
Ag stróruiġeaċt ar mire atáim!

* *Ceol-sith, fairy music.*

† The death of the sons of Uisneach, in the first century of the

So pure, so fair, so blooming,
  So mild, placid-souled and meek;
So sweet and unassuming
  A maiden 'twere in vain to seek!
Her fair and radiant features,
  Her tall form 'twas bliss to see—
The noblest of God's creatures,
  The loveliest, the best is she!

Her face, her brow of marble,
  Breathed music, oh! far more
Than lays the wild birds warble
  In greenwood glens anear the shore,
Or his whose fairy metre
  Bewitched Uisnigh's sons one day,
More tender far, and sweeter
  Were hers that Christ sent in my way.

I bowed before the Daughter
  Of Light, Love, and Heavenly Song,
And asked her what had brought her
  To us without a warrior-throng.
Had she come o'er the ocean
  To melt our hearts and make us wail?
Or owned she the devotion
  Of Conn's tribes of Inisfail?

"O! I'm thy Fondest-hearted,"
  She said, "though now beneath a ban;
From me in days departed
  Sprang Eoghan and each noble clan,
The sons of Conn the glorious,
  And Neill and Art, who filled the throne
Though now the foe, victorious
  Thus makes me pine so lorn and lone.

Christian era, formed the subject of one of the "Three Sorrows of Story-telling" (*Tri Truagh na Sgealuigheachta*). *See Transactions of the Gaelic Society.* Dublin. 1808.

An t'aon d'ár ċeart le cóir sinn,
Ag deóruiġeaċt amuiċ ar fán ;
'S mé dam' ḟracaḋ ag stróinsíġib,
Do león sinn go h-uile an cás !
An Féinics-ḟlaiṫ do ṗór Gaoiḋeal,
Ní mór díb a ċur ar fáġail,
Le faoḃar-neart frasaḋ fóirniḋe,
Go fórsuiġeaċ go d-tigiḋ am ḋáil.

'Tá céadta ag teaċt dam ṫóruiġeaċt,
O ċóistiġiḃ na cruinne lán ;—
Le h-aon do'n treiḃ ní ġeaḃaḋ mé,
'S ní láṁṫaoi a ċur am ṗáirt ;—
An féinneaċ is fearr clóḋ 's gnaoi,
D'ár túismiḋ ar ḟuirinn Aḋaiṁ,
Réiġfiḋ ar trí c'róinniḋe,
Le Móirín Ní Chuillionnáin !

CUISLE NA h-EIGSE.

Seáġan Ua Tuama, cct.

A ċuisle na h-éigse ! * éirgiḋ suas ?
Is tuirseaċ a n-éag-ċruiṫ mé gan suan,
Gan duine san t-saoġal
Ag innsint sgéal,
Ar ṫurus an té 'tá 'g-céin ar cuairt,
'S Eire mo ċroiḋe 'tá m'intinn ort !

Do b'aite liom súd óm' úr-ġas óg,†
Gearraḋ 'gus brúiṫ' na m-búr go feór ;
Is fada mé ag súil
Go ḃ-feicfinn a ġnúis,
An sarraire fiúntaċ, fionn, a g-c'róinn.
'S Eire mo ċroiḋe, 7c.

* A beautiful invocation—"Pulse of the bards, awaken!"

"Our Prince and true Commander
  Is now, too, an exile far.
Alas! we both must wander
  Until the avenging Day of War;
But through what distant regions
  I know not, till the Gaels shall come
And with their victor legions
  Lead him and me in triumph home.

"Crowds throng to seek and find me—
  Of lovers I have many, in truth,
But none of all shall bind me
  In Wedlock's bands but one brave Youth.
A Hero bold and portly
  As ever graced the name of Man
Will share Three Crowns full shortly
  With his Moirin Ni Chuillionain."

SPIRIT OF SONG.

BY JOHN O'TUOMY.

O, Spirit of Song, awake! arise!
  For thee I pine by night and by day;
With none to cheer me, or hear my sighs
  For the fate of him who is far away.
      O, Eire, my soul, what a woe is thine!

That glorious youth of a kingly race
  Whose arm is strong to hew tyrants down,
How long shall it be ere I see his face,
  How long shall it be ere he wins the Crown?
      O, Eire, my soul, &c.

† *Ur-ghas og, Fresh young branch.* Charles Edward Stuart.

Corruiġ go léir a n-éifeaċt duan,
A's seinniḋ-si dréaċt do réir na sluaġ;
Sin ċúġaiḃ an t-aon
Le fuirionn don ḟéinn,
'S as stuirmeaċ tréan do ḋéanfas buairt.
'S Eire mo ċroiḋe, 7c.

'Tá Pilib 's Séamus * glé, 's a sluaġ,
'S na Riġṫe le ċéile a téaċt le buaḋ,
Tiocfaid go léir
A ḃ-fuinnioṁ 's a ḃ-faoḃar,
'S an Innis geal Eilge réiġfid cuan.
'S Eire mo ċroiḋe, 7c

Brisfid 's raobfaid,—déanfaid ruaig,
Air ḃruiṫinis ḃaoiṫ an ḃéarlaḋ ḋuairc;
Cuirfid na Gaoiḋeil
'Na n-ionnadaiḃ féin,
Sin mise le m' rae 's an éigse suas.
'S Eire mo ċroiḋe, 7c.

Ba ḃinne liom súd a rún 's a stór,
An gloine go h-úr dá ḋiúga ar bórd;
Cuidioċta ṡúgaċ,
Mhuirr'neaċ, ṁúinte,
'S go m-brisfear an ceann ná cóġanfaċ leó!
'S Eire mo ċroiḋe, 7c.

A Mhuire na Naoṁ! naċ aoraċ, suairc,
An brisiḋ seo téaċt ar Bhéir an uaḃair;
Biaḋ fuirionn de'n Chléir
Ag seinnim na d-Téad,†
'S gaċ bile do'n éigse ag déanaṁ duan.
'S Eire mo ċroiḋe, 7c.

* *Pilib agus Seamus*, Philip V. of Spain, and James Francis Stuart, whom the native Irish recognized as King James III.

† *D-Fead*, *i. e.*, Te Deum.

Why, Bards, arise ye not, each and all;
  Why sing ye not strains in warlike style?
He comes with his heroes, to disenthral
  By the might of the sword, our long-chained isle!
      O, Eire, my soul, &c.

Kings Philip and James, and their marshalled hosts,
  A brilliant phalanx, a dazzling band,
Will sail full soon for our noble coasts,
  And reach in power *Inis Eilge's* strand.
      O, Eire, my soul, &c.

They will drive afar to the surging sea
  The sullen tribe of the dreary tongue;*
The Gaels again shall be rich and free;
  The praise of the Bards shall be loudly sung!
      O, Eire, my soul, &c.

O, dear to my heart is the thought of that day!
  When it dawns we will quaff the beaded ale;
We'll pass it in pleasure, merry and gay,
  And drink shame to all sneakers out of our pale.
      O, Eire, my soul, &c.

O, Mother of Saints, to thee be the praise
  Of the downfal that waits the Saxon throng;
The priests shall assemble and chant sweet lays,
  And each bard and lyrist shall echo the song!
      O, Eire, my soul, &c.

* The old Irish detested the language of the stranger; they would not, they said, "writhe their mouths with clattering English," which they considered a senseless jargon.—*Stanihurst's Description of Ireland*, 1586, p. 13, and *De Reb. in Hib. Gest.*, 1584.

OL-ḊAN SHEAGHAIN UI THUAMA.

Fonn :—Sean Bhean Chríon an Ḋrantáin.

Ar duine mé ḋíolas liún lá,
'S ċuirios mo ḃuiḋin ċum ran-gáir,
Muna m-beiḋeaḋ aṁáin duine
Am ċuiḋioċtaḋ ḋíolfaḋ,
Is mire ḃeiḋeaḋ ṡíos leis an am-tráiṫ.

Taosgaiḋ ḃúr n-dóiṫin de'n m-bran-dán,
Bhúr n-deoċaḋa ná toṁasaiḋ le ban-láṁ ;*
Tá 'gamsa sgillings,
Le leigion san ḃ-fíon n-glan,
'S as fearr ioná 'n ḃuiḋin ḃíḋeas ag dran-tán.

* *Ban-lamh*, Bandle; a measure two feet long used at country fairs by dealers in frieze, flannel, &c.

O'TUOMY'S DRINKING SONG.

AIR:—"*The Growling Old Woman.*"

THE song which we lay before our readers was written by O'Tuomy amid those festive scenes for which his house was remarkable; and a reply to it, by the witty *Mangaire Sugach*, will be found on the next page.

This pleasing air, though quite common in Munster, has, we believe, escaped the notice of Bunting. Like Moirin Ni Chuillionain, the poets made it a general theme for their effusions, some of which are in our collection, and rank high among the Jacobite class peculiar to the middle of the last century. The circumstance which gave rise to this air is rather singular.

A peasant who had the misfortune to be yoked "for better for worse" to a scolding wife, who never gave him a moment's peace, composed a song to which the air owes its name. The first stanza runs thus:—

"A shean-bhean chrion an drantain,
Ni bhion tu choidhche acht a cam-rann,
Leath-phunt tobac do chur ann do phiopa,
Ni chuirfeach ad chroidhe-si aon t-solas."

"O, you withered, growling old woman,
You never will cease scolding;
A half pound of tobacco to smoke in your pipe,
Would not make your heart merry or joyful!"

I sell the best brandy and sherry,
To make my good customers merry;
But, at times their finances
Run short, as it chances,
And then I feel very sad, very!

Here's brandy! Come, fill up your tumbler,
Or ale, if your liking be humbler,
And, while you've a shilling,
Keep filling and swilling,
A fig for the growls of the grumbler!

Do b'ait liomsa ceólta 'na d-tiom-pán,
Do b'ait liomsa spórt agus bran-dán;
Do b'ait liomsa an gloine
Ag Muirrainn dá líonaḋ,
'S cuideaċta ḟaoiṫe gan ṁeaḃ-rán.

Ag aiṫris eólais na sean-dáṁ,
Carḃas, ól, agus aḃ-rán;
Fuirrion an ġliocais,
Ag imirt na laoiṫe,
Súd mar do ġníḋin-si gaċ ion-tlás.

FREAGRADH AINDRIAIS MHIC CRAITH.

Air Sheáġan Ua Thuama.

Fonn:—"Sean-ḃean Chrion an Drantáin."

Is duine tu ḋiolas liún lá,
Buirinn gan ḃríġ agus bran-dán;
'S ċuireas do ċuidioċtaḋ,
Ar uireasbaḋ cuiṁne,
'S a n-inċinn líontaḋ do ṁeaḃ-rán!

Is deiṁin a rís go meall-ḟáḋ,
Go minic do ḃuiḋin le sleaṁ'nán;
'S go g-cuirir gaċ n-duine,
Ar giodam ċum baoise,
le glugar gan ċríċ, 's le stan-cárd!

Ní'l binneas ad laoiṫe,—ná'd ḟean-dáin,
'S ní milis dar linn do stran-cáin,
Bion iomad do ṫuise
Do ġloine, gan lionaḋ,
'S d'uisge na dríbe ad stan-cán!

I like, when I'm quite at my leisure,
Mirth, music, and all sorts of pleasure.
When Margery's bringing
The glass, I like singing
With bards—if they drink within measure.

Libation I pour on libation,
I sing the past fame of our nation
For valor-won glory,
For song and for story,
This, this is my grand recreation!

ANDREW MAGRATH'S REPLY TO JOHN O'TUOMY.

AIR:—"*The Growling Old Woman.*"

O, Tuomy! you boast yourself handy
At selling good ale and bright brandy,
But the fact is your liquor
Makes every one sicker,
I tell you that, I, your friend Andy.

Again, you affect to be witty,
And your customers—more is the pity—
Give in to your folly,
While you, when you're jolly,
Troll forth some ridiculous ditty.

But your poems and pints, by your favour,
Are alike wholly wanting in flavour,
Because it's your pleasure,
You give us short measure,
And your ale has a ditch-water savour!

Buirinn dá díol mar líon lá,
'S Murrainn dá líonaḋ 'na gann-ċáirt,
Ní sultṁar do'n ḟuirion,
Siḃse dá insint,
Go ruiṫid dá ḃríġ sin ċum ran-gáir!

Is minic do líonuis lom-ċáirt,
'S ċuiris fá ṁaoil í le cúḃar-án;
Do ċuir isi sinne
Gan ċumas ar ṡuiġe,
Ná imṫeaċt san t-sliġe gan tean-tán!

Cia mursanta ṡuiġir a g-ceann cláir,
'S do ċuirfeaḋ tú síos gaċ gann ċáirt;
Muna m-beiḋeaḋ sgillinġ;
Ag duine do ḋíolfaḋ,
Cuirfir do ḃuiḋin ċum stran-cáin!

Tigir go fíor ag lúġ-táil,
A g-coinne gaċ aon dá n-gaḃan sráid;
Gloine má ṫugair,
Do ḋuine gan díol;
San m-bille beiḋ ṡíos air an am-tráiṫ!

Ar imṫeaċt a ris an deaṁan cáirt,
Do ġeaḃaiḋ gan díol, nó geall-tán;
'S as cumaḋ cá h-ionad
A ruiṫfiḋ, cá díg,
Iona d-tuitfiḋ fá ṫrí iona láṁ'cán!

Is é ċluinnim ar ḋís de d' ċam-ċeárd,
Go millid an tír le sleaṁ'nán
Slibiríḋe an Ḋroiċid,
'Gur sib-si go n-díolfaḋ,
Ar ġloine nó trí, ḃúr g-com-pán!

Vile swash do you sell us for porter,
And you draw the cask shorter and shorter;
    Your guests, then, disdaining
    To think of complaining,
Go tipple in some other quarter.

Very oft in your scant overfrothing,
Tin quarts we found little or nothing;
    They could very ill follow
    The road, who would swallow
Such stuff for their inner man's clothing!

You sit gaily enough at the table,
But in spite of your mirth you are able
    To chalk down each tankard,
    And if a man drank hard
On tick—oh! we'd have such a Babel!

You bow to the floor's very level,
When customers enter to revel,
    But if one in shy raiment
    Takes drink without payment,
You score it against the poor devil.

When quitting your house rather heady,
They'll get nought without more of "the ready."
    You leave them to stumble
    And stagger, and tumble
Into dykes, as folk will when unsteady.

Two vintners late went about killing
Men's fame by their vile Jack-and-Gilling;
    Now, Tuomy, I tell you
    I know very well you
Would, too, sell us all for a shilling.

Cuisle mo ċroiḋe na sean-dáiṁ,
Ní h-ionann 's laoiṫe 's meang Sheáġain!
    Mursaire buile,
    Tá ar mire dáiririḃ;
'S a ḃruinniḃ gur líontaḋ d'feall-sán!

AN CNOICIN FRAOICH.

Fonn:—An Cnoicín Fraoiċ.

The Old Bards never vainly shall woo me,
But your tricks and your capers, O'Tuomy,
Have nought in them winning—
You jest and keep grinning,
But your thoughts are all guileful and gloomy!

THE LITTLE HEATHY HILL.

THIS delightful air is a great favorite in Munster; and the *Cnoicin Fraoich* which formed the theme of the bardic muse must be some romantic hill situate in Cork or Kerry. We subjoin the first stanza of the original song, with our own literal translation; and we would feel obliged to any of our Munster friends for a perfect copy:—

" Is ro-bhreagh an tam e air theacht mi na Bealtaine,
Aig feachaint u nun air mo Chnoicin Fraoich;
'S grian-gheal an t-samhraidh aig cur teas is na geamhartha,
'S duilleabhar glas na g-crann a fas le gnaoi;
Bion lacha ann, bion bardal—bion banamh aig an g-crain ann,
Bion searrach aig an lair ann 's leanbh aig an mnaoi;
Bion bradan geal ag snamh ann, san breac aig eirghidhe 'nairde
'San te do bheidheach air phonc bais ann d'eirgheodhach aris!"

" What joyful times! merry May is approaching,
I will gaze over on my little heathy hill;
The summer sun is warming the fields and the corn,
And the foliage on the trees looks blooming and green;
There the mallard and the wild duck sport and play together,
The steed and its rider, the mother and her babe;
The speckled trout and salmon springing in its waters,
And the sick that is dying, health there will find."

AN BHEITH.

Seáġan Ua Tuama, cct.

Fonn :—Béiṫ Eirionn Í.

Am aice cois Máiġ, 'tá'n ṁánlaḋ, ḃéasaċ, ṁín,
Is deise tar ṁnáiḃ, 's as álainn, spéireaṁuil, í;
A carnḟolt táclaċ, breáġ-dear, dréimrioċ, buiḋe,
'S gur b'ísi mo ġráḋ tar ṁnáiḃ, 'bé'n Éire í!

THE MAIDEN.

BY JOHN O'TUOMY.

The subject of this song was a young woman who kept an inn on the banks of the Maig, in the county of Limerick. There is also another song to the same air by Eoghan Ruadh O'Sullivan, of Sliabh Luachradh, in Kerry, beginning.—

" San Mainistir la a d-tigh tabhairne am aonar bhios,
'S beath-uisge ar clar am lathair fein gan suim ;
Do dhearcasa bab thais, mhanladh, mhaordha, mhin,
'Na seasamh go tlath san t-sraid cois taobh an tighe.

" In Fermoy, one day, in an ale-house I chanced to be,
And before me on the table plenty of wines were laid ;
I beheld a babe, soft, comely, mild and meek,
Standing most feeble in the street close by the house."

A maiden dwells near me by Maig, mild, meek to see,
A beauty transcending all speech, all thought, is she ;
Her golden hair floweth like waves along the sea,
O! she is my love and my light, whoe'er she be

AN FREAGRADH AIR AN M-BEITH,

An Mangaire Súgach, cct.

Fonn:—"An Bhéiṫ Eire Í."

Sguir feasda dod' ṗlás, ná tráċt go h-éag a ris,
Ar t-aingir cois Máiġ, cé áluin, spéireaṁail, í;
As fearaċ nár ṫárlaiḋ ad ḋáil-si an ḃéiṫ do ríḋim,
An ḃarr-ḟionn-tais ḃláiṫ do ġráḋas, 'bé'n Eire í!

'Tá a carn-ḟolt cárnaċ, ceásraċ, craoḃaċ, cruinn,
A pearsa uile 'tá gan ċáim, gan taom, gan teiṁiol;
Ní'l maiṫeas le fáġail, ní'l cáil ná méinn a mnaoi,
Naċ feasaċ san m-báb do ġráḋas, bé'n Eire í!

Cé fada le fán me, 's gur ṫárlaiḋ am réic gan ċríċ!
Gan aitios, gan fáġail, gan áird, gan sgéiṁ, gan gnaoi;
'Na ḃ-feacaḋ de ṁnáib níor ṫáṫaiḋ saoġad am ċlí',
Gur ċeanglas páirt le m' ġráḋ, 'bé'n Eire í!

Cé fada le fán me, 's gur ṫárlaḋ óm' ċéill ar baois,
Le taiṫnioṁ do'n m-báin-ċneis ṁánlaḋ, ṁaorḋa, ṁín;
Ní sgarfad go ḃráṫ léi "Bláṫ na Féile," is í,
'Tá m'aice cois Máiġ, is í ġráḋas, bé'n Eire í!

Gluaisig a ċáirde, le gárdas gléastar píb,
Buailig an clár, 's tráġaig go h-éasgaḋ fíon;
Suaṫaig an ċáirt le h-áḋaċt, 's glaoḋaig a ris,
Fae ṫuairim sláinte na mná, bé'n Eire í!

A REPLY TO THE MAIDEN.

BY THE MANGAIRE SUGACH.

AIR:—"*The Maid Eire is She.*"

Have done with your praises! palm not such style on me,
Your maiden may be, if you please, gay, mild, and free—
But she whom *I* love it was ne'er your lot to see,
The beautiful girl of my heart, whoe'er she be!

O! only to gaze on her locks, that reach the knee—
Her loveliest figure, that speaks her high degree,
Nought brilliant or noble hath e'er been met by me,
To match her illustrious worth, whoe'er she be!

Long, long has my lot been as that of a blighted tree,
For Fortune and I, to my woe, could ne'er agree,
But I never till now in my life was made to dree
Such pangs as my darling hath caused me, whoe'er
she be!

Long, long, from one spot to another, in pain I flee—
For love of this fair one I rove o'er land and sea,
The Flower and Queen of all maids in sooth is she,
Who dwells by the meadowy Maig, whoe'er she be!

Then strike up the music, my friends—dull churls are we
If we drain not the goblet of wine right merrilie!
Red cup after cup will we quaff—and this be our plea,
That we drink to the Maid of the Maig, whoe'er
she be!

LEIR-RUATHAR WHIGGIONA.

An Mangaire Súgach, cct.

Fonn:—Plancam Peirḃig.

A ḃile de'n ḟuirion nać gann,
Ba ċurata an am gać cluiṫċe-neirt:
Ná tuigṫear do ṁirneać go fann,
'S a ġoireaċt duit caḃair 's cuideaċta.

Ar osgarḋa ag cosgairt a naṁad,
Le ḟuinnioṁ gać croḃaire cineaḋ-Scoit;
Sgriosfar ar Innis gać Gall,
'S ar sinn a ḃeiḋear teann na ḃ-fionna-Bhroig.

A WHACK AT THE WHIGS.

BY THE MANGAIRE SUGACH.

AIR:—"*Leather the Wig.*"

THE reader has to thank the Whigs for this soul-stirring air, which was never before printed. From the time of the Revolution, this party seem to have been an object of hatred and contempt to the native Irish. The following chorus must be sung after each stanza:—

Will you come plankum, plankum,
Will you come plankum perriwig;
Will you come plankum, leather, and plankum,
Will you come plankum perriwig.

The words "plankum perriwig" mean to thrash with all your might the Wig, which in Irish is synonymous with Whig.

The Jacobite poets of Scotland joined their Irish brethren in reviling the Whigs. The following verses are part of a popular song to one of the most ancient Scotch airs in existence:—

"Awa, Whigs, awa, awa, Whigs, awa,
Ye're but a pack o' traitor loons,
Ye'll ne'er do good at a'.
Our thistles flourished fresh and fair,
And bonny bloom'd our roses;
But Whigs came like a frost in June,
And withered a' our posies.
Our sad decay in kirk and state
Surpasses my descriving;
The Whigs came o'er us for a curse,
And we hae done wi thriving.
A foreign Whiggish loon brought seeds
In Scottish yird to cover;
But we'll pu' a' his dibbled leeks,
And pack him to Hanover."

O, heroes of ancient renown!
Good tidings we gladly bring to you—
Let not your high courage sink down,
For Eire has friends who'll cling to you.

Those insolent Sassenach bands,
Shall hold their white mansions transiently,
Ours shall again be those lands,
Long tilled by our fathers anciently!

As dearḃṫa a d-treasaiḃ an dream,
  Go calma, caḃarṫaċ, coimgníoḋṫeaċ;
Go lonnaṁar, lonnarḋa, lonn,
  Fearḋa, foġlaċ, fuinnioṁaċ.

Beiḋ easbairt go fairsing le fonn,
  A m-Banba, 's Lóġa lá Fheil Muire 'guinn;
Beiḋ "psailm na marḃ" a d-Teaṁair,
  Dá cannaḋ 's gan beann ar Mhinisdir,*

Beiḋ luisne o Dhoire go Leaṁain,
  'S an fuirionn-sa teann, 's teine leó;
Ruiṫfiḋ gaċ mursaire raṁar,
  'S ní coimirc do long, ná Luimneaċ!†

Sin é ċúġaiḃ Pilib tar srúill,
  'S an bile naċ dúr san n-imirios;
Go g-cuirid gaċ mursaire ar lúṫ,
  Fá ḃeannaiḃ a ṡúiste ag *Lucifer!*

A ċumainn na g-cumann glac fonn,
  Tigiḋ d'ár g-caḃair le rine-ġoil;
Ag treasgairt gaċ sean-ṗoc raṁar,
  'S bainfiom-na a meaḃair as cuid aca!

'Tá fuirionn ná cuirfear ar g-cúl,
  Ag druidim le ciúṁais na Sionnainne;
Nuair ṫiocfas an fuirionn tar aḃainn,
  Is deiṁin go b-planc-fam *Whiggiona*!

Beiḋ an ġraṫain dá d-tactaḋ lé tnúiṫ
  Beiḋ basga, 'gus brúṫ', 'gus briseaḋ orra;
Is gairid go g-cacfaid na d-triúr,
  Nuair a ḃainfeas ár b-prionsa cluiṫċe asda!

* Pitt, the Prime Minister of England.

† This is an allusion to the first siege of Limerick in 1690, when that town, although in an almost untenable condition, was held by

We'll muster our clans, and their lords,
  And with energy great and thunderous,
With lances, and axes, and swords,
  We'll trample the Saxon under us!

We'll have masses, as always our wont,
  And sweet hymns chanted melodiously;
'Twill go very hard if we don't
  Make the Minister look most odiously!

We'll have bonfires from Derry to Lene,
  And the foe shall in flames lie weltering—
All Limerick hasn't a green
  Nor a ship that shall give them sheltering.

See! Philip comes over the wave!
  O! Eire deserves abuse, if her
Bold heroes, and patriots brave
  Don't now drive their foes to Lucifer!

Up! arm now, young men, for our isle!
  We have here at hand the whole crew of 'em,
Let us charge them in haste and in style,
  And we'll dash out the brains of a few of 'em!

A tribe who can laugh at the jail,
  Have found on the banks of the Shannon aid—
O! how the blue Whigs will grow pale,
  When they hear our Limerick cannonade!

O! pity the vagabonds' case!
  We'll slaughter, and crush, and batter them—
They'll die of affright in the chase,
  When our valorous Prince shall scatter them!

10,000 Irishmen against 38,500 of the finest troops in the world—Dutch, Huguenots, Danish, German, and British veterans, under William III.—*See O'Callaghan's Green Book*, p. 114, Dub. 1844.

Ag taisdiol na mara le fonn,
 'Tá Carolus ċúġainn 's a ċuiteaċta;
Tá *Neptune* ag sgaipeaḋ na d-tonn,
 'S ní stadfaid an fóġa go h-Inis-Loirc!

Beiḋ *Mars* a d-tosaċ an trúip,
 'S an farraire fionn go fuinnioṁaċ;
Ní ċasfaid go leagfaid an dream,
 'S as dearḃ go b-planncam tuille 'ca!

Beiḋ leagaḋ, 'gus gearraḋ, 'gus brúṫ',
 Beiḋ sgaipeaḋ, 'gus sgannraḋ, 's uireasbaḋ;
Gallaiḃ dá g-caiṫioṁ gan ċaḃair,
 Nuair ġreadfas an Francaċ* teine leó!

Nár ċaillioḋ-sa aṁarc mo ṡúl,
 'S nár lagaiḋ mo lúṫ le foirfeaċt;
Go ḃ-feiceaḋ-sa an ġraṫain-si a b-ponc,
 'S an sean-ṗoc dallt gan giolla aige!

* The frequent allusions to France and Spain throughout these popular songs were the result of the dreadful treatment experienced by the native Irish during the early part of the eighteenth century. Oppressed by penal enactments which proscribed the religion, property, and education of three-fourths of the inhabitants of the island, the old Irish longed for an appeal to arms, and earnestly desired the co-operation of their expatriated kinsmen, whose military achievements in foreign countries had won the admiration of Europe.

Coming over the ocean to-day
  Is Charles, that hero dear to us—
His troops will not loiter or stay,
  Till to Inis Loirc they come here to us!

Our camp is protected by Mars,
  And the mighty Fionn of the olden time,
These will prosper our troops in the wars,
  And bring back to our isle the golden time!

Our cowardly foes will drop dead,
  When the French only point their guns on'em—
And Famine, and Slaughter, and Dread,
  Will together come down at once on 'em!

O, my two eyes might part with their fire,
  And palsying Age set my chin astir,
Could I once see those Whigs in the mire,
  And the blind old goat without Minister!

It is now impossible to calculate what might have been the result if some of the Irish military commanders on the Continent had organized a descent on the coast of Munster while the native population were still labouring under the dreadful penal code.

† *An sean-phoc dall, the old blind buck-goat*, i.e., George III., who became imbecile at the close of his life.

AN BHLÁTH-BHRUINNIOLL.

An Mangaire Súgach, cct.

Fonn:—Cailín Deas Crúiḋte na m-Bó.

As í 'n bláṫ-ḃruinġioll, bláṫ-ṁilis, ḃéasaċ,
Bhláṫ-ṁioċain, ḃéaltanna, ṁoḋaṁuil;
Le gráḋ-geal dá bláṫ-ċruiṫ, do ċéas me,
'S d'ḟág mé gan tréine, gan treoir!
Tá a bláṫ-ḟolt go bláṫ-tiuḃ ar daol-ḋaiṫ,
Is bláṫ-ṡnuiḋte a h-aol-ċroḃ, gan smól,
Is bláṫ-ṫuigseaċ ráiḋte na béiṫe,
'S as bláṫ an uile ġéag di go feóir!

THE FLOWER OF ALL MAIDENS.

BY THE MANGAIRE SUGACH.

AIR:—"*Pretty Girl milking the Cows.*"

WE cannot trace the authorship of this delightful air, but such of our readers as have traversed the "sunny South" of a May morning, and heard it sung by the peasant's ruddy-cheeked daughter, in the milking bawn, or at the cottager's hearth of a winter's evening, after the toil of the day is over, must acknowledge its beauty and tenderness of expression. The words are by the witty Andrew Magrath, surnamed the *Mangaire Sugach.*

To it we are indebted for the source of our greatest enjoyments, a love of the language and poetry of our race.

The following stanza which appears as the "*Ceangal*" ("*Binding*" or "*Summing-up*") to the song—a constant custom with our poets in order to protect their compositions from the ravages of "poetical interpolators"—we forgot putting into the hands of our poet, but now give it a place here:—

"A Chumainn na g-Cumann, mo Chumann 's mo Rogha tu is feas,
Mo Chumann gach Cumann ba Chumann le Togha na m-ban
Is Cumann do Chumann, a Chumainn gan cham, gan chleas,
Mo Chumann do Chumann a Chumainn, 's gabhaim-si leat.

"My Love of all Loves, my Love and my Choice you are,
My Love surpassing all Loves—the Love and the Choice of maids
Your Love is a Love, my Love, without guile or stain,
My Love is Thy Love, my Love; and I take your hand."

O, flower of all maidens for beauty,
Fair-bosomed, and rose-lipped, and meek,
My heart is your slave and your booty,
And droops, overpowered and weak.
Your clustering raven-black tresses
Curl richly and glossily round—
Blest he who shall win your caresses,
Sweet Blossom all down to the ground!

A ġráḋ ḋil do ġráḋ-sa tar béiṫe,
'S do ġráḋḟainn dá m'ḟéidir, ní's mó;
Do ġráḋas tu a ġráḋ ḋil mo ċléib-si,
Le gráḋ dil dod' ṁéinn 's dod' ċló:—
O ġráḋas tu a ġráḋ ḋil le géar-ṡearc,
Do ġráḋ-sa ní ṡéanfad le m' ló;
Do ġráḋ-sa 's mo ġráḋ-sa, má raobtar,
Gan gráḋ ceart ag aoin neaċ go deo!

A rún dil! mo rún tu go n'éagaḋ,
Mo rún-sa le m' rae tu, 's mo stór!
'S gur léigios mo rún leat tar aoin-ḃean,
Mo rún tú 's mo ċéile le m' ló:—
A rún dil na rún g-ceart, ní léigfiod,
Mo rún, tuig, le aon ḃean ad ḋeóiġ,
Do rún-sa 's mo rún-sa má sgéiḋtear,
Gan rún ceart ag aon neaċ go deó!

A ċumainn na g-cumann, ná tréig mé,
'S go ḃ-fuilim a n-éag-ċruiṫ ad ḋeoiġ;
'S gur cumann do ċumann ná tréigfiod,
A ċumainn, go d-tiġeaḋ-sa fá'n ḃ-fód!
O ṫugas duit cumann 's géile,
Mo ċumann-sa a ṡéanaḋ, ní cóir,
'S mo ċumann a ċumainn, má ṫréigir,
Gan cumann ag aoin-ḃean go deó!

A ċarraḋ na g-carraḋ le céile,
Do ċarras le saor-ġean ar d-túis;
Mo ċarraid a ċamaḋ do ṫréigfin,
'S do raċainn a g-céin leat na n-deoiġ!
Ní carraid dam carraḋ, ná céib-ḟionn,
Aċd carraḋ na béiṫe-si am ḃreóġ',
'S mo ċarraḋ-sa a ċarraid, má ṫréigir,
Gan carraid ag aoin-ḃean go deó!

A annsaċt na n-annsaċt do ċéas mé,
Le h-annsaċd dod' sgéiṁ 's dod' ċló;
Bideaċ do róġa 'gad mo ṡaṁuil-si ṁar ċéile,
Nó dumsa gan béasa, gan spórt;—

I have loved you, oh mildest and fairest,
With love that could scarce be more warm—
I have loved you, oh brightest and rarest,
Not less for your mind than your form.
I've adored you since ever I met you,
O, Rose without briar or stain,
And if e'er I forsake or forget you
Let Love be ne'er trusted again!

My bright one you are till I perish,
O, might I but call you my wife!
My Treasure, my Bliss, whom I'll cherish
With love to the close of my life!
My secrets shall rest in your bosom,
And yours in my heart shall remain,
And if e'er they be told, O sweet Blossom,
May none be e'er whispered again!

Oh! loveliest! do not desert me!
My earliest love was for you—
And if thousands of woes should begirt me,
To you would I prove myself true!
Through my life you have been my consoler,
My comforter—never in vain,—
Had you failed to extinguish my dolor,
I should ever have languished in pain!

O fond one! I pine in dejection;
My bosom is pierced to the core—
Deny me not, love, your affection,
And mine shall be yours evermore.
As I chose you from even the beginning,
Look not on my love with disdain;
If you slight me as hardly worth winning
May maid ne'er again have a swain!

O, you who have robbed me of Pleasure,
Will *you*, with your mind and your charms,
Scorn one who has wit without measure,
And take a mere dolt to your arms.

A annsaċt ná sanntaig-si baoṫlaċ,
  Ná stúimpaḋ ná réiġfioċ do ḃrón;
M'annsaċt-sa a annsaċt, má ṫréigir,
  Gan annsaċt ná rae 'gad am ḋeoig!

A stóir ḋil! mo stór-sa tar aon tu,
  Mo stór tú go n-éagfad dar n-dóiṫ;
Is stór mé a stóir-ḋil, gan tréada,
  'S gur dóiṫ leó gur réic me gan fód;
Beiḋeaḋ stór ag am stórac, ni baoġal di,
  Beiḋeaḋ bó-laċt gan baoḋaċas, 's fós,
A stóir-ḋil! do stórac, má ṫréigir,
  Gan stórac ná rae 'gad am ḋeoig!

FASTUIGHIM AN MHANGAIRE SHUGAIG.

Fonn:—"An Beinsín Luaċraḋ."*

A ċarraid ċlúiṁ'úil ḋíograis,
  A ṡaoi ġlain de stoc na n-dáiṁ;
Mo ḃeaṫaḋ ċúġad do sgríḃim,
  No 'n diṫ leat mé ḃeiṫ mar 'táim;—
Gaċ aingir ḋeas 'nar ċuibe liom,
  A cuiṁdeaċt le m' ais, le páirt,
Ní ġlacaċ sí, faraoir me!
  Tan ċíḋ mé gan stoc, gan stáit.

Cia ġeallaim-si do'n ḃuiḋin-si,
  Siġile agus Murrainn ḃláiṫ;
Stair do sgrúda, 's laoiṫe
  Do ṡuiġeaċan mar Oilioll fáiġ!
Cleasaḋ lúṫ go liomṫaḋ,
  'S gaċ niḋ eile riaraċ mnáiḃ;
Is fear gur diúltaḋ is díol dam,
  'Nuair ċíd mé gan ċuid, gan ċáin!

* This beautiful air will be found at page 128.

Your beauty, O, damsel, believe me,
  Is not for a clown to adore—
O! if you desert or deceive me,
  May lover ne'er bow to you more!

Yours am I, my loveliest, wholly—
  O heed not the Blind and the Base,
Who say that because of my folly
  I'll never have wealth, luck, or grace.
How much the poor creatures mistake me!
  I'll yet have green acres and gold;
But, O, if you coldly forsake me,
  I'll soon be laid under the mould!

THE MANGAIRE SUGACH'S PASTIME.

AIR:—"*Little Bench of Rushes.*"

My upright and my noble friend,
  My pure son of the Bardic Race,
To you I unveil my life: oh bend
  Your eyes in pity on my case!
Save from the old and ugly now
  I meet, alas! with no regard;
No gay and fair young maid will vow
  Her heart away to a cashless bard!

In vain I seek to win my way
  With Sighile* and each blooming one—
My merry tale, my gladsome lay
  Fall on their ears as rain on stone.
Mine eyes are bright; I am lithe of limb—
  I think myself a dashing blade;
But all still look askance on him
  The bard, without a stock-in-trade!

* *Sighile*, pronounced Sheela. *Anglice*, Celia.

'Deir Caṫal dúr mac Shíomoin,
  A Shíġile! 'nois tuig an cás?
Gaiḃ-si ċúgad mac Fheiḋlim,
  'S máġaisdir na sgoile fáġ?
Is fearr dúinne Taḋg beag.
  Ná sgain-si de'n ḟuil is fearr;
Gan raiṫ, gan clú, gan oiġreaċt,
  Aċt an ṫuill riaṁ gur ṡloig na ḃráġaid!

Ar ġlac mo ġlaic do sgaoilfin,
  Le h-aoiḃneas gaċ corn tráġaim!
Gaċ bean do ġaḃ am liontaḋ,
  Do ċaoinfin go fliuċ am ḋáin.
Gaċ dailc go pras naċ striocfaḋ
  Le rin-dair a ċorp do ċneaṁain,
'S as Mangaire ait le baois me,
  Cia ṡílid gur b'olc mo ċáil!

Aiṫrisim do'n m-buiḋin-si,
  Cia diṫ leó mo ḋul 'na b-páirt
Ar ċaṫasaḋ gur ḋíolas,
  Le h-aoiḃneas, 's go ḃ-fuilim slán.
Gur b'aiṫnid dam na mílte,
  Go cnaoite ná h-iḃeaċ cáirt,
'S an Mangaire ait naċ cinte,
  Na sgain-si go h-iomlán.

Mo ḃruid! mo ḋuig! mo sgíos-ġuirt!
  Mo sgeiṁle, mo ġoin, mo ġáḋ!
Mo lot do loisg mo ċlí 'nam,
  Ar saoiṫe 's a sliocht ar fán!
Gan ċion, gan ċuid, gan oiġreaċt,
  Gan feiḋim-ċeart, gan coṫram stáit,
'S Tuirc, 's Duirc, 's Daoiṫe,
  Go buiḋionṁar, 's Bodaċáin.*

* *Tuirc*, '*s Duirc*, '*s Daoithe*, '*s Bodachain.*
Turks, Churls, Dunces, and Clowns.
By these epithets the poet designates the Williamite settlers who

And Cathal* Mac-Simon says,—the ass!
  Come, Sighile,† now! you have some sense—
Mac Phelim is your man, my lass!
  That pedagogue has no pretence!
Wed some industrious youth, who shows
  He profits by the lore he learns,
And scout the bard in finest clothes,
  Whose throat engulphs whate'er he earns!

Well! true:—my brain was oft a-whirl
  From whiskey—or, perhaps, the moon!
And if I met a pleasant girl,
  I didn't like to leave her soon.
And if I gave her face a slap
  Whene'er she frown'd, what harm the while?
For I'm a jovial pedlar chap,
  Though some suppose me full of guile!

Some good folks, whom I don't much thank,
  Look down on me—but what of that?
I always paid for what I drank—
  And gave, and still give, tit for tat
I have known a many a screw, and dust,
  That wouldn't buy one drop of drink;
The Jolly Pedlar surely must
  Be better than such sneaks, I think!

But oh! my wound, my woe, my grief,
  It is not for myself or mine—
My pain, my pang without relief,
  Is noting how our nobles pine!
Alas for them, and not for me!
  They wander without wealth or fame,
While clowns and churls of low degree
  Usurp their gold, their lands, their name!

obtained the estates and titles of the Irish Jacobites, after the latter sailed for France in 1691.

* Pronounced *Cahal* (Charles). † *Sighile*, pronounced *Sheela*.

REALTAN CHILL-CHAINNICH.

Aoḋagán Ua Raṫaille, cct.

Atáid éisg ar na srúilliḃ ag léimriḋ go lúṫṁar,
Tá 'n t-Eclips gan fiúntar ag imṫeaċt;
Tá Phoebus ag músgailt 's an t-éasga go ciuin-ġlan,
A's éanlaiṫ na cóige go soiṫiṁ.
'Táid sgaoṫ-beaċaḋ ag túirlinġ, ar ġéagaiḃ is úr-ġlas,
Tá féar agus drúċt ar ár mongaiḃ;
O's céile do'n m-Brúnaċ* í, Réaltan na Múṁan,
'S gaoḋal gar do'n Ḋiuic o Chill-Chainniċ.

Tá biogaḋ ann gaċ táṁ-lag, 's groiḋe-ċnoic go láidir,
'S an n-geiṁriḋ tig bláṫ ar gaċ bile;
Cill Chais ó ṫárlaiḋ, i g-cuiḃreaċ go gráḋṁar,
Le Ríġ Chille h-Airne ár g-Curaḋ;
Ní'l éagcóir dá luaḋ 'guinn, tá faoṫaḋ 'ge trua-ḋaiḃ.
O'n sgéal núaḋ sa luaḋtar le druingiḃ;
Ar ṗéarla óg mná uaisle (a Ḋhe ḋil tabair buaḋ ḋi),
An ċraoḃ ċúbra is uaisle a g-Cill Chainniċ.

Tá'n Rioġ-ḟlaiṫ na gárdaiḃ, ar isliḃ 's ar árdaiḃ,
'S na milte dá ḟáiltiúġaḋ le muirinn;
Tá'n taoide go h-áḋbaraċ, 's coill ġlas ag fás inn,
'S gnaoi teaċt ar ḋántaiḃ gan milleaḋ:—
Táid cuantaḋ ba ġnáṫaċ faoi buan-stoirm ġrána,
Go suaiṁneaċ o ṫárlaiḋ an snuiḋmeaḋ,
Tá cnuastar ar ṫráiġ 'guinn, naċ luasgan an t-sáile,
Ruacain, 's Báirneaċ, 's Ḋillios g.

* This song was written in commemoration of the nuptials of Valentine Browne, third Viscount Kenmare, who married, in 1720, Honoria,

THE STAR OF KILKENNY.

BY EGAN O'RAHILLY.

The fish in the streamlets are leaping and springing,
  All clouds for a time have rolled over;
The bright sun is shining; the sweet birds are singing,
  And joy lights the brow of the lover.
The gay bees are swarming, so golden and many,
  And with corn are our meadows embrowned,
Since she, the fair niece of the Duke of Kilkenny,
  Is wedded to Browne, the renown'd.

The hills are all green that of late looked so blighted;
  Men laugh who for long lay in trouble,
For Kilcash is, thank Heaven, in friendship united
  With Browne of Killarney, our Noble!
Our poor have grown rich—none are wronged or o'er-
    laden,
  The serf and the slave least of any,
Since she came among us, this noble young maiden,
  The Rose and the Star of Kilkenny!

Her Lord, the proud Prince, gives to all his protection,
  But most to the Poor and the Stranger,
And all the land round pays him back with affection—
  As now they may do without Danger!
The ocean is calm, and the greenwoods are blooming,
  As bards of antiquity sung us,
And not even one sable cloud seems a-looming,
  Since he we so love came among us!

daughter of Thomas Butler, of Kilcash, in the county of Tipperary, and great grand-niece of James, first Duke of Ormond.—*Vide* "Burke's Peerage."

Táid uaisle Chill-Airne go suairc ag ól sláinte,
'S buan-ḃíoṫ na lanáṁann a g-cumann ;
Táid suan-ṗoirt 's dánta dá m-bualaḋ ar ċláirsig,
Gaċ suan-ṗort ar áilleaċt, 's ar ḃinneaċt,
Tá claoċloḋ ar ċruaiḋ-ċeirt 's an t-aon cóir ag buaḋ'ċann,
Tá gné-núaḋ ar ġruaḋ'naiḃ gaċ n-duine,
Tá'n spéir ṁór ar fuaimeant, 's an rae fós go suaiṁnioċ
Gan caoċ-ċeó, gan duartan, gan daille.

INGHION UI GHEARAILT.

Aoḋagán Ua Raṫaille, cct.

Fonn :—" Tonn re Calaiṫ." *

A ṗéarla gan sgamal, do léir-ċuir mé a g-caṫaiḃ,
Éisd liom gan ḟearg go n-innsiod mo sgeól !
'S gur faoḃraċ do ċaiṫis gaoṫaḋ 'gus darta,
Tré m' ċréaċtaḋ 'na g-ceaṫaiḃ, do ṁeill mé gan treoir !
Gan ḃréagnaḋ do raċfainn do'n Égipt tar calaiṫ,
'S go h-Éire ní ċasfainn coiḋċe dam' ḋeoin ;
Ar tréanṁuir, ar talaṁ, a n-géiḃionn, a n-aitios,
Níor léan liom a ḃeiṫ farat cois Inse, gan stór !

Is craoḃaċ 's as casda,—'s dréimrioċ 's as dlaṫaċ,
Is niaṁraċ 's as leaḃair,—a dlaoiṫiḃ mar ór !
Is péarlaċ a dearca—mar réaltan na maidne,
Is caol ceart a mala mar sgríoḃ pinn a g-clóḋ;

* We have no recollection of ever having met this air ; but such of our readers as have, will oblige by giving us some information about it.

The Lords of Killarney, who know what the wrongful
  Effects of misrule are, quaff healths to the pair—
And the minstrels, delighted, breathe out their deep songful
  Emotions each hour in some ever-new air.
The sun and the moon day and night keep a-shining;
  New hopes appear born in the bosoms of men,
And the ancient despair and the olden repining
  Are gone, to return to us never again.

THE GERALDINE'S DAUGHTER.*

BY EGAN O'RAHILLY.

AIR: — "*Sea and Shore.*"

A Beauty all stainless, a pearl of a maiden,
  Has plunged me in trouble, and wounded my heart:
With sorrow and gloom are my soul overladen;
  An anguish is there, that will never depart.
I could voyage to Egypt across the deep water,
  Nor care about bidding dear Eire farewell,
So I only might gaze on the Geraldine's Daughter,
  And sit by her side in some pleasant green dell.

Her curling locks wave round her figure of lightness,
  All dazzling and long, like the purest of gold;
Her blue eyes resemble twin stars in their brightness,
  And her brow is like marble or wax to behold!

* Such of our readers as wish to become acquainted with the history of the Geraldines need only consult a work bearing that title, edited by the Rev. C. P. Meehan, for "Duffy's Library of Ireland."

Sgéiṁ-ċruiṫ a leacan aolda mar ṡneaċta,
  Go h-aoraċ ag casṁaint tre lonnraḋ an rós;
Tug Phoebus 'na raṫaiḃ,—tar ḃéiṫiḃ ad t-aṁarc,
  'S t-éadan ar lasaḋ le díograis dod' ċlóḋ !

Is gléigiol a mama,—mar ġéisiḃ cois calaiṫ,
  A h-aolċorp sneaċta is faoileanda snóġ ;
Ní féidir a maiṫios do léir-ċuir a b-pratainn,
  Caoiṁ-lili ċneasda, 's mín-sgoiṫ na n-óg.
Is croiḋeang mar ḃalsam, a déid-ġeal gan aiṫis,
  Do ṡaorfaḋ o ġalar mílte daṁ' ṡórt ;
Saor-ġuṫ a teangan léiġionntaḋ gan stapṫaḋ,
  Bheir tréan-ṗuic tar beannaiḃ le mílseaċtaglór!

Phéinics d'ḟuil Ghearailt,—Gréagaig an ċalaiṫ,
  Séiṁ-ṡiúr ċlanna Mhileaḋ na slóġ ;
Laoċraḋ gan taise, traoċtaḋ le Gallaiḃ,
  Gan tréine, gan talaiṁ, gan ríoġ-ḃrog, gan stór!
Gan ḃréag noċ gur sgagag a b-Paoraig 's a m-Barraig,*
  'S tréan-ċoin Bhunraite ṫríd-sa faoi ḋó,
Ní'l saor-ḟlaiṫ ná dragan do ṗréiṁ ċlainne Chaisil,
  Gan gaoḋal ris an aingir ṁíonlaḋ gan smól.

Ní léir ḋam a saṁuil i n-Eire 'ná a Sagsan,
  A n-éisfioċt, a b-pearsaḋ, a n-intleaċt 's a g-clóḋ.
An ḃéiṫ ċlisde is fearra tréiṫe, 'gus teasdas,
  Ná Helen le'r cailleaḋ mílte san n-gleó!
Ní'l aoin-ḟear na ḃeaṫaḋ d'ḟéaċaċ ar maidin,
  Na h-éadan gan ṁairg, ná sgéiṫfioċ a ḃrón,
Mo ġéiḃion! mo ḋeacair! ní ḟéadaim a seaċain,
  Tré m' néalaiḃ am aislinġ oiḋċe, ná ló!

* *Paoraig agus Barraig*, Powers and Barrys, two ancient and respectable families in the county of Cork.

The Powers are descended from Robert le Paure, or Poer, Marshal to Henry II., from whom, in 1177, he obtained a grant of Waterford, the city itself and the cantred of the Ostmen alone excepted. So early as the fifteenth century the descendants of Le Poer renounced the English legislature, and embraced the Brehon law and Irish customs.

The radiance of Heaven illumines her features,
Where the Snows and the Rose have erected their throne;
It would seem that the sun had forgotten all creatures
To shine on the Geraldine's Daughter alone!

Her bosom is swan-white, her waist smooth and slender,
Her speech is like music, so sweet and so free;
The feelings that glow in her noble heart lend her
A mien and a majesty lovely to see.
Her lips, red as berries, but riper than any,
Would kiss away even a sorrow like mine.
No wonder such heroes and noblemen many
Should cross the blue ocean to kneel at her shrine!

She is sprung from the Geraldine race—the great Grecians,
Niece of Mileadh's sons of the Valorous Bands,
Those heroes, the sons of the olden Phenicians,
Though now trodden down, without fame, without lands!
Of her ancestors flourished the Barrys and Powers,
To the Lords of Bunratty she too is allied;
And not a proud noble near Cashel's high towers
But is kin to this maiden—the Geraldine's Pride!

Of Saxon or Gael there are none to excel in
Her wisdom, her features, her figure, this fair;
In all she surpasses the far-famous Helen,
Whose beauty drove thousands to death and despair.
Whoe'er could but gaze on her aspect so noble
Would feel from thenceforward all anguish depart,
Yet for me 'tis, alas! my worst woe and my trouble,
That her image will always abide in my heart!

The male race of the Powers, Viscounts Decies and Earls of Tyrone, became extinct by the death of Earl James in 1704. His only daughter, Lady Catherine Poer, married Sir Marcus Beresford, Bart., who was created Lord Viscount Tyrone by George II.

The Barrys are descended from Robert Barry, who came over in 1169 with Fitz-Stephen.

AN SEAN-DUINE SEOIRSE.*

An t-Athair William Inglis, cct.

Fonn:—An Seanduine.

Is ro-dhian do sgreadan an sean-duine Seoirse,
O Dhia! Cá rachainn? ní'l agam Hanover;
'Ná fós Hesse Cassel, 'na baile beag cómhgair,
Ná fód mo shean-athrach, táid airicthe, dóighthe!

* This beautiful air, of which we give our readers two different settings, is a great favourite in Scotland, where it is known under the name of "The Campbells are Coming." It owes its birth to the *Mangaire Sugach* (see p. 20).

The song which we now present is the only one we have met to this air, if we except the two versions by the *Mangaire Sugach*, referred to at p. 20, where we gave the opening stanza of one, but omitted the chorus supplied at foot of next page, which should be sung after each verse of the original.

GEORGEY THE DOTARD.

BY THE REV. WILLIAM ENGLISH.

Fonn :—An Seanduine.

Alas for old Georgey—the tool of a faction !
"GOD ! what shall I do ?" he exclaims in distraction.
Not one ray of hope from Hanover flashes—
The lands of my fathers lie spoiled and in ashes !

"Oro sheanduine leatsa ni gheabhadsa,
Oro sheanduine basgadh 'gus breodh ort ;
Oro sheanduine leagadh 'gus leonadh ort,
'S cupla duig ionat chuirfeadh faoi an bh-fod tu !"

"Oh, my old dotard, with you I'll not tarry,
Oh, my old dotard, that the plague may seize you,
Oh, my old dotard, that your doom may soon hasten,
The tomb lies open ready to receive you !"

H

Tá fuadar caṫa go tapa ar bóċnaḋ,
Duaḋ ar ċrannaḋ, agus ar ḟeóltaḋ!
Uaisle Shagsan go h-eaglaċ, óṁanda,
A g-cuanta beiḋ creaċta, 'sa m-bailte beiḋ tóġṫa.

Ní díon dam Breatan, ná féarḟonnaiḃ Fóḋla,
Ní dílis dam Albain ó ġearras a sgórnaċ;*
Ní dílis dam Danair,—ní'l carraid am ċóṁgar,
Fuigiḋ mé marḃ—'s caiṫiḋ faoi 'n ḃ-fód me!

Mo ċiaċ! mo lagar! ní ḟeadar cá n-geoḃaḋ-maoid!
Iarṁar Chalḃin, do ḟeaċain na cóṁaċtaḋ,
A m-bliaġ'na beiḋ 'm basgaiḋṫe, leacaiġṫe, leointe,
'S cliar ċliste Pheadair 's a m-beaṫaḋ go deó 'ca.

Is suairc ar maidin 'na g-cealla, 's am nóna,
Siansna psalm, 's aifrionn glórṁar;
Briaṫraḋ na n-abstal dá g-canna go ceólṁar,
'S an gliaḋaire tan ainim† san m-baile 'gus c'róinn air.

* An allusion to the massacre of the Mac Donalds, at Glencoe, in 1691.

† *Gliadhaire gan ainim* (literally a Hero without name) allegorically, Charles Edward Stuart, of whom it was treason to sing.

The Jacobite bards felt peculiar satisfaction in reviling the house of Hanover. The following is the first stanza of one of the most popular Scotch songs of this period:—

"The thunders of Battle boom over the ocean--
On all sides are Conflict and stormy Commotion;
Black Brunswick is shaken with terrors and troubles,
And the cities are pillaged on Saxony's nobles!

"Nor England nor Eire will yield me a shelter;
And Alba remembers the base blow I dealt her,
And Denmark is kingless—I've none to befriend me—
Come, Death! weave my shroud, and in charity end me!

"But vain is our sorrow, thrice vain our beseeching;
Alas! we forsook the True Church and her teaching,
And hence the o'erwhelming and bitter conviction
Of *her* triumph now and *our* hopeless affliction!"

Yes, George! and a brilliant career lies before us—
The God we have served will uplift and restore us—
Again shall our Mass-hymns be chanted in chorus,
And Charley, our King, our Beloved, shall reign o'er us.

"Wha the deil hae we gotten for a king,
But a wee wee German lairdie?
And when we gade to bring him hame,
He was delving in his kail-yardie;
Sheughing kail, and laying leeks,
Without the hose, and but the breeks;
And up his beggar duds he cleeks,
The wee wee German lairdie."

Hogg's "*Jacobite Relics of Scotland*," p. 83. 1st series. 1819.

SIGHILE NI GHADHARADH

Taḋg (Gaoḋalaċ) Ua Súillioḃáin, cct.

Fonn :—Síġile Ni Ghaḋaraḋ.

Ar maidin a néi is déanaċ do ḃíosa,
Go caṫaċ am aonar ag déanaṁ mo smaointe ;
Do ḋearcas ag pléiríoċt go h-aoraċ am ṫimċioll,
Alaḋ ba ḟéiṁe, ba ċlaoine, ba ċaoine ;
Do ṗreabas, do ruiṫios, do ḋruidios 'na cóir,
Do ṁeasas, do ṫuigios, nár ṁisde ḋam ḟórt,
A blaise go milis a n-iomall a beoil,
Le taiṫnioṁ, le gile, le finne na h-óige,
Le maise, le glaine, le binneaċt a glórṫa.

SIGHILE NI GARA.

BY TIMOTHY O'SULLIVAN (SURNAMED GAODHLACH).

THE first peculiarity likely to strike the reader is the remarkable sameness pervading those Irish pieces which assume a narrative form. The poet usually wanders forth of a summer evening over moor and mountain, mournfully meditating on the wrongs and sufferings of his native land, until at length, sad and weary, he lies down to repose in some flowery vale, or on the slope of some green and lonely hill-side. He sleeps, and in a dream beholds a young female of more than mortal beauty, who approaches and accosts him. She is always represented as appearing in naked loveliness. Her person is described with a minuteness of detail bordering upon tediousness—her hands, for instance, are said to be such as would execute the most complicated and delicate embroidery. The enraptured poet inquires whether she be one of the heroines of ancient story—Semiramis, Helen, or Medea—or one of the illustrious women of his own country—Deirdre, Blathnaid, or Cearnuit, or some Banshee, like Aoibhill, Cliona, or Aine, and the answer he receives is, that she is none of those eminent personages, but EIRE, once a queen, and now a slave—of old in the enjoyment of all honor and dignity, but to-day in thrall to the foe and the stranger. Yet wretched as is her condition, she does not despair, and encourages her afflicted child to hope, prophesying that speedy relief will shortly reach him from abroad. The song then concludes, though in some instances the poet appends a few consolatory reflections of his own, by way of finale.

The present song is one of the class which we have described, and *Sighile Ni Ghadharadh* (Celia O'Gara), in the language of allegory, means Ireland. The air must be played mournfully, and in moderate time.

Alone as I wandered in sad meditation,
And pondered my sorrows and soul's desolation,
A beautiful vision, a maiden, drew near me,
An angel she seemed sent from Heaven to cheer me.
Let none dare to tell me I acted amiss
Because on her lips I imprinted a kiss—
O! that was a moment of exquisite bliss!
For sweetness, for grace, and for brightness of feature,
Earth holds not the match of this loveliest creature!

Is grianṁar, dréimreaċ, niaṁraċ, frainseaċ,
Bhí a carn-ḟolt craoḃaċ, na ṡlaoda a síneaḋ;
Go baċallaċ, péarlaċ, go réaltaċ, go soillseaċ,
Go camarsaċ, craoḃaċ, go niaṁ'raċ aoiḃinn;
Ag feacaḋ, 's ag filleaḋ, 's ag sileaḋ na deoig,
Na m-beartaiḃ, na sraṫaiḃ, 'na muirear go feór,
Go h-altaiḃ, go h-uileaḋ, go friṫir a g-cóṁad,
Go slámaraċ, cumaraċ, omraċ, órḋa,
Na sraṫaiḃ ag tuitim go h-iomallaċ, omraċ.

Do ċaiṫfioċ a ḃ-féadfaċ a réiġtioċ a buiḋinne,
Go banaṁail, saorḋa, go maorḋa, go mionlaḋ;
Go flaṫaṁail, déarcaċ, go séadṁar, go síoṫṁar,
Go rabairneaċ, gaoḋ'laċ, go féastaċ, go fiontaċ;—
Ar ḋragaiḃ, ar ḋrongaiḃ, ar ċóngnaṁ ár leóġan,
Ar lannaiḃ, ar longaiḃ, ar iomarcaḋ slóiġ,
Ar ṁarcaiḃ, ar ġairge, ar ċuraḋ na n-gleó,
Do ċartaċ gaċ sruimile cuirire, crón-duḃ,
Do leag, 's do ṫurraic an iomarcaḋ bróin sinn!

Is eagnaċ, éasgaḋ, do léiġ'fioċ an Bioblaḋ,
Startaċa Chéitinn, 's tréiṫe na n-draoiṫe;
A Laidion 's a n-Gréigis, a d-téxionnuiḃ diaḋaċta,
Le sean'ċas tréanṁar na Trae ṡoir go lioṁṫa.—
Go gasda, go cliste, go h-oilte, go leór,
Go snasda, go snuiġte, go snaimṫe, go móḋaṁuil,
Go h-altaḋ, go h-uileaḋ, go friṫir a g-cóṁard,
'Na g-ceaċdannaiḃ sult-ṁara, lonnarḋa, snóḋa-ṁuil,
A tagairt a tuirse ar uirearbaḋ núaḋċair!

Már carraig a g-céill tú, a n-éifioċt 's a n-inn-tleaċt,
A b-pearsainn, a m-bréiṫriḃ, a ngnéi, 's a ngníoṁ-arṫaiḃ;
Aiṫris dam féin sin an réimionnaiḃ ríogḋa,
A ċarraḋ an tú *Helen*, no Déirdre Naoisi?

Her eyes, like twin stars, shone and sparkled with
lustre;
Her tresses hung waving in many a cluster,
And swept the long grass all around and beneath her;
She moved like a being who trod upon ether,
And seemed to disdain the dominions of space—
Such beauty and majesty, glory and grace,
So faultless a form, and so dazzling a face,
And ringlets so shining, so many and golden,
Were never beheld since the storied years olden.

Alas, that this damsel, so noble and queenly,
Who spake, and who looked, and who moved so serenely,
Should languish in woe, that her throne should have
crumbled;
Her haughty oppressors abiding unhumbled.
O! woe that she cannot with horsemen and swords,
With fleets and with armies, with chieftains and lords,
Chase forth from the isle the vile Sassenach hordes.
Who too long in their hatred have trodden us under,
And wasted green Eire with slaughter and plunder!

She hath studied God's Gospels, and Truth's divine
pages—
The tales of the Druids, and lays of old sages;
She hath quaffed the pure wave of the fountain Pierian,
And is versed in the wars of the Trojan and Tyrian;
So gentle, so modest, so artless and mild,
The wisest of women, yet meek as a child;
She pours forth her spirit in speech undefiled;
But her bosom is pierced, and her soul hath been
shaken,
To see herself left so forlorn and forsaken!

"O, maiden!" so spake I, "thou best and divinest,
Thou, who as a sun in thy loveliness shinest,
Who art thou, and whence?—and what land dost thou
dwell in?
Say, art thou fair Deirdre, or canst thou be Helen?"

D'ḟreagair an bruinnioll a n-dlíġṫiḃ gan ṁóid,
Naċ aiṫne duit mise 'nois, buime na d-treoin ;
Do basgag, do milleag, do cuireag, tar feoir,
Le dalla, le daille, le buile na g-cóbaċ,
Do ṁalartaig mise le duine gan ċóṁḟogus.

Is gairid gur aontaig an *Phœnix* ar insint,
Do laḃarṫa géara na ḋéig sin do ḃíḋ 'guin ;
Go blasda, go bésaċ, go néata, go naoiḋeanda,
Gur b'ainim di Eire boċt ! céile na Stíoḃart ;
Ag trearsgarnaċ, brursgurnaċ, tiubaisdeaċ, d'reoil,
Daṁ ġearraḋ, daṁ iṫeaḋ, daṁ ċreime, daṁ ḋeól,*
Go d-tagaig am ċoinne le cuman, mo stór !
Do leagfas, do briosfios, a n-dlíġṫiḃ 's a g-cóṁaċta,
Do ṡealbaiḋ ionad mo ċloinne le fórsa !

Már caraid duit Séarlus mac Shéamuis, a Ríogain,
Is gairid go d-téarnaiḋ tar tréanṁuir ad ċoiṁ-
deaċt ;
Le gasaraḋ ġléir-ċaṫaiḃ ġaoḋalaċ, ḋeiġ-ġníoṁaċ,
Ag sealbaḋ do ṡléiḃtiḃ, do ċoiṁṫiḃ, 's do ċoilltiḃ,
Ag treasgairt gan tuirsle le tuinsneaċt na
d-treon,
'S ag tasgaḋ na droinge d'ḟúig sinne san m-brón !
Go g-caiṫfior, go g-cluinfior, le fuinnioṁ na slóġ,
A g-caṫraċaiḃ cumais tá tuilte do ṡeoidiḃ,
Do ṫabairt ar ċoimirc do ċumainn 's do ċ'róin-
neaċ.

* Since the arrival of the English, in 1169, the native Irish have suffered much for political and religious offences. They have been massacred (Leland), tortured (Leland), starved to death (Leland), burned (Castlehaven), broiled (Carte), flayed alive (Barrington), sold to slavery (Lynch), compelled to commit suicide (Borlase), and to eat human flesh (Moryson). In one century their properties were four times confiscated (Leland). They were forbidden to re-

And thus she made answer—" What! dost thou not see
The nurse of the Chieftains of Eire in me—
The heroes of Banba, the valiant and free?
I was great in my time, ere the Gall* became stronger
Than the Gael, and my sceptre passed o'er to the
Wronger!"

Thereafter she told me, with bitter lamenting,
A story of sorrow beyond all inventing—
Her name was Fair Eire, the Mother of true hearts,
The daughter of Conn, and the spouse of the Stewarts.
She had suffered all woes, had been tortured and flayed,
Had been trodden and spoiled, been deceived and betrayed;
But her Champion, she hoped, would soon come to her
aid,
And the insolent Tyrant who now was her master
Would then be o'erwhelmed by defeat and disaster!

O, fear not, fair mourner!—thy lord and thy lover,
Prince Charles, with his armies, will cross the seas over.
Once more, lo! the Spirit of Liberty rallies
Aloft on thy mountains, and calls from thy valleys.
Thy children will rise and will take, one and all,
Revenge on the murderous tribes of the Gall,
And to thee shall return each renowned castle hall;
And again thou shalt revel in plenty and treasure,
And the wealth of the land shall be thine without
measure.

ceive education at home or abroad (Irish Statutes). Their language, dress, and religion, were proscribed (ibid.), and their murder only punished by fine (ibid.) They were declared incapable of possessing any property, and, finally, compelled to pay large sums to their worst oppressors (ibid.)

* *Gall*, the stranger; *Gaels*, the native Irish.

SUIRGHE PHEADAIR I DHOIRNIN.

Fonn:—Sliab Féilim.

Aingir ċiuin na g-ciab,
Déinfi liomsa triall,
Air aisdior go Sliab Féilim ?
Mar nár ṫig' 'nár n-diaig,
Carraid 'ná cliar,
'Ná neaċ ar biṫ faoi ċion a m-buairioṁ !
Beiḋeaḋ mé ḋuit am sgiaiṫ,
Chosantaḋ ann gaċ gliaiḋ
A lile mar ġrian ag éirgiḋe.
Mharḃfainn ḋuit mar ḃiaḋ,
An torc-allaḋ 'gus an fiaḋ,
'S ḋéanfain caṫair ḋuit do'n ḟiar-ċraobaig !

PETER O'DORNIN'S COURTSHIP.

AIR:—" *The Hill of Feilim.*"

Sliabh Feilim (the Hill of Feilim, from which this song takes its name) is the largest of a group of hills situated about two and a-half miles north-west of the parochial chapel of Kilcommon, partly in the parish of Abington, in the barony of Owney and Arra; and partly in the parish of Dolla, barony of Upper Ormond, in the county of Tipperary. It rises 1783 feet above the level of the ocean. On the top of it is a curious conical-shaped pile of stones, of the slate kind, about forty feet in height. Its first name was *Sliabh Eibhlin*, from *Eibhle*, the son of *Breogan*, one of the forty chiefs who came to be avenged for the death of *Ith*, as is recorded in the eighth verse of a poem in the *Leabhar Leacan* (Book of Leacan, col. i., fol. 288, beginning *Seacht mic Breoguin*, &c. (Seven Sons of Breogan, &c.)

Within the last twenty years several urns, containing bones, were discovered by a peasant named Tierney, near a *Leaba Dhiarmuid 's Ghrainne* (the bed of Diarmuid and Grainne), on the townland of Knockeravoola, parish of Upperchurch, about four miles east of this mountain.

Sliabh Feilim is now called *Mathair Sleibhe* (*i. e.*, Mother, or Parent mountain), from the fact of its being the largest of the surrounding hills, on which also are many *Crom Leacs* now to be seen. At Ahon Mor, there is a *Crom Leac*. At Cnocshanbrittas, there are two *Crom Leacs*, and a *Giant's grave*. At Logbrack, a *Leaba Dhiarmuid 's Ghrainne*. At Cnoc *na Banshee*, a *Crom Leac* and pillar stone. At Grainiva, a *Crom Leac*.

Maid of the golden hair!
Will you with me repair
    To the brow of the Hill of Feilim?
Whither we go shall know
Neither a friend nor foe,
    Nor mortal being nor fairy—
I'll guard and shield you there,
I'll banish from you all care,
    O, Lily, that shine so paly
I'll slay for you the deer,
And for you, my love, I'll rear
    A bower of roses daily!

Dá d-téiġin-si leat siar,
Go talaṁ ṡíl m-Brian;
Is iad mo ṁacnaiḋ beiḋ 'm ḋiaiġ go buarṫa!
Níor aibiḋ mo ċiall,
Níor b-fearaċ ḋam riaṁ,
Ceannaċ ná díol do ḋéanaṁ!
B'olc ár n-gnóḋ ar ṡliaḃ
Feilim, gan biaḋ.
Mun a b-faġamaois aċd fiaḋ fioḋḃa!
Chuirfin a b-facaḋ riaṁ,
Go n-goilfin mo ṫriall,
Sul a g-cóṁnuiġinn ann bliaġain do laeṫiḃ!

A ċuisle! 'gus a stóir!
Ná ceisniḋ go deó,
An faid ṁairfios mo ṁór-léiġion liom,
Is deas do ċuirfin bróg,
'S culaiṫ do'n t-sróll,
'S as stuamaḋ ar gaċ sórt saor me.
Chuirfin long duit faoi ṡeól,
Ní'l ealaḋan dam naċ eól,
Beagán di ar dóiṫ a ḋéanaṁ;
'S ná ceisniḋ-si go deó,
Go d-tuitfiḋ orrainn brón,
Ar mullaiċ sléiḃ mór Féilim!

O ṫárlaiḋ go b-fuil tú stuamaiḋ,
Ar gaċ ealaḋan dá g-cualais,
Is é ṁeasaim-si gur cluain Ṁhuiṁneaċ! *
Chuirfeáḋ orm dá n-gluaisfin,
Leat do'n tír úd ṡuar,
A b-fad ó m' ċuaird ṁiosa.

* A Momonian trick.

Could you give me your plighted hand,
And lead me to Brian's land,
'Tis my kin that would be wailing!
For knowledge of worldly ways
I merit but slender praise—
I am always falling and failing.
Sad, should we fare on the hill
With nothing to cook or kill—
Though I never much fancied railing,
I should bitterly curse my fate
To stop there early and late
In trouble for what I was ailing.

My *Cuisle*,* my life and soul,
Give up your heart's deep dole!
For nought shall trouble or ail you—
'Tis neatly I'd make full soon
For you silk dresses and shoon,
And build you a ship to sail in.
There's not a trade in the land
But I thoroughly understand—
And I see its mystery plainly;
So, never at all suppose
That lives like ours would close
On the brow of the Hill of Feilim!

O! cajoler from the South,
'Tis you have the girl-winning mouth!
Momonia's arts are no fable!
Long, long, I fear, should I rue
My journey to Munster with you
Ere the honeymoon were waning

* *Cuisle*, pulse. *Cuisle mo chroidhe*, Pulse of my heart.

Mo ṫaḃairt ó ṫuairim,
An baile úd a b-ḟuairis,
    Macnas gan fuaċt, 's aoiḃneas,
B'ḟearr ḋam fuireaċ uait
A n-aice na g-Cruach,
    'Ná ḃeiṫ ag filleaḋ óm' ruaig ḋíoṁaoin!

A ċuisle! 'gus a stór,
Is deise fá ḋó,
    Na *Helen* le'r leónaḋ an tréin-ḟear!
Gur binne liom go mór,
'Nuair ċluinim guṫ do ḃeól,
    Nó seinneaḋ do ṁeór ar ṫéadaiḃ.
Triall liom ann-sa ród?
Ná fulang mé a m-brón!
    A lile, 's gur tu ḃreoiḋ 's ḃuar' me!
Gheaḃair imirt agus ól,
Do roġa do'n uile ṡórt,
    Ar mullaiċ sléiḃ mór Féilim!

Tá do ġeallaṁnaḋ ró ṁór,
Le na g-cóiṁlionaḋ go deo,
    A radaire, ḃreóiḋ agus ḃuar me!
Imirt agus ól,
Meaḋair agus spórt,
    Do ġnoḋṫaiḋ-si, 's do ṁór-léaġan!
Mar ḃiḋ mise ró óg,
Ba ṁaiṫ leat me ṫaḃairt,
    A b-ḟad óm' ṁór-ġaoḋaltaiḋ!
Imṫeaċt leat san ród,
An áit naċ aiṫneóċain neaċ beó,
    Ar mullaiċ sléiḃ mór Féilim!

You would take me away from the sight
Of the village where day and night
    They banqueted and regaled you.
Begone, deceiver, begone!
I'll dwell by the *Cruach's* alone,
    And not on the Hill of Feilim!

My *Cuisle*, my beaming star!
Twice lovelier, sure, you are
    Than Helen, of old so famous.
No music ever could reach
The melody of your speech,
    So sweet it is and enchaining.
O! hear me not so unmoved!
O! come with me, Beloved!
    'Tis you, indeed, who have pained me!
Your choice of every sort
Of banqueting and sport
    You'll have on the Hill of Feilim!

Ah! no more of your promises, cheat!
You tell me of things too sweet,
    I know you want to betray me.
By pleasure, and mirth, and joy,
Ah! though you seem but a boy,
    Your learning would soon waylay me!
Because I am innocent and young,
You have wheedled me with your tongue
    Afar from those who would claim me,
To travel with you the road
Where I'd know no soul or abode
    To the summit of the Hill of Feilim!

A ḃruinnioll gan smuaid,
Nár meallaḋ le cluain,
  A réalt-eólais mar ġrian ag éirġiḋ!
Ġeaḃair meaḋair ar d-túis,
Séis gan ċúṁaḋ,
  Le gaḋar-ċoin ċiuin, ḃéil-binn.
Biaiḋ d'eaċraiḋ ar lúiṫ,
Leatsa ċum siúḃail,
  Chum geataiḋe gaċ Dúna raobaḋ;
Le h-aitios do'n ċúis,
Le sparsaiḋ caoin, dlúiṫ,
  Ar d'aisdior go dúiṫċe Fhéilim!

A ċiuin-ṁarcaig ṡéiṁ,
Is neaṁ-ṁeónaċ, réiġ,
  A ċannas do ċéim liomṫa?
Dá g-cluinfeaḋ an ċléir,
Go m-biaḋmaois a g-céin,
  Sgarfaiḋe ó ċéile a raon sinn!
Má ṫiġeaḋ tusa a g-céin,
Le feaḃas do ṁór-léiġin,
  Ġeaḃair cuiṁdeaċt ó'n g-cléir naoṁṫa;
Biaiḋ mise liom féin
'S mo ṁacnaiḋ gan réim,
  Ag filleaḋ 's mé 'm aonar coiḋċe!

A ċuisle rúin mo ċléiḃ,
Ná ceisniḋ go h-éag,
  Go ḃ-fillfeaḋ tú leat féin ad t-aonar!
Ġeaḃair cuideaċta ó'n g-cléir,
Biaiḋ tu a g-cumann na naoṁ,
  'S ní h-eagal duit céim ḋúrtain!
Ma ċreidion tú mo sgéal,
Is ró-ġearr go m-béiḋir,
  'S do ṁacnaiḋ ar réim ḋiomsaċ;
Ar eaċraiḋ ciuin séiṁ,
Ag brosdúġaḋ do ċuiḋ gaḋar,
  Mar *Paris* ar ṡliaḃ *Ida*.

O! Damsel, O, purest one!
O! morning star like the sun!
    No soul could mean you betrayal!
You will know all pleasures on earth—
We'll revel in music and mirth,
    And follow the chase unfailing!
All over the neighbouring ground
You will spur your palfreys round,
    The nobles on all sides hailing!
As happy as the Blest you'll be,
And pleasantly live with me
    For your visit to the Hill of Feilim!

O! Cavalier, meek and brave!
Of mind so noble and suave!
    Have you, then, no fear as a layman?
If here we plighted our troth,
By the Church we should speedily both
    Be brought to the chancel's railing!
Yet, still, if you leave me alone,
And depart to another zone,
    Where your learning will glow so flaming,
I cannot but weep and mourn
For I never shall see you return
    To the pleasant high Hill of Feilim!

O! Pulse and Life of my soul,
Abandon your ceaseless dole,
    You'll never be left a-wailing;
Our priests and the saints of Heaven
Will never behold you bereaven,
    So fear not slander or fables.
O! only believe my tale,
And you, of the race of the Gael,
    Will again rise proud and famous—
You shall gallop on bounding steeds
Over hills and dells and meads,
    As the heroines of olden ages.

Naċ me ḃeiḋ millte go deó,
Dá d-téiġinn leat san ród,
  Do neaṁ-ċead mo ṁór-ġaoḋaltaḋ;
Gan capall, gan bó,
Gan ciste, gan stor,
  Aċd beaġán beag do lón éadaiġ;
Gan caraid am ċóir,
Maidion ná nóin,
  'S tusa beiṫ ar an nós céadna;
Nuair a ċruinneóċaḋ an ceó,
Tuitfimíd a m-brón,
  Ar ṁullaċ sléiḃ mór Féilim!

A ċóm seang séiṁ,
An úr-ċroiḋe réiġ,
  Rug bárr ar an saoġal le crionnaċt;
Is leanbaḋ an focal béil,
A ċeangalfaḋ sinn a raon,
  Naċ ḃ-faġfaiḋe go h-éag ár sgaoileaḋ:
Ní'l aon neaċ faoi 'n n-gréin,
Naċ ḃ-faġaḋ tú an éadan,
  Mór-ċuid dá ṁéinn sgrioḃṫa;
Aiṫreas ort dá m-béiḋeaḋ,
Go d-tiocfaḋ an t-éag,
  Fuasgailt od' ṗéinn ní ḃ-faġaḋ tu!

But, woe is me! if I leave
My kindred at home to grieve
'Tis bitterly they will blame me!
O! what a fate will be mine,
Without gold, or gear, or kine,
Or a single friend to stay me!
And you, too, night and morn,
Would meet but Poverty and Scorn.
When it came on dark and rainy
Oh! where should we find a friend—
Our sorrows would never end
On the brow of the Hill of Feilim!

Mild maid of the slender Waist—
Chaste girl of Truth and Taste,
Excelling all other maidens,
What a few sweet Words of Life
Would make us man and wife,
With happiness never waning!
I gaze on your lovely brow,
And from Eve's bright day till now
The soul shines out in the features.
O! only take me as yours,
And as long as Life endures
My Love, it is you shall sway me!

MOIRIN NI CHUILLIONNAIN.*

Tá sgamal duiḃ 's ceó draoiḋeaċt',
  Ná tógfuiġear go bruinn' an ḃráṫ'!
Air ḟearann ḟairsing, ḟód-ċloinn,[1]
  O ṡeóil CRIOSD an fuirionn smáil:—
Tar sleasaiḃ mara ag tóruiġeaċt,
  Le gleó-cloiḋiṁ do ċuir ar fáġan!
Ar n-dragain ṁeara, ṁór-ḃuiḋean,
    O Mhóirín Ní Chuillionnáin!

D'easgaḋ an ṗeacaḋ, fa-rior!
  Do ṡeoil sinn faoi ḋliġṫiḃ náṁad;
Gan flaṫas Airt ag pór Gaoiḋeal;
  Gan seoid puinn, gan cion, gan áird!—
'S gaċ báṫlaċ bracaċ, beól-ḃuiḋe,
  Do'n ċóip ċríon do ruiṫ tar sáil,
A g-ceannas flaiṫ, 's a g-cóiṁṫiġear,
    Le Mhóirín Ní Chuillionnáin!

Do ḋearcas neaċ ar ċló 'n aoil,
  Do ró-linn ó neaṁ am ḋáil;
'S d'aiṫris dam go beól-ḃinn,
  Gan ró-ṁoill go d-tuitiḋ pláiġ:—
Air *Amsterdam* na seól slim,
  Ar Sheón Stiall† 's ar Philib Sáill,
'S nár ḃ-fada ceart na Seóirsiḋe,
    Air Mhóirín Ní Chuillionnáin!

* I copied this song from a MS. of 1732, now in the possession of Sir William Betham.

† *Seon Stiall* (John Steele), *Pilib Saill* (Philip Sall), two obnoxious characters.

MOIRIN NI CHUILLIONNAIN.

A gloomsome cloud of trouble,
  A strange, dark, Druidic mist,
Lowers o'er Fāil * the noble,
  And will while Earth and Time exist.
Across the heaving billows
  Came slaughter in the wake of Man—
Then bent our Chiefs like willows,
  And fled Moirin Ni Chuillionnain!

Alas! our sad transgressions
  First brought us under Saxon sway,
The power and the possessions
  Of Eire are the Guelphs' to-day.
The churls who crossed the surges
  Six ages back, and overran
Our isle, are still the scourges
  Of mild Moirin Ni Chuillionnain!

I saw, in sleep, an Angel
  Who came, downward, from the moon,
And told me that some strange ill
  Would overtake the Dutchman soon.
On Amsterdam's dammed city
  On Steele and Sall their lies a ban;
'Tis God, not George, can pity
  Our poor Moirin Ni Chuillionnain!

* *Innisfail*, one of the names of Ireland—*the Isle of Destiny*.

AISLING CHONCHUBHAIR UI RIORDAIN.

Fonn:—An Spealadóir.

Tráṫ 's tréiṁse ṫaisdiolas,
Aṁ ṫiṁċiollaiḃ saoġail ;
O Ráṫ Loirc* tré gaċ aċaran,
Go laoi-ṡruiṫ† a n-éisg ;
Go d-tárlaiḋ a n-gaorṫaḋ gleanna glais,
Na b-feaḋḃa réiḋ nár ċrapaiġṫe,
Ba ḃreáġṫaḋ sgéiṁ dá b-feacaḋ-sa,
De ċoillṫiḃ na g-craoḃ !

* *Rath Loirc*, Charleville.

CONOR O'RIORDAN'S VISION.

AIR :—"*The Mower.*"

CONOR O'RIORDAN, author of this song, was a native of West Muskerry (Muscraidhe), in the county of Cork, and flourished A. D. 1760. He followed the occupation of parish schoolmaster in his native district, whence he obtained the appellation of "*Conchubhar Maister*" (Conor Master), by which he is better known at this day, and from which many of his compositions, current among the peasantry of Cork, take their name. He had a son named Peter, who "lisped in numbers," but not with that inspiration which fired the father's poetic muse. He followed the profession of his father, and went by the name of *Peadair Maister* (Peter Master), but we cannot tell when, or where, either of the Riordans closed his earthly career.

The present song is adapted to the air of a pleasing pastoral love ballad of great beauty, very popular in the south, of which the following is the first stanza:—

"Ata paircin bheag agamsa,
Do bhan, mhin, reigh;
Gan cladh, gan fal, gan falla lei,
Achd a h-aghaidh ar an saoghal;
Spealadoir do ghlacfainn-si,
Ar *task* no d'reir an acradh,
Be aco sud do b'fearr leis,
No padh an aghadh an lae."

"A little field I have got,
Of smooth meadowy lea;
Without a hedge, a wall, or fence,
But exposed to the breeze;
A mower I would hire on task,
Or by the acre, if it pleased him best,
Or if either would suit him not,
I'd pay him by the day."

Once I strayed from Charleville,
As careless as could be;
I wandered over plain and hill,
Until I reached the Lee—
And there I found a flowery dell
Of a beauty rare to tell,
With woods around as rich in swell
As eye shall ever see.

† *Laoi-Shruith.* The river Lee.

Gáir ar ġéagaiḃ cantannaḋ,
　　Ba ḃinn, ṁioċair, séis;
Breáġṫaċt sgéiṁ, 's daṫannaḋ,
　　Ar gaċ mion-alt de'n ḟéar;
Luċt páise, péinne, 's peannaide,
Gearrṫaḋ créaċt, 's galaraig;
A g-cás go d-tiġeaḋ ar dear'mad,
　　Le h-aoibneas na n-éan.

Do ṫárlaiḋ taom dá ḋeasgaḋ ḋam,
　　Le'r ṡinear go faon!
Is gearr gur éirgiḋ aisling ḋam,
　　Le'r ḃiogus tar éis,
Tháiniḋ réaltan ṁalla-roisg,
Ba ċáblaċ, craoḃaċ, casda-foilt;
'S páirde caoċ na h-aice 'ci,
　　Do ṁeallfaċ an saoġal!

Is gráḋṁar, séiṁ, do ḃeannaiḋ ḋam,
　　An cruinn-ġiollaḋ caoċ!
'S a láṁ gur léig ar armaiḃ,
　　An rín-ċoilg ġéar!
Do ráiḋ an ḃéiṫ go carṫannaċ,
Cur deárnaḋ fae na ċeal'gaiḃ;
Gráin mo ċléiḃ a ḋartaire,
　　Ar do ṡaiġeadaiḃ, ná déin?

A ġráḋ, a laoġ, 's a ċarraid ċumainn,
　　Ḋiograis mo ċléiḃ!
Ná fág mé n-éagmais t-ainime,
　　Le h-innsint tar h-éis!
Ḋáilid Eire 's Banba,
Clár Loirc Eibear gairmid,
Cé 'táimse d'éis na b-fearra-ċon,
　　Gan ċuiṁneaḋ! gan ċéill!

Wild birds warbled in their bower
    Songs passing soft and sweet;
And brilliant hues adorned each flower
    That bloomed beneath my feet.
All sickness, feebleness, and pain,
The wounded heart and tortured brain
Would vanish, ne'er to come again,
    In that serene retreat!

Lying in my lonely lair,
    In sleep medreamt I saw
A damsel wonderfully fair,
    Whose beauty waked my awe.
Her eyes were lustrous to behold,
Her tresses shone like flowing gold.
And nigh her stood that urchin bold—
    Young Love, who gives Earth law!

The Boy drew near me, smiled and laughed,
    And from his quiver drew
A delicately pointed shaft
    Whose mission I well knew;
But that bright maiden raised her hand,
And in a tone of high command
Exclaimed, "Forbear! put up your brand,
    He hath not come to woo!"

"Damsel of the queenly brow,"
    I spake, "my life, my love,
What name, I pray thee, bearest thou
    Here or in Heaven above?"
—"Banba and Eire am I called,
And Heber's kingdom, now enthralled,
I mourn my heroes fetter-galled,
    While all alone I rove!"

Is gearr gur éirgiḋ sean'ċas,
D'ár g-cointinn a raon ;
Ag casaṁ tréad na ranna suilt,
Dá n-diog' as an saoġal,*
Gan tráċt ar sgéal, ná eaċtraḋ,
Acd clára faoḃair 's spealanaḋ,
Bánta réiḋ 'gus aċarainn,
'S Innseaċaḋ féin !

Tá 'gaṁ sgéal le h-aiṫris,
'S innsim duit é ;
Gur gearr go réiġfeaḋ an t-Aṫair-Mhac,
De ġeiṁleaċaiḃ Gaoḋail ;
Tá garda laoċ fá armaiḃ,
Go dána ag teaċt tar fairge,
Ní gáḋ ḋiḃ téarmaḋ ar ṫalaṁaiḃ,
'S ná coingṁiḋ ḃúr léis?

Beiḋ lá tar éis go h-aiṫreaċ
Ag daoiniḃ na g-claon !
Arsaċt, léiṫeaċt, craipiḋṫeaċt,
'S crinneaċt a téaċt !
An bás mar ċéile leapṫaḋ 'ca,
'S as grána gné an ṗeacaḋ orra ;
A láṫair Dé gaċ ain'ḃeart,
Dá n-gníoṁarṫaiḃ le léaġaḋ !

Táim cráiḋte ag béarlaḋ Sagsannaċ,
San tír ar gaċ taoḃ !
'S táid na Gaoiḋeil cóṁ gangaideaċ,
'S a n-inntin is claon !
Lán do ṫréiġṫiḃ mallaiġṫe,
Gan táḃaċt a n-déirc, ná g-carṫannaċd,
'S grása Dé go n-dearmaid,
Le díograis do'n t-saoġal !

* Here the poet laments the persecutions suffered by his brethren of the bardic profession at this period; because of the exposure which they made of the delinquencies of state officials and men in authority,

Together then in that sweet place
In saddest mood we spoke,
Lamenting much the valiant race
Who wear the exile's yoke,
And never hear aught glad or blithe,
Nought but the sound of spade and scythe;
And see nought but the willow withe,
Or gloomy grove of oak.

"But hear! I have a tale to tell,"
She said—"a cheering tale;
The Lord of Heaven, I know full well,
Will soon set free the Gael.
A band of warriors, great and brave,
Are coming o'er the ocean-wave;
And you shall hold the lands God gave
Your sires, both hill and vale.

"A woeful day, a dismal fate,
Will overtake your foes,
Grey hairs, the curses of deep hate,
And sickness and all woes!
Death will bestride them in the night—
Their every hope shall meet with blight,
And God will put to utter flight
Their long-enjoyed repose!

"My curse be on the Saxon tongue,
And on the Saxon race!
Those foreign churls are proud and strong,
And venomous and base.
Absorbed in greed, and love of self,
They scorn the poor:—slaves of the Guelph,
They have no soul except for pelf.
God give them sore disgrace!"

they were looked upon as the greatest evil the supreme power had to contend with.

AN CHUILFHIONN.

Fonn :—An Chúil-Fhionn.

A ḃ-ḟacaḋ tú an Chúil-ḟionn 's í ag siúḃal ar na bóiṫre,
Maidion ġeal drúċta 's gan smúit ar a bróga;
Is iomḋa ógánaċ súil-ġlas ag tnúṫ le í ṗósaḋ,
Aċd ní ḃ-ḟaġaḋ siad mo rún-sa ar an g-cúntas is dóiṫ leó.

A ḃ-ḟacaḋ tú mo ḃábán, lá breáġ 's í na h-aonar,
A cúl dualaċ, dris-leánaċ, go slinneán síos léiṫe;
Mil ar an óig-ḃean, 's rós breáġ na h-éadan,
'S as dóiṫ le gaċ spriosán gur leanán leis féin í!

A ḃ-ḟacaḋ tú mo spéirḃean 's í taoḃ leis an toinn,
Fáinniḋe óir ar a méaraiḃ 's í réiḋtioċ a cinn;
Is é dúḃairt an Paoraċ ḃí 'na ṁaor ar an loing,
Go m'ḟearr leis aige féin í, 'ná Eire gan roinn!

THE CUILFHION.

THE Coolun, or *Cul fionn*, literally means *The maiden of the fair flowing locks*. In Hardiman's "Irish Minstrelsy," vol. i. p. 251, will be found another version of this song in six stanzas, with a translation by Thomas Furlong, the original of which has been attributed to Maurice O'Dugan (*Muiris Ua Duagain*), an Irish bard who lived near Benburb, in the county of Tyrone, about the middle of the seventeenth century, but is probably of much greater antiquity.

The air of this song is by many esteemed the finest in the whole circle of Irish music, and to it Moore has adapted his beautiful melody "Though the last glimpse of Erin with sorrow I see."

The three stanzas here given are all that we have been able to procure, after a diligent search in Munster, where our version is in the hands of every peasant who has any pretensions to being a good songster.

Have you e'er seen the Cuilfhion when daylight's declining,
With sweet fairy features, and shoes brightly shining?
Though many's the youth her blue eyes have left pining,
She slights them, for all their soft sighing and whining.

Have you e'er on a summer's day, wandering over
The hills, O, young man, met my beautiful rover?
Sun-bright is the neck that her golden locks cover—
Yet each paltry creature thinks *she* is his lover!

Have you e'er seen my Fair, on the strand, in her bower,
With gold-ringed hands, culling flower after flower?
O! nobly he said it, brave Admiral Power,
That her hand was worth more than all Eire for dower.

MOIRIN NI CHUILLIONNAIN.

Tomás Meic Coitir, cct.

Cia h-í an ḃean! nó an eól díḃ,
  Do seólaiḋeaḋ anois am láiṁ?
Thrg ciall na ḃ-fear air mór-ḃaois,
  Ba ḋóiġ linn naċ tiocfaid slán:—
Glan-ḃiaḋ 'gur searc na n-óg í,
  'S stór-croiḋe gaċ n-duine an ḃáb,
Geal-ġrian na m-ban air ló í,
        Móirín Ní Chuillionnáin!

'Tá "Ghlaḋaire Caṫa"* air deóraiḋeaċt,
  San Eórup fá ċomairc ċáich:
Do'n ġrian-ḟuil Alban ṁór-ríoġ,
  'Gur fós, ní ḃ-fuil fuil is fearr;—
San m-bliaḋain re fear naċ dóiṫ linn,
  Le fórsaiḋiḃ go h-Innis Fáil;
Beiḋ'n triaṫ-si teaċt ag tórnġeaċt,
        Air Mhóirín Ní Chuillionnáin!

Beiḋ 'n Ríoġ-ḟlaiṫ aguinn pósda,
  Gan mór-ṁoill i n-Innis-Fáil;
'S clíar ag teaċt o'n Róiṁ leis,
  A g-cóir guiḋe eision ḃeiṫ slán:—
Déanfaḋ áċt an ṁór-ġrinn,
  Ag tórnġeaċd air ċuid na mná;
'S ní iarrfaiḋ aċt trí c'róinníḋe,*
        Le Móirín Ní Chuillionnáin!

* *Tri Coroinnidhe. Three Crowns, i. e.*, of Ireland, England, and Scotland.

MOIRIN NI CHUILLIONNAIN.

BY THOMAS COTTER.

But who is she, the maiden,
  Who crossed my path but even now?
She leaves men sorrow-laden,
  With saddest heart and darkest brow.
O! who she is I'll tell you soon—
  The pride of every Irishman—
Our heart, our soul, our sun, our moon—
  Is she—Moirin Ni Chuillionnain.

A great and glorious warrior
  Is now struggling fierce in fight—
And yet will burst the barrier
  That severs Ireland from the light!
He will combine each scattered host—
  He will unite each creed and clan—
Ah, yes! we have a Queen to boast,
  In our Moirin Ni Chuillionnain!

Hurrah! hurrah! I see him come—
  He comes to rescue Inisfail—
And many myriad priests from Rome
  Will aid him—for, he cannot fail!
Search hamlets, villages, and towns,
  Tempt all the best or worst you can,
But, ere twelve moons go by, Three Crowns
  Will deck Moirin Ni Chuillionnain!

AN BEINSIN LUACHRADH.

Fonn :—Beinsín luaċraḋ.

Lá dá raḃas go h-uaigneaċ,
  Ag dul suas go Conntae an Chláir ;*
Mo ġadairín beag go h-uaiḃreaċ
  Ag ual-puirt, 's mo ġun am láiṁ ;
Cia casfaiḋe orm aċt stuaiḋ-ḃean,
  Na gruaige finne, gile, breáġa ;
'S aḋḃar beinsín aice buainte,
  De'n luaċair ba ġlaise d'ḟás.

* See note, page 130.

THE LITTLE BENCH OF RUSHES.

THIS song will be found at p. 334, vol. 1, of Hardiman's "Irish Minstrelsy," where it is left untranslated. The meaning of the word "*Beinsin*" (little Bench) is mistaken by some of our most eminent writers, who suppose it to mean a *Bunch*. In the days of our boyhood it was a general custom with the peasantry to go on midsummer's eve to the next bog, and cut a *beart luachra* (a bundle of rushes), which would be as much as a stout lad could carry home on his back; and this they strewed on benches of stones made for the purpose outside their cottages, where the youth of the neighbourhood spent the evening in their usual pastimes. The custom generally prevailed in our own day, but probably has now died away. The heroine of this song must have been on an excursion of this kind, in "milk-white Clare," and from the simplicity of the language, it appears to be the composition of an early period.

Monsieur Boullaye Le Gouz, who travelled through Ireland in the middle of the seventeenth century, tells us that " Les Irlandois ornent leur chambres de iong, dont ils font leur lits en eté, et de paille en hiver, ils mettent un pied de iong autour de leur chambres, et sur leur fenestres, et plusieurs d'entr'eux ornent leur planchers de rameaux.—"*Les Voyages et Observations du Sieur Boullaye Le Gouz.* 4to. A Paris, 1657. 476.

One day I journeyed lonely
  Along the road to milk-white Clare,
My dog beside me only,
  My gun in hand, and free from care;
When, lo! I met a maiden
  Of bright and golden shining hair—
With greenest rushes laden,
  To make a bench—this fairest fair!

A ċailín big na luaċraḋ,
An léigfeáḋ do ḃeart ar lár;
No a d-tiocfáḋ liom an uaignios,
Faoi ḃruaċ na coille is glaise bláṫ?
Sagairt ní ḃ-faġaiḋ sgéal air,
Ná aon neaċ dá ḃ-fuil le fáġail;
Go d-tiocfaḋ caint do 'n ċéirseaċ,
'S Gaoiḋeilge do 'n lon-duḃ breáġa!

A ċailín big na luaċraḋ,
Glac suaiṁnios 's fan go réiḋ
Ní cáil duit a ḃeiṫ uaiḃreaċ,
An uaigneas 's tú leat féin!
Má sgaip mé do ċuid luaċraḋ,
Is dual go ḃ-fuil cuid tar h-éis,
Bainfiod beinse mór ḋuit,
A's ualaċ mar ṫuille léis.

The County of Clare is proverbial for its bad buttermilk; as may be seen by the following quatrain illustrative of the peculiarities of four southern counties, from which our poet gave it the appellation of "milk-white Clare."

Conntae an Chlair na blathaighe breine
Conntae Chiarraidhe ag flafruighe a cheile
Conntae Chorcaighe is gortaighe n-Eire
'S Conntae Luimne ag piocu na deise.

The County of Clare, of the stale buttermilk;
The County of Kerry, of brotherly love;
The County of Cork, the hungriest in the land;
And the County of Limerick, gleaners of the corn-fields.

"O girl of greenest rushes,
  This burden suits you not too well—
I fain would spare your blushes,
  But come with me to yonder dell:
The priests will never know it,
  Until the songful, soulful thrush
Speak Gaelic as a poet,
  The blackbird from the greenwood bush.

"My darling girl, my own dear,
  Don't pout, but lay your rushes by,
You know you are here alone, dear,
  And have no friend to help you nigh.
I've tossed your rushes rather,
  But more remain uncut behind—
And I'll hie off, and gather
  For you a larger bench, you'll find."

With respect to Cork—we find the following stanza in reference to the town of Bantry, in Angus O'Daly's Satires.

Tri h-adhbhair far sheachain me,
Duithche Bheanntraighe 's Bheara ;
Croinmhil bhoga gan bhlas,
Cuibhreun fada 'gus anglais.

Three reasons there were why I lately withdrew
  In a hurry from Bantry,
  Its want of a pantry
Was one; and the dirt of its people was two.
  Good Heavens! how they daub and bespatter
Their duds! I forget the third reason. No matter.

CAITILIN NI UALLACHAIN.

Uilliam Dall Ua h-Earnáin, cct.

Fonn :—Caitilín Ni Uallaċáin.

Measamaoid, naċ calm rin, do'n ḃrairt san Sbáinn,
Aċd mealla slíġe, ċum caṫa cloiḋiṁ, do ṫabairt a
d-tráiṫ ;
Béiḋ Galla a rís, dá leagaḋ síor, le lúṫ ár láṁaiḃ,
Agss mac an Ríġ, ag Caitilín Ni Uallaċáin !

CAITILIN NI UALLACHAIN.

BY WILLIAM HEFFERNAN (THE BLIND).

SEVERAL imperfect versions of this song are already before the public, and were we not anxious to preserve the best copy, we might pass it over in silence. *Caitilin Ni Uallachain* (Catharine Holahan) is another of those allegorical names by which Ireland is known in Irish song; and for an account of the author, *Uilliam Dall O'Hearnain* (William Heffernan, the Blind), we have only to refer our readers to p. 92 of our "Reliques of Irish Jacobite Poetry." With respect to the prefix "*Ni*," used before surnames in the feminine gender, we may quote the following extract from Conor Mac Sweeny's "Songs of the Irish," No. VI., where he says, "It is proper here to warn Irish ladies that they commit a blunder in writing their names with *O* or *Mac*, instead of *Ni*. They should bear in mind that O'Neill, Mac Carthy, O'Loghlen, O'Connell, are not surnames like the English Baggs, Daggs, Scraggs, Hog, Drake, Duck, Moneypenny, &c., but simply mean *Son of Niall*, *Son of Connell*, *Son of Loughlin*, &c., as the Jews say, Son of Judah, Son of Joseph, &c., and that a lady who writes *O* or *Mac* to her name calls herself son, instead of daughter. What should we say of a Hebrew lady who should write herself 'Esther *Son* of Judah?' and yet we do not notice the absurdity in ourselves. I therefore advise every Irish lady to substitute *Ni*, pronounced *Nee*, for *O* or *Mac*. Julia Ni Connell, Catharine Ni Donnell, Ellen Ni Neill, will at first sound strange, but they are not a whit less euphonious than the others, and use will make them agreeable. In Irish we never use O or Mac with a woman's name, and why must it be done in English?"

Fully coinciding in these observations of our esteemed friend Mr. Mac Sweeny, we adopt the prefix "*Ni*," in preference to the *O* in surnames of the feminine gender, throughout this book.

In vain, in vain we turn to Spain—she heeds us not.
Yet may we still, by strength of will, amend our lot.
O, yes! our foe shall yet lie low—our swords are
drawn!
For her, our Queen, our *Caitilin Ni Uallachain!*

Geallaim díb, naċ fada a rís, gur buaḋarṫa an ġáir,
Ag arm faobair, dá g-ceapaḋ linn, 's sradar láṁaig;
Is tapa cruinn do ṗreabfamaois, 's as buacaċ, árd,
Dá m-beiṫ mac an Ríġ, ag Caitilín Ní Uallaċáin!

Is fada sinn, ag faire air, le fuasgail d'ḟáġail,
Nár stalairiḋe, gan balcaisiḋe, 'ná luaḋ 'nár láiṁ;
Beiḋ barca líonta air barra taoide, 's fuaim air sáil,
Le mac an Ríġ, ċum Caitilín Ní Uallaċáin!

Ná measadaois, gsr caile ċíor, ár stsaire stáid,
Ná caillíċín, 'na g-crapadaois, a cuaill-beag cnáṁa;
Cia fada luiġe ḋí, le fearaib ċóiṁṫeaċ, gan suaiṁneas d'ḟáġail,
Atá sáiṫ an Ríġ, a g-Caitilín Ní Uallaċáin!

Is fada a dlaoiṫe, casda cíorṫa, 's a sguab-ḟolt bán,
'S a dearca rín, ag aṁarc Gaoiḋeal, cois cuanta breáġ;
Is blasda binn, do ċanan sí, gur buan ḃíos páirt,
Idir ṁac an Ríġ, 'gus Caitilín Ní Uallaċáin!

Ná measadaois, na sprealairiḋe, gur buan ár b-páis,
'S gur gearr a ḃíd, na glasa a sgaoile, 'nuair is crraiġ an cás;
Go n-deárnaḋ Dia, roiṁ ṗobul *Israel*, de'n mór-ṁuir tráiġ,
'S go ḃ-fóireaḋ an Ríġ ort, a Ċaitilín Ní Ualla-ċáin!

Yield not to fear! The time is near—with sword
in hand
We soon shall chase the Saxon race far from our
land.
What glory then to stand as men on field and bawn,
And see all sheen our *Caitilin Ni Uallachain!*

How tossed, how lost, with all hopes crossed, we long
have been!
Our gold is gone; gear have we none, as all have
seen.
But ships shall brave the Ocean's wave, and morn
shall dawn
On Eire green, on *Caitilin Ni Uallachain!*

Let none believe this lovely Eve outworn or old—
Fair is her form; her blood is warm, her heart is
bold.
Though strangers long have wrought her wrong, she
will not fawn—
Will not prove mean, our *Caitilin Ni Uallachain!*

Her stately air, her flowing hair—her eyes that far
Pierce through the gloom of Banba's doom, each like
a star;
Her songful voice that makes rejoice hearts Grief
hath gnawn,
Prove her our Queen, our *Caitilin Ni Uallachain!*

We will not bear the chains we wear, not bear them
long.
We seem bereaven, but mighty Heaven will make us
strong.
The God who led through Ocean Red all Israel on
Will aid our Queen, our *Caitilin Ni Uallachain!*

A Mhuire dílis! a ċarad ċaoin-ruisg, gaċ uair nár
  b-páirt,
Agal Iosa! ar son na n-Gaoiḋeal-boiċt, is cruaiġ
  an cás!
Luċt an ísbirt, do ċur ar díbirt, ár stuaire mná,
'S a céile fír-ċeart, do ṫeaċt tar taoide, gan
  buairt na dáil!

Ceangal.

Tá gné ġlan air *Phoebus*, 's lonnraḋ ṫriḋ,
Tá an rae 'gus na réalta a g-cúrsa ċruinn;
Tá na spéarṫa fá sgéiṁ-ġlan, gan smúit, gan
  téiṁiol,
Roiṁ Réx ceart na féinne, 's a ṫrúp tar toinn.

Tá ár g-cléire a g-caoiṁ-ġuiṫ, a súil le Críost,
'S ar n-éigsi go réimeaċ, 's a g-cuṁa dul díoḃ:
Gaoḋail boċt Innis Eilge, go súgaċ, síoḋaċ,
Roiṁ Shéamus* ṁic Seamuis, 's an Diuic tar
  toinn.

* In the first stanza, the poet alludes to the regal honors paid James Francis Stuart, at Madrid, in 1719, when Cardinal Alberoni and the Duke of Ormond planned the expedition to Scotland in his favour. He committed a fatal mistake in not making a descent upon Ireland where the old Irish and northern Presbyterians were most anxious to have "The auld Stuarts back again."

O, Virgin pure! our true and sure defence thou art!
Pray thou thy Son to help us on in hand and heart!
Our Prince, our Light, shall banish night—then
beameth Dawn—
Then shall be seen our *Caitilin Ni Uallachain !*

SUMMING-UP.*

Phœbus shines brightly with his rays so pure,
The moon and stars their courses run;
The firmament is not darkened by clouds or mist,
As our true king with his troops over the ocean comes.

Our priests are as one man imploring Christ,
Our bards are songful, and their gloom dispelled;
The poor Gael of Inis-Eilge in calm now rest
Before James,† the son of James, and the Duke‡
who over ocean comes.

Had he accomplished his design of sending the Duke of Ormond and General Dillon to Ireland, the Irish government could not have sent the troops to the Duke of Argyle, which dispersed the Scotch Jacobites in 1716. *Hooke. Stuart Papers.*

* We have given a literal translation of these two stanzas, as Mr. Mangan omitted to versify them.

† The Chevalier de St. George.

‡ James, second Duke of Ormond.

FAILTIUGHADH RIGH SEARLUS.

Uilliam Dall, cct.

THE HUMOURS OF GLYN.

A Pháḋraig na n-árrann! a g-cluin' tú na gárrṫa,
  A g-cluinir an plé-ráca,* an siosmaḋ, 's an gleo?
Ar ċualais mar ṫáiniġ go cóige Ullaḋ an gárda,
  Thurot† na ṡláinte le h-iomarcaḋ sgóip!

* *Ple Raca* means a row, such as would occur in a country shebeen house. It is derived from *ple*, contention, and *raca*, an

A WELCOME FOR KING CHARLES.

BY WILLIAM HEFFERNAN (THE BLIND).

AIR:—"*Humours of Glynn.*"

THIS air is very popular in the town and vicinity of Clonmel. The Glynn, from which it takes its name, is a small romantic country village, situated at either side of the Suir, midway between the towns of Carrick and Clonmel.

Having, from our infancy, heard this air traditionally ascribed by the peasantry of the district, to a celebrated piper named Power, a native of the locality, we, some time ago, wrote to John R. O'Mahony, Esq., of Mullough, for information on the subject, and the following extract from his letter will probably satisfy our readers.

"Glynn," says Mr. O'Mahony, "was more than a century ago the residence of a branch of the Powers, to which family it still belongs. One of them, Pierse Power, called *Mac an Bharuin* (the Baron's Son, for his father was the '*Barun*,' or Baron, of an annual fair held here), was celebrated as a poet and musician; and there is a tradition among his descendants, that he was the author of the popular air of 'The Humours of Glynn.'"

O Patrick, my friend, have you heard the commotion,
The clangor, the shouting, so lately gone forth?
The troops have come over the blue-billowed ocean,
And Thurot commands in the camp of the North.

epithet by which a country public house is known among the natives.

† Commander Thurot (whose real name was O'Farrell) and Colonel

Preab! bíḋ ad ṡeasaṁ! glac meanṁnaḋ 's bíoga 'nois?
  Griosaig na seaḃaic-si ad t-aice ċum spóirt,
Beiḋeaḋ puicíḋe dá séide le cloiḋeaṁ a m-beiḋeaḋ
    faoḃar air,
  'S racam a n-éinfeaċt faoi ḃrataiḃ ár leóġain.

Eisdig a ġaoḋail-ḃoiċt 'tá cráiḋte 'ge méirlig,
  Glacaig ḃúr d-tréan-airm gairge 'n-ḃúr n-dóid,
Bioċ *Hurrah* go súgaċ! anois o tá 'n prionnsa
  'S a ġárdaiġe go dúbaltaḋ ag tarraint 'n-ḃúr
    g-cóir?
Hurroo gan doċmaḋ! bioċ deoċ ar an m-bórd
    agaiḃ,
  Suigíḋe go socṁaḋ le soiliḃios ceoil?
Tá'n báire ag ár muintir, 's an lá 'co ar an
    naṁaide,
  'S go bráṫ beiḋ ár saoiṫe ag imirt 's ag ól.

Atá 'n Rúta* sa láidir más fior gaċ a ráiḋtear,
  An croḃaire ceann-árd 's a ḃuime gan ḃrón;
Seoirse go lán-lag—'s *Cumberland* cráiḋte,
  Pitt ann sa *Pharliament* caite air a ṫóin!

Cavenac landed with 700 French troops near Carrickfergus in 1760, according to the old song—

> "The twenty-first of February, as I've heard the people say,
> Three French ships of war came and anchored in our bay;
> They hoisted English colours, and they landed at Kilroot,
> And marched their men for Carrick, without further dispute."

They immediately took possession of the town, and remained in it for five days, after which they sailed away, having obtained the supplies of provisions and water, for which they had landed.

On the 28th the French vessels were attacked and captured, off the Isle of Man, by three English frigates, commanded by Captain Elliot.

Up, up, to your post!—one of glory and danger—
  Our legions must now neither falter nor fail:
We'll chase from the island the hosts of the Stranger,
  Led on by the conquering Prince of the Gael!

And you, my poor countrymen, trampled for ages,
  Grasp each of you now his sharp sword in his hand!
The war that Prince Charlie so valiantly wages
  Is one that will shatter the chains of our land.
Hurrah for our Leader! Hurrah for Prince Charlie!
  Give praise to his efforts with music and song;
Our nobles will now, in the juice of the barley,
  Carouse to his victories all the day long!

Rothe marshals his brave-hearted forces to waken
  The soul of the nation to combat and dare,
While Georgy is feeble and Cumberland shaken,
  And Parliament gnashes its teeth in despair.

Thurot was killed in the action, after a most heroic but ineffectual defence against a vastly superior force. The contemporary ballad tells us that,—

> "Before they got their colours struck, great slaughter was made,
> And many a gallant Frenchman on Thurot's decks lay dead;
> They came tumbling down the shrouds, upon his deck they lay,
> While our brave Irish heroes cut their booms and yards away.
> And as for Monsieur Thurot, as I've heard people say,
> He was taken up by Elliot's men, and buried in Ramsey Bay."

This affair has been greatly misrepresented. Thurot merely landed to procure provisions, as his men were almost starved, having only one ounce of bread daily to live upon.—M'Skimmin. "*Life of Thurot*," by T. C. Croker.

* One of the Rothes of Kilkenny, then in the French service.

Na *Heelans* * dá d-tarraingt faoi ṗlaidiḃ na d-triúsannaiḃ
'S a b-píbionaḋ fada dá spreaga ċum ceoil,
Rainnce ar gaċ maol-ċnoc—le h-áṫus na sgléipe;
Ag cur fáilte roiṁ Sḣéarlus a baile 'na ċ'róinn.

As é 'n ríġ-ráḋ dáiríre é—an plé-raca, 's an t-aoiḃ'neas,
An sgéal breáġa le n-innsint faid ṁairfiom gaċ ló;
Na cóbaig go claoiḋte—gan fóiṫ'rin, gan fionta,
Gan ceólṫaḋ, gan saoiṫe, gan bailte, gan lón!
Raobaig gaċ Galla-ṗoc,—leagaig 's rúsgaig iad,
Cuirig as talaṁ búr n-aiṫreaċ an ċóip,
Tá Seoirse 's a ṁuintir go brónaċ lag claoiḋte,
'S c'róinn na d-trí ríoġaċda ní ċasfaidgo deo!

AN BHAIN-TREABHACH 'S AN MHAIGHDION.†

As maiġdion 's as bain-treabaċ do rinn Dia go h-óg diom,
Ni binn liom an ċreiḋill-si gabail timċioll mo nuaḋċair;
Ba bean-ṗósda ar maidin mé, o'n Eaglais ċoṁaċ-taċ,
'S as bain-treabaċ m'ainim ar ṫeaċt do'n tráṫ-nóna.

* *Heelans*, the Highlanders.

† We cannot trace the author, or rather the *authoress*, of this song. That it was composed during the campaign of King James in Ireland

The lads with the dirks from the hills of the Highlands
Are marching with pibroch and shout to the field,
And Charlie, Prince Charlie, the King of the Islands,
Will force the usurping old German to yield!

O, this is the joy, this the revel in earnest,
The story to tell to the ends of the earth,
That our youths have uprisen, resolving, with sternest
Intention, to fight for the land of their birth.
We will drive out the Stranger from green-valleyed Erin—
King George and his crew shall be scarce in the land,
And the Crown of Three Kingdoms shall he alone wear in
The Islands—our Prince—the Man born to command!

THE VIRGIN, WIFE, AND WIDOW.

A virgin...and widow...I mourn lone and lowly,
This morn saw me wedded, in God's Temple holy,
And noontide beholds me a lorn widow weeping,
For my spouse in the dark tomb for ever lies sleeping.

need not be questioned. According to the highest authority on that portion of our history, it cost England nearly eighteen millions sterling to overcome the 1,200,000 Irish who took up arms in 1689. *Macariæ Excidium*, edited for the *Irish Archæological Society*, by *J. C. O'Callaghan*.

Tá smúit ar mo ċroiḋe-si ná sgaoilfeaḋ go h-éag de,
Feaḋ ḃeiḋeaḋ drúċt ar na gleanntaḋ, ná ceó ar na sléiḃte ;
Tá cóṁraḋ dá snioṁ ḋuit go caoin deas de'n ċaol dair,
Is é mo lá brón an ċreiḋill-si* dá innsint gur éagais !

Is deas do ṫiocfaḋ cloiḋeaṁ ḋuit ar marcaiġeaċt ar ċaoil-eaċ,
Nó ag séide na h-aḋairce 's do ġaḋair-ḃinne air faoṫar ;
Ṫógfáḋ an ceó ḋe m'intinn 's tú ar ḃeinn-ṁaoil an t-sléiḃe,
Agus áireóċamaoid uainn tú lá buailte Ríġ Séamus !

Is mór mór é m'eagla go ḃ-fuil do ṁuintir a ḃ-fuarán liom,
Mar nár liuġas 's nár sgreadas nuair ċonairc an ḟuil uasal !
D'ḟéaċ tú tar ais orm a ḋian-ġráḋ le truaġ ḋam,
Aċd d'imriġeag an feall ar mo annsaċd an uair úd !

Mo ṁallaċt ḃéarfainn d'aoin-ḃean na m-beiḋeaċ beirt ḟear dá h-iarraḋ,
Ná déanfaċ a diṫċioll gan aon aca riaraḋ ;
Mar is áilleán fír cailce ar ċaill mé mo ċiall leis,
'S fear breáġa-deas ná grána ní ġráiḋfeaḋ ad ḋiaig-si !

* *Creidhill*, death-bell, knell.

On my heart lies a cloud, and will lie there for ever.
Hark! hark to that death-knell that dooms us to sever.
Oh! well may my eyes pour forth tears as a fountain,
While dew gems the valley or mist dims the mountain.

King James mourns a hero as brave as e'er breathed—
O! to see him, when mounted, with bright blade unsheathed,
Or high on the hill-side, with bugle and beagles,
Where his foot was a deer's and his eye was an eagle's.

I shrieked and I cried when his blood gushed like water,
But treachery and baseness had doomed him to slaughter.
He glanced at me fondly, to comfort and cheer me;
Yet his friends love me not, and they never come near me.

Accurst be the maid who can smile on two lovers!
Around me the shade of my lost husband hovers,
And oh! never more can I think of another,
Or feel for a lover save as for a brother!

The first stanza of this poem bears a great resemblance to the following, from Gerald Griffin's beautiful verses on "The Bridal of Malahide."

"Ye saw him at morning,
How gallant and gay!
In bridal adorning,
The star of the day:
Now weep for the lover—
His triumph is sped,
His hope it is over!
The chieftain is dead!

But, oh for the maiden
Who mourns for that chief,
With heart overladen
And rending with grief!
She sinks on the meadow
In one morning's tide,
A wife and a widow,
A maid and a bride!"

SLAINTE RIGH SEARLUS.

Eóġan Ruaḋ Ua Súilleaḃáin, cct., A.D. 1783.

Fonn :—Seáġan O'Duiḃir an Ghleanna.

Mo ċas! mo ċaoi! mo ċeasnaḋ!
An fáṫ ṫug claoiḋte an easbaḋ!
Faiġe, draoiṫe, 's sagairt,
  Daiṁ agus cléir!
Gan dáin da ríoṁ le h-aiṫios,
Gan ráiḋte grínn dá g-cannaḋ;
Gan sáṁ-ċruit bínn dá spreagaḋ,
  A m-bán-ḃrogaiḃ réiḋ!

A HEALTH TO KING CHARLES.

BY EOGHAN O'SULLIVAN (THE RED).

AIR:—*John O'Dwyer of the Glyn.*

THIS Jacobite relic by *Eoghan Ruadh*, is adapted to the well-known air of *Seaghan O'Duibhir an Ghleanna*, of which the original song, with a translation by the late Thomas Furlong, will be found at p. 86, vol. ii. of Hardiman's "Irish Minstrelsy."

Colonel John O'Dwyer, for whom the song was composed, was a distinguished officer who commanded in Waterford and Tipperary, in 1651, but after the capitulations, sailed from the former port with five hundred of his faithful followers for Spain.

The O'Dwyers were a branch of the Heremonians of Leinster, and possessed the present baronies of Kilnemanach, in Tipperary. From an early period they were remarkable for their courage, and after the expatriation of the old Irish nobility, several of the family distinguished themselves abroad in the Irish Brigade. In the last century General O'Dwyer was governor of Belgrade, and Admiral O'Dwyer displayed great bravery in the Russian service.

Source of lamentation!
Bitter tribulation,
That I see my nation
   Fallen down so low!
See her sages hoary,
Once the island's glory,
Wandering without story
   Or solace, to and fro.

Gaċ ráib d'ḟuil Mhílið ċeannais,
Láiḋir, laoċda, ṫapa;
Ba ġnáṫaċ rainceaċ, raṫaċ,
  Lán-oilte air faoḃar!
Gan stát, gan buiḋean,* gan fearann,
Ann is míle measaḋ
Na Seáġan Ua Duiḃir an Ghleanna,
  A ḃeiṫ fágṫaḋ gan *Game!*

Tráiṫ a raoir am leabaḋ,
Ag cásaṁ diṫ† na seaḃac;
Tháiniḋ sguim gan sgaipeaḋ,
  O láṁaiḃ *Morpheus!*
Faoi'm ḋáil go sílteaċ, seasgair,
Táṁaċ, tím, gan taise,
D'ḟág me air ḋíṫ mo ṫapaiḋ
  'Gus d'árdaig mo neul!
Gan spás a tíġeaċt do ḋearcas,
Fáingeaċ ġrínn tre m' aisling,
Go h-áluinn, íogair, aibig,
  Táite le m' ṫaoḃ.
'S gur ḃreáġṫaḋ línn, gan bladar,
Sgáil 's aoiġir a leacan;
Ná'n ṁánlaḋ ṁin‡ le'r cailleag
  Gárda na Trae!

Ba ċáblaċ, cíorṫa, casda,
Táclaċ, dlaoiṫeaċ, daṫaċ,
Sgáinneaċ, trinseaċ,§ fada,
  Fáingeaċ go feur,
A bláṫ-ḟolt ḃinneaċ, leaḃair,
Cárnaċ, bíseaċ, snamaċ;
O árd a cinn na n-dlaṫaiḃ,
  Táiṫ-leaḃair, léi.

* Readings in other copies—maoin. † éag.
‡ Helen. § Frainnseaċ.

Mileadh's* offspring knightly,
Powerful, active, sprightly,
They who wielded lightly
  Weighty arms of steel,
Left with no hopes higher,
With griefs ever nigher,
Worse woes than O'Dwyer
  Of the Glens could feel!

Last night, sad and pining,
As I lay reclining,
Sleep at length came twining
  Bands around my soul;
Then a maiden slender,
Azure-eyed, and tender,
Came, me dreamt, to render
  Lighter my deep dole.
Fair she was, and smiling,
Bright and woe-beguiling;
Vision meet for wiling
  Grief, and bringing joy.
None might e'er compare her
With a maiden fairer—
O! her charms were rarer
  Than the Maid's of Troy.

Like that damsel's olden
Flowed her tresses golden,
In rich braids enfolden,
  To the very ground;
Thickly did they cluster
In a dazzling muster,
And in matchless lustre,
  Curled around and round.

* *Mileadh*, pronounced *Meeli*, Milesius.

Bhí sgáil na g-caor' air lasa,
Tre ḃáine an liṫ 'na leacain;
Mándaċt, míne, 's maiseaḋ,
  Táite 'na sgéiṁ!
'S a sáiṁ-rosg rín le'r ċealg,
Táinte laoiċ gan tapaḋ!
Sásta 's ionann mala
  Ard-ṡnuiḋte, caol.

A bráġa mar ġnaoi na h-alann,
An tráṫ do luiġean air aḃainn;
Nó snáṁ na taoide mara,
  Air ḃán-ṫonnaiḃ tréan,
A bán-ċroḃ aolda, leaḃair,
Is sáṁ do ríṁeaċ air ḃrataiḃ;
Cága, míoltaḋ, seannaig,
  Róinte 'gus éisg.
Cárnaḋ 's coiṁeasgair seaḃac,
Gáir na g-cloiḋeaṁ dá n-greada,
Bláṫ na g-craoḃ 's ealta,
  A m-bárr-ċluṫair géag,
'S gur ḟáiṁe linn gaċ airde,
'S dáin gan fuiġeall dá g-cannaḋ;
A ráiḋtiḃ grinn le blaise
  Ná sáṁ-ċruit *Orpheus!*

Táim, ar sí, le sealad,
Fágṫaḋ air diṫ mo ċarrad;
Faoi ṫáir ag drioḋar Danar,
  D'árdaig mo leun!
Gan ċáin, gan ċríċ, gan ċeannas,
Gan árus ríġ mar ċleaċtas,
Gan táin, gan buiḋean, gan fearann,
  Ardaċt,* ná réim!

* Ard-ṁeas.

The red berry's brightness,
And the lily's whiteness,
Comeliness and lightness,
  Marked her face and shape.
She had eye-brows narrow,
Eyes that thrilled the marrow,
And from whose sharp arrow
  None could e'er escape.

Her white breasts were swelling,
Like the swan's while dwelling
Where the waves are welling
  O'er the stormy sea;
And her fingers, pat in
Broidering upon satin
Birds at early matin
  Warbling on the tree,
Fishes, beasts, and flowers,
Fields, and camps, and towers,
Gardens, lakes, and bowers,
  Were so fine and white!
Wandering through the mazes
Of her lyric phrases,
I could chant her praises
  All the day and night!

"O! thou land of bravery!"
Cried she, "sunk in slavery,
Through the tyrant knavery
  Of the stranger foe—
Tribeless, landless, nameless,
Wealthless, hostless, fameless
Wander now thine aimless
  Children to and fro.

Ani ċráin boċt ċnaoite, ċaite
Ag tál go fuiġeaċ o'n ḃallaiḃ,
Air áḋal gaċ daoiste d'aicme,
  Shátan, gid' claon!
'S go bráṫ ní cuiḃe ḋuit laḃairt,
Páirt ċum grinn do ṫaḃairt;
Le m'áirioṁ d'ḟuiġ'leaċ airm,
  Gárda agus maor.

Dar Párán, diḃ do ṁeasas,
Gur plás gaċ níḋ do laḃair;
Mar ḟál ó'n n-gníoṁ 'nar ḃeartas,
  Páirteaċ ḃeiṫ léi;
Gan spás do'n ríoġ gur aiceas,
Fáṫ a tíġeaċt dam aice,
A rás, a craoiḃ, 's a h-ainim,
  Farraḋ a béas.
D'éis lán-toċt caoi gur aiṫris
Arr na saoiṫe* ṡnamaig;
An áitreaḃ críċe Chaisil,†
  Cháiġ, ċumaisg, léi.
'S tar sáil go sgiordfaḋ aicme,
Dhána, ḋíomsaċ, aibiġ,
A craḋ 'sa ḋíoṫ-ċur Danar,
  Ḋána, as a réim.

* The total extirpation of the Irish natives was strongly advocated in the English political pamphlets of the seventeenth century. One of them, printed at London, in 1647, contains a tirade against the Irish too brutal for quotation, and concludes by invoking an imprecation on all who would not make their swords "starke drunk with Irish blood." Two years afterwards, Oliver Cromwell observed this advice so religiously, that his name among the Irish peasantry is still synonymous with murder, ruin, and desolation.

† In 1647, Cashel was sacked by the Earl of Inchiquin's troops.

Like a barren mother
Nursing for another
Cubs she fain would smother,
So feel I to-day.
Sadness breathes around me,
Sorrow's chains have bound me,
They who should have crowned me
Perish far away!"

Could I, think you, waver?
No!—these words I gave her—
"O, thou fair enslaver,
Thou hast won my heart.
Speak on, I entreat thee,
I may never meet thee,
Never more may greet thee,
Speak, before we part!"
So she then related
How our land was hated,
Cashel devastated,
And its chieftains slain.
"But," she said, "we are striving,
Hosts are now arriving
Who will soon be driving
Tyrants o'er the main!"

who broiled the Rev. Richard Barry alive, and butchered three thousand persons.

Forty of the Earl's soldiers, concerned in this massacre, afterwards solemnly attested that several of the murdered Irish had tails "near a quarter of a yard long." A tradition still exists among the people that "tails" are peculiar only to persons of Danish descent, among whom are the families of the Hassetts, the Brodars, &c.—Ludlow. D. O'Dalaei Pers. Hæret. 1652. Dr. Nash. Mac Geoghegan. Bruodini Propugnac, p. 715.

Ain páirt-si guiḋeaċ gaċ seaḃac,
Atá gan ċríoċ le sealad ;
Faoi ṫáir na daoirse ag seasaṁ,
Sáir-ṫoile Ḋé!
Gaċ tráiṫ ċuin CRIOSḊ fuair peannaid,
Páis 's ioḋbairt ṡearḃ!
Cráḋ le fioċ 's gearraḋ
Cnáiṁ, agus géag!
An fáġnaċ Ríġ gan ainim,*
Atá do ṡíor fá sgamal ;
Gan spás a ṫíġeaċt a n-gratam,
Aitreaḃ na n-Gaoḋal.
'S an táir-sprot coiṁṫeaċ, meaṁuill,
Atá na suiġe 'nár m-bailte,
Le cárna clóiḋeaṁ do sgaipeaḋ,
Ar cláir leaṫan Néill.

Go h-áitreaḃ Chuinn dá d-tagaċ,
Spáinnigt† ġroiḋe le ceannas ;
'S gárda laoiseaċ ḟearaḋ,
Táin do luċt faoḃar.
Ní ḃ-fuil sráid san ríġeaċt 'ná caṫair ;
Nár ḃ'árd a d-teinte air lasaḋ,
Lán-ċuid fíon dá sgaipeaḋ,
'S gárdaċas pléar,
Ḋáin ag buiḋean na leaḃar,
Ráis 's "rainnce fada ;"
Cláirseaċ ċaoin dá spreagaḋ,
Gárṫa 'gus sgléip!
Ag fáilṫiúġaḋ an Ríġ tar calaiṫ,
'S ní ṫráċtfar linn air ainim,
'S a ċáirde diúgaig fearda,
Sláinte mo Rex!

* *An faghnach Righ gan ainim.* The exiled or wandering King without a name—Prince Charles Edward Stuart.

† "Les Irlandois" (says Boullaye Le Gouz) "ayment les Espagnols

O! Thou who inspirest
Eire's bards, and firest
Heroes' breasts in direst
   Woe through bitter years,
Unto Thee each morning,
Who didst dree such scorning,
Scoffing, scourging, thorning,
   I cry out with tears!
Send him back, and quickly,
Who now, sad and sickly,
Roams where sorrows thickly
   Press and crush him down!
And disperse and scatter
All who in these latter
Times have striven to shatter
   Eire's rightful Crown!

O! the French and Spanish
Soon our foes will banish;
Then at once will vanish
   All our grief and dread,
City, town, and village
Shall no more know pillage,
Music, feasting, tillage,
   Shall abound instead;
Poetry, romances,
Races, and "long dances,"
Shouts, and songs, and glances
   From eyes bright with smiles!
Our King's feasts shall Fame hymn,
Though I may not name him,
Victory will proclaim him
   Monarch of the Isles.

comme leur freres, les François comme leurs amis, les Italiens comme leurs alliez, les Allemands comme leur parens, les Anglois and Ecossois sont leur ennemis irreconcilables."—*Voyages et Observations*, 477.

INGHION AN FHAOIT O'N N-GLEANN.*

Siúḃail a ċuid! bíḋ ag gluaiseaċt,
Gan sgíṫ, gan stad, gan fuaraḋ;
Tá'n oíḋċe ġairid ṡaṁraḋ,
'S bíoḋam a raon ar siúḃal?
Gheaḃair aoiḃneas bailte móra,
'S radarc le m' ṫaoib ar ċuantaḋ;
'S a Chríost nár ró-ḃreáġ an uain í,
Ar an ḃ-Faoiteaċ fada ó'n n-Gleann!

Tá mé lán do náire
Tré gaċ beart dá n-deárnaḋ;
Mar is buaċaill mé ḃíḋ dána;
'S d'imṫig uaim mo ġreann!
Ní beó mé mí 'ná ráiṫċe,
Mar a ḃ-faġaiḋ mé póg 's fáilte,
'S cead síne síos le d' ḃáin-ċneis,
A Inġion an Fhaoit ó 'n n-Gleann!

Is iomḋa cailín barraṁail, spéireaṁail,
Do ġluaisfeaḋ liom na h-aonar;
Mollaim féin a tréiġṫe,
A g-coillte ḃéal áṫ-úir,†
Dá m-beiḋmís agá ċéile,
'S ag ól a n-Durlas Fhéile,‡
Mo láṁ faoi ċeann mo ċéad-searc,
Do ċuirfinn í ċum suain!

* *Gleann* (Glyn), a small village situated on the banks of the Suir, midway between the towns of Carrick and Clonmel. An annual fair is held here on the twenty-eighth of May. The Suir runs direct through the village, dividing it into two—hence, the following proverb among the natives:—

"*Bioch a leath air an d-taobh air nos aonach an Ghleanna.*"

"Let it be fairly divided, like the fair of Glyn."

WHITE'S DAUGHTER OF THE DELL.

Come, let us trip away, love,
We must no longer stay, love,
Night soon will yield to Day, love;
We'll bid these haunts farewell.
We'll quit the fields, and rather
New life in cities gather;
And I'll outwit your father,
The tall White of the Dell!

I am filled with melancholy
For all my bygone folly;
A wild blade and a jolly
I was, as most can tell;
But woes now throng me thickly,
I droop, all faint and sickly,
I'll die, or win her quickly,
White's Daughter of the Dell!

There's many a Kate and Sally
Who'd gladly stray and dally
Along with me in valley,
Or glade, or mossy cell—
O! were we in Thurles together,
And each had quaffed a mether,§
We'd sleep as on soft heather,
My Sweet One of the Dell!

† A large tract of land east or south-east of Carrick, lying near an opening in the hills immediately over the Suir, and not far from the demesne of Tinahalla.

‡ *Thurles*, in the county of Tipperary.

§ Mether, in Irish *Meadar*, a drinking-vessel used by the ancient Irish,—but now it means a churn.

A ċailín barraṁail, spéireaṁail,
'Na d-tug mé searc mo ċléiḃ duit;
Is é 'n gráḋ do ṫug mé 'raoir duit,
Chuir an saoġad-sa tre m' ċoṁ!
Ní beó ar muir ná ar ḟéar me,
'S taosgaim fuil mo ċléiḃe 'maċ;
Is é mo ḃrón gan mé is mo ċéad-searc,
Faoi ḋuilleaḃar glas na g-crann!

Dá m-beiḋinn-si lá breáġ gréine,
Am ṡuiḋe ar ḃeinn an t-sléiḃe;
An lon-duḃ* 's an ċéirseaċ,
Ag seinnim ós mo ċeann;
Ba ḋeas do sgríḃfinn ḃéarsa,
'S b'iongnaḋ leó mar léiġfin,
A n-gráḋ beiṫ sínte taoḃ leat,
A Inġion an Ḟhaoit ó'n n-Gleann!

* *Lon-dubh.* The Blackbird. This bird was a great favorite with our Gaelic Poets. There is a poem attributed to *Oisin* on the Blackbird of *Doire an Chairn* (Derry Carn), in the County of Meath. The following are the two first stanzas:—

Binn sin, a loin Dhoire an Chairnn!
Ni chualas an ard san m-bith,
Ceol ba bhinne na do cheol
Agus tu fa bhun do nid.

Aen cheol is binne fa'n m-bith,
Mairg nach eisdir ris go foil!
A mhic Alphruinn na g-clog m-binn,
'S go m-beartha aris air do noin.

You bright, you blooming Fair, you!
'Tis next my heart I wear you!
The wondrous love I bear you
        Has bound me like a spell!
Oh! both by land and ocean
My soul is all commotion,
Yours is my deep devotion,
        Dear Damsel of the Dell!

Oh! were I seated near her,
Where summer woods might cheer her,
While clearer still, and clearer,
        The blackbird's notes would swell,
I'd sing her praise and glory,
And tell some fairy story
Of olden ages hoary,
        To White's Rose of the Dell!

Melodious are thy lays, O, Blackbird of Derrycarn!
I have never heard in any quarter of the globe
Music sweeter than thine
While perched beneath thy nest.

Music more melodious is not in the world,
Alas! had you but listened to it a while,
O son of Alphruin of the deep-toned bells,
You could again your prayers resume.

See Oisin's poems, where he contends with St. Patrick about the "croaking" voice of his psalm-singers, with which he contrasts the tuneful warbling of the Derrycarn blackbird.

DOṀNALL NA GREINE.

Fonn :—Doṁnall na Gréine.

Comaoin 's *Frolic*—ċuir Artúr de Bhailis
Ar Dhoṁnall na Gréine!
Má ċualaḋ sib a ṫréiġṫe!
Go g-caiṫfeaċ sé seaċtṁain—ag ól a d-tiġ leannaḋ,
'S ná tuitfeaċ néal air,
B'anaṁ dit céille air!

DOMHNALL NA GREINE.

Of Donall na Greine, the hero of this song, little is known. We find the following allusion to him in a Jacobite ballad by the Rev. Patrick O'Brian, which appears at page 258 of this volume.

" Beidh hata maith beabhair,
Air *Dhomhnall na Greine*,
Da chathadh is na speartha le mor-chroidhe."

Domhnall na Greine
Shall have a fine beaver,
Which he will toss to the skies with delight.

Our own opinion is, that *Domhnall* was a fellow who loitered his time idly basking in the sun, as his cognomen *na Greine* (of the sun) would indicate, and consequently became a fitting subject for the poets to display their wit upon.

On this air the Scotch have founded their "Bucky Highlander," which was by some wag burlesqued in an Anglo-Irish rhyme beginning thus:—

Potaties and butter would make a good supper
For Bucky Highlander,
For Bucky Highlander.

Of Arthur Wallace we know little; but we have seen some records of a family of that name living in Cork about a century ago—patrons of poets and poetry—and it is probable that "Arthur" was a distinguished member of this family.

We forgot placing the following stanza in the hands of our poetical translator:—

Bion Domhnall air meisge 's a bhean ag ol uisge,
'S a phaisdighe a beice—'s a phaisdighe a beice

Olfach se a d-tuillean se, 's da m-beidheach a thuille 'ge,
Domhnall na Greine—Domhnall na Greine.

Domhnall is drunk, and his wife drinking water,
And his children are screaming—his children are screaming.

He drinks what he earns, and more if he gets it,
Domhnall na Greine! Domhnall na Greine!

Wild Domhnall na Greine!—his frolics would please ye,
Yet Wallace, confound him,
Came trickishly round him!
He'd sit, without winking, in alehouses drinking
For days without number,
Nor care about slumber!

Do riarfaċ sé ceaṫrar—ní ḋéanfaċ sé casaoid,
B'anaṁ gan gléas é,
Doṁnall na Gréine!
Trodaire, Bucaire—dá ḃ-fuil san ḃ-faision é,
"Cuisle na Féile"
An Spalpaire Tréiṫeaċ!

Do léiġiseaċ sé cailleaċ—ar ṁúċaḋ 's air ċeasaċd,
Sin cuid dá ḃéasa,
Go n-déanaḋ sé réiḋteaċ!
Dá n-bogaḋ 's dá mealla—ó oiḋċe go maidion.
Le bladar 's bréaga,
Eaċtra 's sgéalta!

B'árd a léim-raṫa—'s ba ċruaiḋ a ḃuille ḃata,
Ag teaċt aimsir ḟéaḋma,
Do ṫroidfeaċ sé céadta.
Ba ṡaṁail mo ġearḟiaḋ—le Lúġaiḋ Láṁ-ḟada,
Le Alustrom éaċtaċ,
No *Hercules* Gréagaċ

Ní tréine é ar talaṁ—'ná ar tuinn mara,
Do ṡnáṁṫaċ an Eirne
An stoirm no 'n séide.
Níl aon neaċ dá mairion—nár ṡáraiḋ a g-cleasaḋ,
B'ḟuiris do ḋéanaṁ,
Bhí sé ró ṫréiṫeaċ.

Níl ceárd ná ealaḋan—nár ṡáraiḋ gan doċar,
'S níor cuireaḋ bréag,
Ar Dhóṁnall na Gréine.
Ba ṫáiliúir, ba ġoḃa é—b'ḟear gléasda potaiḋe é,
'S d'ḟiġfeaċ sé éadaċ,
Cotún 's *Cambrick!*

* *Spalpeen* (*rectius*, spailpin), a person following the spade—a spade-officer.

O! jovial and funny—a spender of money—
A prince at his Table,
Was Domhnall the Able!
The Soul of Good-breeding, in fashions his leading
Was copied and stuck to
By tradesman and buck too!

Old crones, of diseases, of coughings, and sneezes,
He'd cure without catsup,
And quarrels he'd patch up.
With flattery and coaxing, with humbug and hoaxing,
And song-singing daily,
He'd pass the time gaily.

O! he was the spalpeen* to flourish an alpeen! †
He'd whack half a hundred,
And nobody wondered!
He'd have taught a right new way to Long-handed
Lughaidh,
Or Great Alexander,
That famous Commander.

On water and land he was equally handy,
He'd swim without fear in
A storm o'er Lough Eirin!
Not a man born of woman could beat him at *coman*, ‡
Or at leaping could peer him,
Or even come near him!

Every artisan's tool he would handle so coolly—
From the plough to the thimble,
Bright Domhnall the Nimble!
A blacksmith and tailor, a tinker and nailer,
And weaver of cambrick,
Was also the same brick!

† *Alpeen* (*rectius*, ailpin), a wattle. Used at country fairs in faction fights.
‡ Hurling.

Gréasaíde nó ṁolta'é—Printéir breáġa leaḃar é,
Dhéanfaċ sé céaċta,—
D'ḟuirseaċ na bréanraḋ*—
Gléiséir ar ḟeaḃas—ba ḋaoine ḃí a g-Corcaiḋ é,
Doṁnall na Gréine
Do ḟeinneaċ air ṫéadaiḃ!

Le h-aol 's le cloċa—do ḋéanfaċ sé obair
Droiċead ar an Éirne,
Nó tárrsna ar an d-tréan-ṁuir!
Bád agus Coite—Do ḋéanfaċ go tapa,
Threaḃṫaċ an tréanṁuir,
A nún ċum na Gréige!

Groom agus marcaċ é—naċ fuair riaṁ a leagaḋ,
Sheinneaċ sé ar ṗíob,
'S ar gaċ sórt siansa.
Bórd agus leabaiḋ—do ḋéanfaċ go tapaiḋ,
'S ḋéanaċ sé brísde,
Do ċroicean na caoraċ.

D'ólfaċ deoċ leanna—'s é féin dá ceannaċ
'S as blasda na briaṫra,
Channaċ go ciallṁar.
Dhéanfaċ sé *Pitcher*—do ṫuiġfeaċ san g-cistin,
Choinġṁeóḋaċ *Geneva*,
D'ólfaċ na *Ladies!*

Le feaḃas a ċuideaċta—ṁeallfaċ sé cuid aca,
Cailíníḋ óga!
Singil 's Pórsda!
Dhéanfaċ sé hata—d'oirfeaċ do 'n Easbog
'S Peiriḃig do 'n Iarlaḋ!
Srian agus Diallait.

* *Fallow.*

He made stout shoes for winter—he shone as a printer,
He'd shape a wheelbarrow,
A plough and a harrow!
His genius for glazing was really amazing,
And how in Cork city
He'd harp to each ditty!

In a week's time, or shorter, with stones and with mortar,
He'd rear a high stronghold,
And bridge that would long hold.
With wood from the valley he'd build a gay galley,
To cleave the deep waters
To Greece of the Slaughters!

He reigned a musician without competition,
And coursed like a jockey,
O'er ground the most rocky.
'Twas he that was able to make bed and table—
And breeches to match you,
Of sheepskin he'd patch you.

No churl and no grumbler, he'd toss off his tumbler,
And chat with a croney,
In speech sweet as honey.
For the Fair and the Richer he'd shape a neat pitcher
For gin or for sherry,
To make the heart merry.

With married and single he'd oftentimes mingle,
And many's the maiden
He left sorrow-laden.
A wig for a noble he'd make without trouble,
Hat, saddle, and bridle—
He couldn't be idle!

Níl ceól dár spreagaḋ—a seomraḋ, no a h-alla,
Nác b-fuil air a ṁéara,
'S ċumfaċ sé béarsa.
Is líoṁṫa a ṫeanga—a m-Béarla nó a Laidionn,
Sgríbṫeaċ sé Gaoiḋeilge
Dutch agus Gréigis!

Níl aon bean a g-Corcaḋ—nác fágfaḋ a n-doċar!
Gan orra aċd sméide!
Do ṫiocfaidís taob leis!
Le méad a ṁisniḋ—Do ṡáraiḋ sé an doṁan,
Sin aguib a ṫréiṫe,
Doṁnall na Gréine!

Fonn:—Bean an Fhir Ruaḋ.

All airs, pure or garbled, that ever were warbled
By harpers or singers,
He had on his fingers!
Greek, Erse, English, Latin, all these he was pat in,
And what you might term an
O'erwhelmer in German!

Long, long, they'll regret him, and never forget him,
The girls of Cork city,
And more is the pity!
What more? By his courage he topped all in our age—
To him, then, be glory!
And so ends my story.

THE RED-HAIRED MAN'S WIFE.

The following is the first stanza of *Bean an Fhir Ruadh* (The Red-Haired Man's Wife), which is quite common among the Munster peasantry:—

Do thugas naoi mi a b-priosun ceangailte cruaidh,
Bulta air mo chom 's mile glas as sud suas;
Do thugasa sigh mar do thabharfuch aladh cois cuain
D'fhonn a bheith sinte sios le Bean an Fhir Ruadh.

I spent nine months in prison fettered and bound,
My body chained and secured with locks,
Bounded as the swan on the wave
In hopes to sit down beside the Red-haired man's wife.

TEACHT NA N-GEANNA FIADHAINE.*

Seáġan Ua Cuinneagáin, cct

Fonn :—Seáġan Buiḋe.

Fanaiḋ go h-éistiom a cceaṫair ar ċaogaḋ,
'S geallaim go réiġfeaḋ an t-Ard Ríoġ !
An ceangalsa air Ghaoiḋeilib, ag Danaraib ċlaonaḋ,
A b-fearannaib Eibear na lán-sgríob :—
Lasfaḋ na spéarṫaḋ,
Le h-annfaḋ an éirlig,
Do ḋearcfar o Bhéara go Tráiġ Liṫ,
'S go calaṫ-port Eirne,
Ag gas'raḋ Shéarluis ;
A treasgairt an tréada sin Sheáġain Bhuiḋe !

* In Bunting's Irish music will be found a beautiful air called "*Geadhna Fiadhaine*" (Wild Geese), with words by Dr. Drennan, the *United Irishman*.

THE RETURN OF THE WILD GEESE.

BY JOHN O'CUNNINGHAM.

AIR :—" *Seaghan Buidhe.*"

THE epithet *Seaghan Buidhe* (Yellow Jack) was applied to the followers of William III. We have no less than ten different songs to this air in our collection; but the true *Seaghan Buidhe* is one in which the accomplishments of an individual with this cognomen are humorously described, and which we give on the next page.

Of the author, *Seaghan O'Cuinneagain*, nothing is known. We possessed some of his MSS., written in 1737, among which we found the following toast, composed for him by a contemporary poet :—

Ag so slainte Sheaghain Ui Chuinneagain,
Fear gan chaim na chroidhe,
Fear geal aluinn, ba chlisde laimh,
Fear le raidhte grinn—
Fear nar bathag an iomarbhaidh
Fear a d-tabhairne dighe,
Fear nar fhag a bhille lan,
Fear le radh, 'gus saoi.

Here's a health to John O'Cunningham,
A man without guile in his heart,
A man fair and comely, with a clever hand,
A man of jovial speech,
A man well versed in his country's lore,
A man he was in the tavern,
Who never left *scores* unpaid,
A man right sage was he.

O, wait till you reach but the year Fifty-four,
And I promise the High God shall free you!
He shall shiver your Sassenagh chains evermore,
And victor the nations shall see you!
The thunder and lightning
Of battle shall rage—
'Twixt Tralee and Berehaven it shall be—
And down by Lough Eirin
Our Leader shall wage
Fierce war to the death against *Seaghan Buidhe!**

* Pronounced *Shawn Bui.*

Casfaiḋ na h-éanlaiṫ dá n-gairmṫear "Géana,"*
  An ainm go gléasda gan spás puinn,
Ag cabair le Séarlus—an caiṫbile is tréine,
  Dár ḟeasaiṁ o d'éagadar cnáṁa Fhinn !
          Creaċfaid 's céasfaid,
          'S sgaipfid na bréan-toirc,
Leagfaid 's raobfaid a n-gárdaiġe,
          Leagfar na péirse,
          Tá ċeal'gaċ, craosaċ,
Gan faice, gan éadaċ, gan Seáġan Buiḋe !

SEAGHAN BUIDHE.

Air maidin de domhnadh ag gabhail sios an bothar,
Go hatuirseach, bronach, gan or puinn;
Casag orm oigbhean bhi suighte go corach,
'S i faire air an roguire *Seaghan Buidhe!*

Ba thailiuir, ba ghobha e, ba phrinteir breagha leabhar e,
'S geallaim gan amhras gur breagha sgriobhach,
Dheanfach se fionta de bharraoidh na g-craoibheacha,
'S do shnamhfach an taoide go toin sios!

B'fhearr e ar an maide, 'gus b-fhearr e ar an m-bearrnadh,
B'fhearr e la chasda na suistighe,
B'fhearr e la an earraig ag grafa na m-banta,
'Gus b-fhearr e ar binse na giuistis,

Cuirfeadsa an roguire feasta dha fhoguirt,
A g-Corcaidh, a n-Eochuill, 's a d-*Tralee*,
Ni leomhthadh aon oig-bhean gabhail thoruinn an bothar
Le he-agla an roguire *Seaghan Buidhe!*

* The departure of the Irish Jacobites, in 1691, still spoken of by the people as "The Flight of the Wild Geese," marks one of the most mournful epochs in our sad history. It was indeed a memorable and mournful spectacle; women and children severed from their husbands, and the ties of nature rent asunder. The parting sails were pursued by moans and lamentations, that excited even the sympathies of the English and foreign troops, and still find a mournful echo in the

The "Wild Geese" shall return, and we'll welcome
them home—
So active, so armed, and so flighty
A flock was ne'er known to this island to come
Since the years of Prince *Fionn* the mighty—
They will waste and destroy,
Overturn and o'erthrow—
They'll accomplish whate'er may in man be;
Just heaven! they will bring
Desolation and woe
On the hosts of the tyrannous *Seaghan Buidhe!*

SHANE BWEE.

One Sunday morning as I rambled on the road,
Sorrowful, gloomy, and penniless,
I happened to meet a comely young maiden,
A watching the thief known as *Seaghan Buidhe.*

He is a smith and a tailor—a fine printer of books,
And I have no doubt he can write well;
He can make wines from the blossom of trees,
And can swim and dive in the ocean.

He is the best at the cudgel—the first in the gap,
The first to thresh his corn:—
The first in spring to till his land,
And more skilled in the law than a judge!

Henceforth I'll proclaim this wandering rogue,
In Cork, and in Youghal, and in Tralee,
For none of our maidens dare travel the road,
For fear of the sly rogue called *Seaghan Buidhe!*

breasts of the Irish people. It is said that the weather was unusually gloomy, as if the sun itself had been unwilling to behold so sad a spectacle of fathers torn from their children—husbands from their wives, and, more touching still, of brave men torn from the bosom of their native land, to fill the world with the fame of their valour, and the glory of that nation which they were never to revisit.—"Military Memoirs of the Irish Nation," by M. O'Conor. Dub. 1845, p. 192.

Le feartaiḃ an aon-Mheic—d'ḟulaing peannaid
dár saoraḋ,
Go d-tagaiḋ mo ḃriaṫra le grάḋ, a g-críċ;
Ar n-eaglais naoṁṫa—go g-caraid a n-éinḟeaċt,
A g-cealla na saor-sgolaḋ sáir-ḃinn!
Dá mairinn dá éis sin
Aċt seaċtṁain de laeṫiḃ,
'S gan labairt air ċlaon-dliġṫe Sheáġain Bhuiḋe!
Le h-atal ba aonaċ,
Mear, acfuinneaċ, éadtrom,
Do ġlanfainn do léim tar an m-bán laoi!

SEBEAL NI BHRIAIN.*

Aoḋ Buiḋe Mac Cuirtín, cct.

A Ġhéis ġarṫa ġléigiol—a ḃéiṫ ṁaiseaċ ḃéasaċ,
A ċraoḃ-ċneasda ċéim-leas do ṁaṫaiḃ síol Táil;†
A aon-lasair sgéiṁe na n-aol-ḃan le ċéile,
A ḃéal-tanna an déid-ġil na laḃarṫa sáṁ.

Is tréan teaċt do ṫréiṫe le féiḋim-ṁaiṫ na féile,
'S t-aol-ċroḃ le daonnaċt is taḃarṫaċ társ,
Do 'n tairtiollaċ tréiṫ-lag—do 'n aimid gan éirioċt,
Do 'n lagar le h-aostaċt is tú a g-caḃair 's a sgáṫ.

* We have no means of ascertaining who this fair one, Isabel Ni Brian was. She must have been of the house of Thomond from the fact of Hugh Buidhe (the Yellow) Mac Curtin—a Clare poet who flourished early in the last century—having made her the theme of his muse.

† Tail. Cas, the son of Conall Eachluaith, on whom, after the

And oh! may the God who hath kept evermore
  This isle in His holy protection—
Bring back to His temples His priests as before,
  And restore them to Eire's affection!
      To end! may I sooner
      Be slaughtered in war,
Or lie sunk in the waves of the Grand Lee,
      Than with spirit for Freedom,
      E'er cease to abhor
The detestable statutes of *Seaghan Buidhe!*

ISABEL NI BRIAN.

BY HUGH BUIDHE (THE YELLOW) MAC CURTIN.

O, Swan of bright plumage! O, maiden who bearest
  The stamp on thy brow of Dalcassia's high race,
With mouth of rich pearl-teeth, and features the fairest,
  And speech of a sweetness for music to trace!

O! how shall I praise thee, thou lovely, thou noble!
  Thou prop of the feeble, thou light of the blind!
Thou solace and succour of wretches in trouble,
  As beauteous in body as bounteous in mind!

death of Corc, Criomhthan, monarch of Ireland, conferred the sovereignty of Munster, was surnamed *Dolabhra Mac Tail*, from his foster-father, who was a smith, is the original founder of the Dalcassians, whose posterity is called *Clann Tail.*—See "O'Flaherty's Ogyg." Part III. p. 310.

Mar bárr ar ġac léan-lot do ṁearaḋ mo
ċéadfaḋ,
'S d'ḟág dealḃ gan ċéill mé am ṁeaṫaċ mar
'táim,
Gur ċailliosaḋ laoċraḋ ba ċaḃair dam éigion,
Fearr'ċoin éaċtaċ Chaisil 's Chláir.*

Do ċeanglas le núaḋċar, flaṫ ceannsa do'n ċúainne,
O Anntruim na n-guais-beart, 's o Albain árd;
Do 'n ċlainn sin Cholla Uais ṁir, fuair Teaṁair 's
Tuaṫ-Mhuṁain,
A n-dán sin 's a n-dualgas na n-aiṫreaċ ó'n ḟás.

Cread daṁsa ná luaḋfainn an lann-ṁarcaċ uasal,
An "crann-caṫais"† cnuasaċ gan casaḋ ar a láiṁ;
Gan fann-beart, gan truailleaċt, aċt ceannsaċt
le cuallaċt,
An plannda do ṡuaṫaḋ tre ċaise d'ḟuil Táil.

* Charles O'Brian, Lord Clare, who fell at the battle of Ramilies, in 1706, where he commanded a regiment of infantry.

† *Crann caithis*, a May-pole.

Alas! these are woes from which nought can defend me,
My bosom is loaded with sorrow and care,
Since I lost the great men who were prompt to befriend me,
The heroes, the princes of Cashel and Clare!

But, glory and honour to thee!—thou hast wedded
A chieftain from Antrim, of chivalrous worth,
Of the great *Colla-Uais* the Swift—they who headed
So proudly the conquering tribes of the North!

To that bold cavalier hast thou plighted thy duty,
And *he* is a hero whom none can surpass—
His valour alone was the meed of thy beauty,
Thou Rose of the Garden of golden Dal Cas!

AN PAISDIN FIONN.

Séamus ṁic Consaidín, cct.

Fonn:—An Páisdín Fionn.

Atá sgéal beag agam le h-áirioṁ diḃ,
Air réaltan ṁaiseaċ do ċráḋaiġ mo ċroiḋe,
Le h-éigion taiṫniṁ 's gráḋ tá gnaoi,
  A n-géibionn galair gur ḟág me!
Is péarlaċ, baċallaċ, tá gaċ dlaoi,
'Na craoḃ-ḟolt craṫaċ, go fáinngioċ síos,
Gné na h-alan a snáṁ ar ling,
  'Na h-éadan geanaṁail, náireaċ!

THE FAIR-HAIRED CHILD.

BY JAMES CONSIDINE.

JAMES CONSIDINE, of *Ath na g-Caorach* (Sheepford) in the county of Clare, author of this beautiful song, flourished about the close of the last century.

A lady from the south (a Tipperary girl) kindly gave us the following fragment of a much older version, which is generally sung by the peasantry about Cahir, Clogheen, and Clonmel, and of which we give a literal translation at the close of this song:—

A g-Cluain geal Meala ta 'n Paisdin Fionn,
A bh-fuil a croidhe 's a h-aigne ag gaire liom;
A dha pluc dhearg mar bhlath na g-crann,
Is truagh gan i 'dir mo dha lamha 'gam.
Is tusa mo mhaon-sa, mo mhaon-sa, mo mhaon sa,
Is tusa mo mhaon-sa, 's mo ghradh geal,
Is tusa mo mhaon, 's carra mo chroidhe,
Is truagh gan tu 'dir mo dha lamha 'gam.

Da m-beidhin-si seachtmhuin an ait a m-beidheadh greann,
No dir dha bharraille lan de leann;
Gan aon am aice acht mo Phaisdin Fionn,
Go deimhin duit d'olfain a slainte.
Is tusa, &c.

Da m-beith sud agamsa airgiod 's or,
Ba boga geala 's caoire ar moin,
An charraig ud Chaisil na piosaidhe oir,
Do mhalairt ni iarfuin mar cheile.
Is tusa, &c.

The air must be played with spirit, and the chorus sung after each stanza.

A maiden there is whose charmful art
Has fettered and bound my love-sick heart;
From thence her image will never depart,
But haunts it daily and nightly.
How glitters and curls each lock of her hair,
All golden over her bosom fair!
As the swan on the wave, so it on the air
Floats hither and thitherward brightly.

N

Is caol a ṁala ar ḃláiṫ-ḋearc rín,
Chuir saoġad go daingion am lár go tínn;
Na caora a sbairinn le sgáil an aoil,
Go tréan na leacain ġlain ṁánlaḋ.
A béal is tanna 's as áilne gnaoi,
A ḋéid-ṁion ċailce gan ċáim a ṁnaoi,
Is léir gur binne ná cláirsioċ ċaoin,
Gaċ ḃéarra ċanan an ḃáin-ċneis.

Venus, banaltra ḃláiṫ, na gnaoi,
'S Helen ġreanta ṫug ár na Traoi;
Déirdre* ṁaiseaċ re 'r fágḃaḋ Naois
Go faon a n-Eaṁainn, 's a ḃráiṫre!
A sgéiṁ, 's a b-pearsainn, ní táire ḋíoḃ,
An ḃéiṫ-si ċanaim ṫug bárr o ṁnaoi,
'S as baoṫ an dearmad Bláiṫnid ġrinn
Thug eag do Churaiġ ṁic Dáire!

Tá gléire an t-sneaċta gaċ tráiṫ 'na píb,
'S gné na mama-ḋeas ḃláṫṁar, ċruinn;
Sgéiṁ a seanga-ċuirp áluinn ċaoil,
'S an t-aol a taiṫnioṁ na bán-ċroiḃ.
Ní 'l éisg le h-aṁarc go bráṫ ar ling,
Ná éanlaiṫ seasaṁ ar ḃárr na g-craoiḃ,
Ní 'l gné ná saṁuilt le fáġail air tír,
Naċ léir di ṫarruint ar bán-ḃrait.

Do léiġfin seanċas ċláir na n-Gaoiḋeal,
'S réim na Breatan do ċráḋaig mo ċroiḋe!
Léiġim na psalm ba ġnáṫ go binn,
Ag cléire ag cantuin a d-tráṫa.
Ar ṫéada sbreagainn go gáiḃṫeaċ Reel,
Do leiġisfinn galaraiḃ sláinte croiḋe,
Ar ṫaoḃ na faiṫċe níor ṫláṫ mo ġníoṁ,
Ag déanaṁ airte ná tráċtaim!

* *Deirdre.* For the fate of Deirdre, Naoise, and his brethren, at Eamhain (Emania), see Transactions of the Gaelic Society, Dub. 1808.

From her piercing eye, so blue and bright,
Shoot arrows on arrows of Love's own light,
And the red rose vies with the lily's white
In her brilliant queenly features;
No pearls can rival her dazzling teeth,
Her lips are like coral above and beneath;
And never was harp on a wild wood heath,
Like the voice of this fairest of creatures!

Not she, that dame who was Eire's pride,
Not Helen of Troy, famed far and wide,
Not Deirdre, who when King Naoisi died,
No more in Emania would tarry,
Could vie in features, figure, or air,
With this young damsel of beauty rare,
Not even the maiden, Blanaid fair,
Who slew brave Curigh Mac Daire.*

Her heaving bosom and beauteous neck
Are white as the snow, and as pure from speck,
Her arms are meet for gems to deck,
And her waist is fine and slender;
And there never was seen, by sea or land,
Beast, bird, or fish, but her delicate hand
Could broider it forth on silk so grand,
And glowing, yet soft and tender!

I have pondered, with tears, the rueful tale
Of the Saxon's conquest over the Gael;
I have heard the chant, the melodious wail
Of the priest in his matin duty;
I have played my land's harp o'er and o'er,
And was pierced with grief to my bosom's core,
But nothing could touch or move me more
Than the charms of this young beauty!

* Curaigh Mac Daire's tragic fate is related in Keating's Ireland, Haliday's edition, p. 405, Dub. 1811.

Féaċ-sa a ċaraḋ cia b'ḟearr duit sinn,
Gan spré, gan fearan mar táim, gan ḃuiḋin,
Ná créice searḃ ḃeiḋeaċ lán do ṗuimp,
  Do ḃéarfaċ aiṫis 's cáin duit!
Dá réir sin tarraing an ḋáil, gan sgiṫ,
'S déin mo ċaḃair ó 'n m-bás so am ċlaoiḋe,
'S an té do ċeannaig le grása sinn,
  Béarfaḋ caiṫiom 's fáġail dúinn.

In gay Clonmel dwells the fair-haired child,
Whose heart and soul at me have smiled;
Her two rosy cheeks like the red apple shine,
My grief, she is not in my arms!
  You are my fond one—my fond one—my fond one,
  You are my fond one and *gradh croidhe!*
  You are my fond one—my heart's only treasure,
  My grief you are not in my arms!

REIDH-CHNOC MNA SIGHE.

Seoirse Robairt,* cct.

Is fada mé ag gluaiseaċt ar ṫuairisg mo ġráḋ,
Ar fuaid coillte dúḃa uaigneaċ am ruagaḋ le fán;
A saṁuil ní ḃ-fuaras—giḋ' ċuarduiġeas a lán,
O Ghlaise na Tuaṫa go bruaċ geal na Máig.

Do seólaḋ me 'n uaignios ċnoic uaisle mná síġe,
Do casaḋ orm stuaire na sguab-ḟolt na suiġe;
Ba ċas, dlaoiṫeaċ, dualaċ, a cuaċa lé sios,
Ar gaċ taoḃ dá guaille dá luasgaḋ ag an n-gaoiṫ.

* We cannot trace the history of George Roberts, to whom the authorship of this beautiful fairy song is attributed.

Not belonging to that peculiar race of beings—the "good people," we cannot, dare not, say anything about their movements, for such

O! come then unto me, darling dove!
I am sure I can make you a better love,
Than a pompous, purse-proud fellow would prove,
Though I neither have lands nor treasure.
O! come to my arms, my Fond, my True!
'Tis a step, I vow, you never will rue,
For He who died for both me and you
Will give to us bliss without measure.

Were I for a week where mirth prevails,
Or 'twixt two barrels of foaming ale,
No one beside me but my *paisdin* fair!
Her health I would quaff in a bumper.
You are my fond one, &c.

If I had plenty of silver and gold,
Herds, and cattle, and lands to boot,
That huge Rock of Cashel in bits of gold,
No other I'd take but you, love!
You are my fond one, &c.

THE DARK FAIRY RATH.

BY GEORGE ROBERTS.

Long, long have I wandered in search of my love,
O'er moorland and mountain, through greenwood and grove.
From the banks of the Maig unto Finglas's flood
I have ne'er seen the peer of this Child of the Wood.

One bright Summer evening alone on my path,
My steps led me on to the Dark Fairy Rath;
And, seated anear it, my Fair One I found,
With her long golden locks trailing down on the ground.

as meddle in their affairs are said to seldom escape unscathed. Any of our readers, anxious about their "doings," may consult Crofton Croker, historian to the Munster fairies, and only illustrator of Irish fairy mythology before the public.

Do casaḋ mo ġráḋ orm, 's ba nár liom gan suiġe,
Do ċuirear mo láiṁ ar a bráġaid 's ar a cíċ;
Is é 'dúḃairt sí liom, " fág me? ní h-áḋḃar ḋuit
     sinn,
Mar is bean dúḃaċ do 'n áit me do ṫárlaiḋ san
     m-Bruiġin!"

Cá tuaiṫ, nó cá h-oilean duit, nó 'na g-Clár Luirc
     do ḃíḋir?
Nó má 's buairt duit suiḋ láiṁ liom, 's taḃair slán
     faoi gaċ buiḋin?
An tu 'n stuaire geal Bláṫnaid ṫug an saiġead-sa
     tre'm ċroiḋe
No 'n ċuaċ ṁilis, ṁánlaḋ,—ṫug Paris do 'n Traoi!

" Ní h-aoin neaċ do'n dréim sin me féin" a dúḃairt sí
Aċt cailín caoin gaoḋ'laċ ó 'n taoḃ ṫall do'n tír;
Nár ṡín sios a taoḃ dear le aoin ḟear san t-saoi-
     ġeal,
Bog díom do ġéagaḋ, 'táim déanaċ ó 'n m-Bruiġin?"

Is dúḃaċ 's as léan liom tú a ċéad-searc mo
     ċroiḋe,
Do ġruaḋ'na mar ċaora, dá léasa ag an sín;
Is iad sluaiġte Chnoic-Gréine do ṫárlaiḋ ad lion,
Do ruaig tú ód' ġaoḋalta go réiġ-ċnoc mná síġe!

Do ċuirfin le m' ċroiḋe steaċ mo ċaoin ġaiṫlion
     mná,
Mo ḋá láiṁ 'na timċioll 's do b'aoiḃinn liom í ḟáġail;
Ba ḃreáġa dear a braoiġṫe dúḃa, caola, gan ċáim,
Mar ṗlánait na h-oiḋċe, 's gan d'aois aici aċt lá.

Do ċuirear mo ġéagaḋ ar a caol-ċom mar ṡnuiḋim,
As san dá réir sin go méaraiḃ a troiġe;
Sínte le na taoḃ dear ba ṁéinn liomsa luiġe
Aċt uaimse gur léim sí mar éan ar an gcraoiḃ!

When I met her, though bashfulness held me in
check,
I put my arm gently around her white neck;
But she said, "Touch me not, and approach me not
near;
I belong to this Rath, and the Fairy Host here."

"Ah!" I spake, "you are burdened with sorrow and
care;
But whence do you come? From Clār Luirc or else-
where?
Are you Blanaid the blooming, the queenly, yet coy,
Or the dame brought by Paris aforetime to Troy?"

"I am neither," she said, "but a meek Irish maid,
Who years ago dwelt in yon green-hillocked glade,
And shone all alone, like a lamp in a dome.
Come! take off your arms! I'll be late for my
home!"

"O, Pearl of my soul, I feel sad and forlorn
To see your bright cheeks fairy-stricken and worn.
From your kindred and friends far away were you
borne
To the Hill of Cnoc-Greine,* to languish and mourn!"

And I said to myself, as I thought on her charms,
"O, how fondly I'd lock this young lass in my arms!
How I'd love her deep eyes, full of radiance and
mirth,
Like new-risen stars that shine down upon earth!"

Then I twined round her waist my two arms as a
zone,
And I fondly embraced her to make her mine own;
But, when I glanced up, behold! nought could I see.
She had fled from my sight as the bird from the tree!

* *Anglicised* Knockgreny, *i. e.*, The Hill of the Sun.

BEAN DUBH AN GHLEANNA.

Fonn:—Bean Ḋuḃ an Ġhleanna.

Atá bó 'gam ar an sliaḃ,
'S táim le seal na diaig,
O ċailleas mo ċiall le núaḋċar!
Ḋa seóla soir 's siar,
Ann gaċ áit dá n-gaḃaḋ an ġrian,
Go d-tionntuiḋeann a niar am ṫráṫnóna!
Nuair ḟéaċaim féin ann súd,
Ann gaċ áit a m-bíḋ' mo rún
Ruiṫean óm' ṡúil sruṫ deóra!
A Ríġ ḋil na g-cóṁaċt!
Go b-fóirir ar mo ċúis,
Mar is Bean Ḋuḃ ón n-Gleann do ḃreóḋaig
me!

THE DARK MAIDEN OF THE VALLEY.

We cannot ascertain the authorship of this air, but the words which accompany it are attributed to *Emonn an Chnoic* (Ned of the Hills), who flourished about the year 1739, and of whom we shall have occasion to speak hereafter.

The allusion to "Georgey" in the third stanza, meaning the second monarch of that name, shows it to have been composed early in the eighteenth century.

There is much simplicity in the style and composition of this song; perhaps more than in any other in our volume; from which we may infer that it is the production of a peasant of the humbler class of society.

The air must be played in slow time, and rather mournfully.

On the hill I have a cow,
And have herded it till now,
        Since a fair maiden stole my reason.
I lead her to and fro,
Wheresoever the winds blow,
        Till the sun shines at noontide in season.
I glance above afar,
Where my true-love shines a star—
        My spirit sinks, hardly to rally.
O, mighty King and Lord,
Thy help to me accord,
        To win the Dark Maiden of the valley!

Bean Duḃ an Ghleanna!
An Bhean Duḃ do b'ḟearra!
  Bean Duḃ ba ḋeise gáire
Na b-fuil a gruaḋ mar an alaḋ,
'S a píb mar an sneaċta!
  'S a com seang, singil, álainn,
Ní 'l ogánaċ cailce,
O Bhaile Áṫa Cliaṫ go Gailliṁ;
  Ná ar súd go Tuama Ui Mheára!
Naċ b-fuil ag triall 's ag tarraing,
Ar eaċaiḃ donna deasa
  Ag tnúṫ leis an m-Bean Duḃ álainn!

Gheaḃainn-se bean sa Múṁain,
Triur ban a Laiġeann,
  Agus bean o ríġ geal Seoirse,
Bean na lúbaḋ buiḋe
D'ḟáisgioċ mé le na croiḋe,
  Bean agus dá ṁíle bó lé,
Inġion óg an Iarlaḋ
Ata go tinn duḃaċ diaċraċ,
  Ag iarraiḋ mise d'ḟáġail le pósaḋ!
'S dá b-faġainnse féin mo roġa!
De ṁná deasa an doṁain
  As í an Bhean Duḃ ó 'n n-Gleann do b'ḟearr liom.

An té ċíḋfeaċ mo ṫeaċ,
'S gan do ḋíon air aċd seasg,
  Na ṡuiġe 'muiċ cois taoiḃ an ḃóṫair!
Nuair éirgiḋeann an ḃeaċ,
Agus ḋéingion a nead,
  Le grian 's le teas an t-saṁraiḋ!
Nrair éirgiḋeann suas an t-slat
Ní ḟanan uirṫe aon ṁeas,
  Aċd ag tnúṫ leis an m-brainnse is óige,
Mo ċailín plúraċ, deas,
D'éalaiḋ uaim le spreas,
  Mo ċúig céad slán go deó lé!

Dark maiden, first and best,
Who hast robbed me of my rest,
O, maiden, most beautiful and tender;
With swan-like neck so bright,
With bosom snowy-white,
With waist so delicate and slender,—
Not a youth from Dublin town
Unto Galway of renown,
Or thence to Toomevara, but is laden
On steeds bounding free,
With love-gifts to thee,
My loveliest, my Dark own Maiden!

In Momonia* I could find
Many damsels to my mind,
And in Leinster—nay, England, a many,
One from Georgey, without art,
Who would clasp me to her heart,
And a beauty is the lass among many.
The daughter of the Earl,
Who walks in silk and pearl,
Would fain have me netted in her thrall yet,
But could I have my choice,
How much would I rejoice
To wed thee, my Dark Maiden, of all yet!

My hut may stand unseen,
But 'tis thatched with rushes green,
And around it the bee is a hummer;
And it shines day by day,
In the glory and the ray
Of the Eire-loving sunlight of Summer.
But when maidens grow old,
They are viewed with glances cold,
And we chuse, then, the gay and youthful-hearted.
Thou hast left me, blooming flower,
In a dark and evil hour,
But I mourn thee as one who has departed.

* Munster.

INGHION UI GHEARAILT.

Doṁnall na Buile, cct.*

Atá lile gan sgamal d'ḟuil Ghearailt na sáir-ḟear,
  Is soinneanda a teasdas ag fáiḋiḃ iuil,
Ní ḟaicim a saṁuil ag taisdiol na sráide,
  A n-inniolltaċt pearsan—a g-cáil 's a g-cló,
Grád na rún í an múirnín margalaċ,
  Bláṫ na n-úḃall í a d-túis an t-saṁraḋ
Lúibín laċanta—alaḋ an ċuirp báin,
  An ḟinne-ḃean ḟada-ċroiḃ áluinn óg!

Is mogullaċ, muirearaċ, uilleannaċ, ómbraċ,
  Coċallaċ, cluṫair, ag fás go feór;
A carn-ḟolt craipinneaċ, fionna-ġeal, fáinneaċ,
  Cnotaċ ag tuitim go bárr a bróg:—
Go trínseaċ, táclaċ, tláiṫ-tiuḃ, taiṫnioṁaċ,
  Ciorṫa, cárnaċ, cáblaċ, camarsaċ,
Biseaċ, barra-ḃog, baċallaċ, bláiṫ,
  Dlaoiṫeaċ, drollaċ, 's a sgáil mar ór.

Bion Cupid na h-aṫaḋ go geanaṁuil, gráḋṁar,
  Is firrean an leanḃ d'ḟuig Paris dóiḃ;
Is follus na leacain ag caismirt go dána,
  Lonnraḋ an t-sneaċta le sgáil an róis.
Rin-rosg réiḋ-ġlas, péarlaċ, geaṁaraċ,
  Braoiṫe caolaḋ air éadan leanabaċ,
Cruinn-ċíċ córa is geanamnaiġe ġnáiṫ,
  'S gile an ċuim-ċailce í nár láṁuigeaḋ fós.

Is binne guṫ geann-ġuib, ḃalsam-ḃuig, ṁánlaḋ,
  An leinḃ-ṡi ċanann le sáṁ-ġuṫ ceól;
Ag seinnim-cirt Gall-ṗort ċeapaidis dáiṁe,
  An fuireann do ṫeagaisg an ċláirseaċ dóiḃ;

* Of *Domhnall na Buile*, (i. e. Domhnall the mad or crazy) the reputed author of this ballad, we have nothing to say, except that his claim to the authorship is disputed, some asserting it to be the joint production

THE GERALDINE'S DAUGHTER.

BY DOMHNALL NA BUILE.

There's a beauteous lily, a blooming flower,
A damsel of the Geraldine's race—
I know not her peer in city or bower,
For comely figure or lovely face;
The love of my soul, my life and my light she is!
Sweet as the apple-tree blossom, and bright she is,
A dazzling, a white-breasted, white-plumaged swan,
Is she, this wonder of radiance and grace!

Her tresses fall down in many a cluster,
Braided, yet free, on the emerald ground,
Shining with glorious and golden lustre,
And bright green ribbons flowing all round,
They beam on the sight serenely and shiningly—
O! I have gazed on them fondly and piningly!
Gracefully plaited and braided they are,
Yet in luxuriance flowing unbound!

Love glows and sparkles from all her features,
And all the graces that Love bestows—
You see in the face of this first of creatures
The brightness of snow, the bloom of the rose;
Her blue eyes shine ever tender and tenderer,
And her fair eye-brows ever seem slenderer,
And pure is the bosom, and pure is the heart
Of this fairest flower of any that blows.

The songs of her fallen land she singeth
Sweetly and softly, with tone and fire—
Each glorious air and melody ringeth
Forth all silvery from her lyre.

of *Seaghan Clarach Mhic Domhnaill*, and *Uilliam Dall O'Hearnain*, celebrated poets, who, it is said, composed each half stanza alternately.

Faoileann ṁaorḋa, béasaċ, banaṁúil,
  Naoiḋeanda, tréiġṫeaċ, ḋéarcaċ, greannaṁar,
Ṁilis-ḃean urramaċ, ṁioċair, gan ċáim,
  'S d'ḟeartaiḃ a cumainn tá táin gan treoir!

Is mursdar do'n ainnir a h-aṫair go fáiṫ-ġlic,
  Doineanda, draganta, a m-bearrnain gleó,
'S as tuille dá maṫar ceangal le Seáġan geal,
  Curaḋ nár ḃ'aindis a d-tábairne an óil :—
A máṫair úir-ċéiḃ, ċiuin-ċaoiṁ, ċarṫannaċ,
  Thug Sirriam Conntae, 's Túrnae laidionda;
Chúġainn, 's marcra calma, cáiġ,
  Chum searaṁ a g-coṁrac, 's a n-gárda slóġ.

Dá d-tagaċ fear forrusda, fonnḃar, fáiṫ-ġlic,
  Cumasaċ, neartṁar, faoi lán an t-seoil;
Fionn-ḟlaiṫ ḟonuis do ġlacaċ le gráḋ í,
  A n-dliġe na h-eaglais an báin-ċneis, ṁodaṁuil :—
Lucy ġléigiol féin Ní Gheasuilt í,*
  Do ċrú na n-Gréagaċ d-trean, seaḋ d'easgair sí,
Seang-ḃean ṁaiseaċ, na labarṫa sáiṁ,
  Fuair clú 'gus beannaċt ó'n n-dáiṁ go deo.

* At page 26 there is a slight allusion to the heroine of this ballad —a lady named Fitzgerald, a native of Ballykenely, in the county of Cork, which was a portion of the family estate at the time, and is still held by their descendants. So captivating were her personal charms that she became the theme of the Munster poets, by whom she was celebrated in more than a thousand and one ballads, two of which we have given in our present volume. She had a brother named Pierse, a celebrated poet, of whom many anecdotes are related by the peasantry of his native district, one of which is as follows:—

One day passing a nook, close by his land, where the tide flowed

A maiden she is of rich hospitality,
Noble, and gifted with every high quality,
Innocent, good, but so lovely withal,
That her beauty has wrought desolation most dire!

She hath a pride in the fame of her father—
A hero fierce on the battle-plain—
And her lover, who never was slow to gather
Bright wreaths amid the festival train,
And her mother, the bold, the learned, the meek-minded,
Shield and support of the feeble and weak-minded;
One, who if battle threatened the land,
Would stand unmoved 'mid its reddest rain.

May there soon come a hero to seek her—
Some stalwart lord of a kingly race—
None could he find higher-minded, yet meeker,
None of more beautiful figure and face.
From the grand Geraldines, foes of iniquity,
Sprang she, this maiden of Grecian antiquity;
Blessings are on her from poet and sage,
And her glory all Time can never efface!

in from the main ocean at high water, and meeting a brother bard he accosted him thus:—

Ceisd agam ort a shair-fhir,
Os tu is deanaighe d'fhag an cuan;
Ca mheid galun saile
San g-Crampan sa Chill Moluadh?

To which he received the following sarcastic reply:—

Ni feidir a thomhas le cairtibh,
Ata se laidir luath;
San mheid na faghadh slighe san Ath dhe,
Geabhadh se an fanadh o thuaig.

It would be impossible to convey the extraordinary wit of this answer in an English version.

LEATHER AWAY WITH THE WATTLE, O!

Tomás ṁic Coitir, cct.

A raoir 's mé go déanaċ,
  Air ṫaob cnoic re h-ais an Ċóiḃ; *
Do ṡuiġ mé seal ag éisdeaċt,
  Le guiṫ na n-éan ag cantuin ceóil;
Le m' ṫaoiḃ gur ḋearcas spéirbean,
  Ba ṡaoḋṁar, snuiḋte, snasda, a snóġ;
'S a dlaoi-ḟolt craṫaċ péarlaċ
  Air fad ag téaċt go h-alt na deóig.
Ba ġeal a gné mar ṡneaċta sléiḃ,
  Ba ḋeas a sgéiṁ, a cneas, 's a cló,
'S as pras do sgreag ar ṫéadaiḃ,
  " Leather away with the Wattle, O!"

* Cove of Cork, now Queenstown.

LEATHER AWAY WITH THE WATTLE, O!

BY THOMAS COTTER.

THIS spirited air escaped the notice of our most eminent collector, Bunting, and probably would have never been in print had it not fallen into our hands.

The words are the production of a violent Jacobite. By leathering away with the wattle, he implies his determination to decide all political differences by an appeal to "physical force."

The wattle was a stout cudgel, or *Ailpin*, in frequent requisition at country fairs and faction fights early in the present century.

Cearnaid, or Cearnuit, referred to in the third stanza, was a beautiful female bondmaid of Cormac, King of Ireland in the third century. She was obliged to grind a certain quantity of corn every day with a quern, or handmill, until the king, observing her beauty, sent across the sea for a millwright, who constructed a mill on the stream of Nith, which flows from the fountain of *Neamhnach*, to the north-east of Tara; and all ancient authorities and traditions agree that this was the first mill erected in Ireland.—See *Petrie's* "*Essay on Tara Hill*," 4to. Dublin: 1839. *Keating's Ireland*, vol. i., p. 418. Dublin: 1809.

Last night, when stars did glisten,
By a hill-side near the Cove,
I sat awhile to listen,
The sweet birds' pleasant lays of love.
A damsel tall of stature,
With golden tresses long and low,
Which—loveliest sight in nature!—
Down to the bright green grass did flow;
And breast as fair,—as snow in air,
Without compare for beauteous show,
Stood near, and sang me sweetly,
"Come, Leather away with the Wattle, O!"

A braoiṫe cearta, caola,
  Air a h-éadan tais, gan snas, gan smól,
Ba rín a rosg mar ḃraon glas,
  Ag sile o'n aeḋar ar ḃárr an ḟeóir:
Sneaċta geal gan aoluing,
  Go géar a g-caṫ le daiṫ an róis
'S níor ḃ'aiṫnid do 'n éigse,
  Cia 'co staon na leacain óig;
As cneasda caoiṁ—d'aiṫris sgéal,
  Go m-beiṫ an Régs ag teaċt a g-coróin,
Le'r ḃ-fonn a ḃeiṫ seal ag éisdeaċt,
  Le "Leather away with the Wattle, O!"

D'ḟiafraiġeas féin do'n spéirḃean,
  An féidir gur tu an ḃruingioll óg;
A maċaire na laoċ mear,
  A g-caṫ na TRAE le'r milleaḋ treoin,
Nó'n ainnir ṁilis Déirdre,
  O EIRE rug clann Uisneaċ mór,
No'n ḃean dá n-goirṫear Cearnuit,
  Air caise ġéar ċuir milion dóiḃ,
Melpomene,—Cassandra ḟéin,
  Muirinn, Meiḋḃ, nó'n ainnir óg
'S gur binne liom do ḃriaṫra,
  Ná "Leather away with the Wattle, O!"

D'ḟreagair dam an spéirḃean,
  A m-briaṫra binne, blasda, beoil;
A d-teangain ṁilis gaoiḋeilge
  Do ċuir go caoiṁ an ceart a g-cóir;
Cia file tu le h-éisteaċt
  A n-gleire goil na m-bruingioll óg,
M'ainim-si ní léir ḋuit;
  Ar feaḋ an ṁéid do ċanais fós.
Mise an ṁéirdreaċ—Innis Eilge,
  Le fada a b-péinn fá ġlasaiḃ bróin!
Ag tnuiṫ go g-cloisfin glaoḋaċ feasda,
  Air "Leather away with the Wattle, O!"

Her eyebrows dark and slender,
  Were each bended like a bow;
Her eyes beamed love as tender
  As only poets feel and know;
Her face where rose and lily
  Were both pourtrayed in brightest glow;
Her mien, so mild and stilly,
  All made my full heart overflow.
A tale she told,—of that Prince bold
  Whose crown of gold the Gael doth hold.
I hearkened all delighted
  To "Leather away with the Wattle, O!"

I asked this lovely creature
  Was *she* Helen famed of yore:
(So like she seemed in feature)
  Whose name will live for evermore—
Or Deirdre, meekest, fairest,
  Whom Uisneach's sons wrought direful woe—
Or Cearnuit, richest, rarest,
  Who first made mills on water go—
Or Meadhbh the young,—of ringlets long,
  So sweet her song along did flow,
Her song so rich and charming,
  Of "Leather away with the Wattle, O!"

And thus in tones unbroken,
  While sweet music filled her eye,
In accents blandly spoken,
  The damsel warbled this reply—
Albeit I know and blame not
  Your marvellous poetic lore,
You know my ancient name not,
  Though once renowned from shore to shore;
I am *Inis* famed,—*of Heroes* named,
  Forsaken, lost in pain and woe,
But waiting for a chorus,
  To "Leather away with the Wattle, O!"

Cia treasgaraḋ go faon lag,
Na céadta d'ḟuireann Airt 's Eoġain;
Do balbaiḋ ár n-éigse
'S do cuireaḋ ár g-cléir ar easbaḋ lóin;
Air ṫaisdiol do 'n ḃ-flaiṫ éaċtaċ,
Go h-Eire tabarṫaig fearda coróin,
'S ruacfaiḋ ruic an béarla
Le ceaṫa pléar tar calaiṫ fós,
'S as fearaṁuil, féasdaċ,—soilb, saorḋa,
Clanna Gaoḋal gan ċeas ag ól
'S go caoin dá spreagaḋ ar ṫéada,
"Leather away with the Wattle, O!"

CAOINE CHILLE CAIS.*

Cread ḋéanfamaoid feasda gan aḋmad,
Atá deire na g-coillte ar lár?
Ní'l tráċt ar Chill Chais ná a teaġlaċ,
'S ní bainfear a clingt† go bráṫ!
An áit úd 'na g-coṁnuiġeaċ an Dia-ḃean,
Fuair gairm 's meiḋir tar ṁná,
Bhíḋeaċ Iarlaiḋe‡ ag tarruing tar toinn ann,
'S an t-aifrionn binn dá ráḋ.

* Kilcash, a small country village situated about six miles east of the town of Clonmel, at the foot of *Sliabh na m-ban* mountain, and formerly the seat of a branch of the Butler family, and a place of note in its time. The only vestiges now remaining to attract the traveller's attention are the walls of the castle.

"This venerable mansion, for many centuries the residence of [a branch of] the Butler family, and attractive theme of travellers and tourists, was finally prostrated in the year 1800, and the materials sold for a trifling consideration to a Mr. James Power, a merchant of Carrick-on-Suir, by (the then) Lord Ormonde, father to the present representative of that noble family."—See Lynch's edition of *Castlehaven's Memoirs*, p. 23, note *. Dublin: 1815.

They died in war for ages,
  The brave sons of Art and Eoghan;
Mute are our bards and sages,
  And oh! our priests are sad and lone.
But Charles, despising danger,
  Will soon ascend green Eire's throne,
And drive the Saxon stranger
  Afar from hence to seek his own.
Then, full of soul,—and freed from dole,
  Without control the wine shall flow;
And we shall sing in chorus,
  "Come, Leather away with the Wattle, O!"

A LAMENT FOR KILCASH.

Oh, sorrow the saddest and sorest!
  Kilcash's attractions are fled—
Felled lie the high trees of its forest,
  And its bells hang silent and dead.
There dwelt the fair Lady, the Vaunted,
  Who spread through the island her fame,
There the Mass and the Vespers were chaunted,
  And thither the proud Earls came!

The song is probably the composition of a student named Lane, whom Lady Iveagh educated at her own expense for the priesthood, and from whose pen another song will be found in Hardiman's "Irish Minstrelsy," vol. ii., p. 267.

† *Cling*, death-bell, or knell.

‡ *Jarlaidhe, Earls.* To escape "the machinations of Shaftesbury and the party who wished to excite another persecution against the Catholics of England, by the fabrication of Popish plots, pretended conspiracies, and meditated assassinations, Lord Castlehaven came to Ireland, and died at his sister's house in Kilcash, county of Tipperary, Oct. 11, 1684."—Lynch's *Castlehaven Memoirs*, p. 26.

Is é mo ċreaċ-ḟada ! 's mo léan-ġoirt !
Do ġeataiḋe breáġa néata ar lár !
An *Avenue* ġreanta faoi ḟaoṫar,
'S gan fosg' ar aon taoḃ do 'n *Walk!*
An Chúirt ḃreáġa a sileaċ an braon di,
'S an ġarraḋ ḟéin go tláṫ,
'S an leaḃar na marḃ do léaġtar
An t-Easbog* 's *Lady 'Veagh !*†

Ní ċluinnim fuaim laċa ná géi ann,
Ná fiolair ag déanaḋ aeḋir cois cuain ;
Ná fiú na m-beaċa ċum saoṫair,
Thabarfaċ mil agus céir do'n t-sluaiġ !
Ní'l ceol binn milis na n-éan ann,
Le h-aṁarc an lae ḋul uainn,
Ná 'n ċuaiċín a m-bárr na n-géag ann,
O's í ċuirfeaċ an saoġal ċum suain.

Nuair ṫigeaḋ na puic faoi na sléiḃte,
'S an guna le na d-taoḃ, 's an líon ;
Féaċan siad a nuas le léan air,
An m-baile fuair *Sway* ann gaċ tír ;—
An ḟaiṫċe ḃreáġa aoiḃinn na raobṫaċa,
'S gan fosg ar aon taoḃ ó'n t-sín,
Páirc an *Phaddock* 'na *Dairy*,
Mar a m-biḋeaċ an eilit ag déanaḋ a sgíṫ!

A tá ceó ag tuitim ar ċraoḃaḋ ann,
Ná glanan ré grian, ná lá ;
Tá smúid ag tuitim o 'n spéir ann,
'S a cuid uisge go léir ag tráġa ;—

* Bishop Butler of West-Court, Callan, a man eminent for his virtues, unaffected piety, and the sanctity of his life.

† *Lady Iveagh*, "Margaret Bourke, eldest daughter of William, Earl of Clanricarde, first married to Brian Magennis, Viscount *Iveagh ;* and secondly to the Hon. Col. Thomas Butler, of Kilcash, county Tipperary, where she died 19th of July, 1744. She was a lady of great personal charms, and a bright example of every female

I am worn by an anguish unspoken
  As I gaze on its glories defaced,
Its beautiful gates lying broken,
  Its gardens all desert and waste.
Its courts, that in lightning and thunder
  Stood firm, are, alas ! all decayed ;
And the Lady Iveagh sleepeth under
  The sod, in the greenwood shade.

No more on a Summer-day sunny
  Shall I hear the thrush sing from his lair,
No more see the bee bearing honey
  At noon through the odorous air.
Hushed now in the thicket so shady,
  The dove hath forgotten her call,
And mute in the grave lies the Lady
  Whose voice was the sweetest of all !

As the deer from the brow of the mountain,
  When chased by the hunter and hound,
Looks down upon forest and fountain,
  And all the green scenery round ;
So I on thy drear desolation
  Gaze, O, my Kilcash, upon thee !
On thy ruin and black devastation,
  So doleful and woful to see !

There is mist on thy woods and thy meadows ;
  The sun appears shorn of his beams ;
Thy gardens are shrouded in shadows,
  And the beauty is gone from thy streams.

virtue. Her piety, charity, and universal benevolence, are eloquently described in the funeral sermon preached after her death, by the Rev. Richard Hogan, and printed in Kilkenny."—Hardiman's "Irish Minstrelsy," vol. ii., p. 417:

The family of Magennis, with whom the subject of this song was connected, are thus described by *O'Dubhagain* (O'Dugan), an Irish topographer of the fourteenth century:—

Ní'l coll, ní'l cuilion, ní'l caor' ann!
Aċd cloċa 'gus maol ċloċáin,
Páirc an ḟorgaois * gan ċraoḃ ann.
'S d'imṫiġ an *Game* ċum fáġain!

Anois mar ḃárr air gaċ mí-ġreann,
Chuaiḋ prionnsa na n-Gaoiḋeal† tar sáil;
A nún re h-aingir na míne,
Fuair gairm san ḃ-Frainc 's san Spáinn—
Anois atá a cuallaċt dá caoine,
Gheiḃeaċ airgiod buiḋe 'gus bán,
As í ná tógfaċ seilḃ na n-daoine
Aċd carraid na ḃ-fior boċdán!

Aitċim ar Mhuire 's ar JOSA
Go d-tagaiḋ sí 'rís ċúġainn slán?
Go m-beiṫ "rainciḋe fada" ag gaḃail timċioll,
Ceól ḃéiḋlinn 's teinte cnáṁ:—
Go d-tógfar an baile-si ár sinnsior,
Cill Chais ḃreáġa 'rís go h-árd,
'S go bráṫ nó go d-tiocfaḋ an dílionn,
Ní ḟaicfear í 'rís ar lár!

"Chief over the noble clan Aodh
Is the exalted and agreeable Magennis;
They settled on the fertile hill;
They took possession of all Ulidia."

They were descended from the famous warrior *Conall Cearnach*, and were the head of the *Clanna Rudhraidhe* of Ulster. Their possessions were the baronies of Iveagh and Lecale, and part of Mourne, in the county of Down.

The hare has forsaken his cover;
  The wild fowl is lost to the lake;
Desolation hath shadowed thee over,
  And left thee—all briar and brake!

And I weep while I pen the sad story—
  Our Prince has gone over the main,
With a damsel, the pride and the glory
  Not more of Green Eire than Spain.
The Poor and the Helpless bewail her;
  The Cripple, the Blind, and the Old;
She never stood forth as their jailer,
  But gave them her silver and gold.

O, GOD! I beseech thee to send her
  Home here to the land of her birth!
We shall then have rejoicing and splendour,
  And revel in plenty and mirth.
And our land shall be highly exalted;
  And till the dread dawn of that day
When the race of Old Time shall have halted,
  It shall flourish in glory alway!

In 1689, Lord Iveagh, husband of the lady commemorated in this song, furnished King James with two regiments of infantry and dragoons. After the war, he entered the Austrian service with a choice battalion of five hundred men.—*Green Book.*

* *Forghaois*, a rabbit burrow.

† *Prionnsa na n-Gaoidheal, Prince of the Gael.* The poet here alludes to the exiled Duke of Ormond.

BINN LISIN AORACH AN BHROGHA.

Brian Ua Flaiṫearta, cct.

Fonn :—Binn Lisín Aoraċ an Bhroġa.

Lá meaḋraċ dá raḃas-sa liom féin,
  Ar binn lisín aoraċ an Bhroġaḋ;
Ag eisdioċt le binn-ġuṫ na n-éan,
  Ag cantainn ar ġéagaḋ cois aḃan :—
An "Breac Taiḋḃrioċ" san líng úd faoi réim,
  Ag rainnce sa n-gaorṫa le fonn,
Már teinn liḃ-si raḋarc súl na béil,
  Tá leiġeas luaṫ ón éag diḃ dul ann!

THE FAIRY RATH OF BRUFF.

BY BRIAN O'FLAHERTY.

THIS song and air take their name from a celebrated fairy fort situated at the town of Bruff, in the county of Limerick, and like many others in this collection, would have probably been lost, or left in the "world of spirits," had it not fallen into our hands.

Brian O'Flaherty, the author, was an humble peasant, a mason by trade, and, for aught we know, he may have been "master-builder" to his friends—the fairies and "good people" of Bruff.

He was a native of Bruff, or its vicinity, but we cannot discover when he lived. It appears he was not numbered among the literary portion of the bards of his day, but was considered rather presumptive in assuming the name, and for such conduct he was cited, prosecuted, and expelled, at one of the Bardic Sessions then held in Munster. However, Brian was not so easily got rid of, and in order to gain favour, he mustered up all the natural talent he was possessed of, and composed the present song.

Bruff is situated on the banks of the river *Camog* (*Anglicised* "The Morning Star"), and lies about fifteen miles from Limerick. Tradition informs us that the banks of this river up to the town were formerly laid out with beautiful gardens, where all species of plants and trees peculiar to this country grew, and was much admired for being the resort of birds of all kinds, from the melody of whose notes it gained the appellation of *Binn* (melodious). At the west side of the town there is a little eminence called *Lios* (Fort), and there is also a castle, or *Brogha*, which is supposed to have been built by the De Lacy family shortly after the English invasion.

The birds carolled songs of delight,
  And the flowers bloomed bright on my path,
As I stood all alone on the height
  Where rises Bruff's old Fairy Rath.
Before me, unstirred by the wind,
  That beautiful lake lay outspread,
Whose waters give sight to the Blind,
  And would almost awaken the Dead!

Níor ċian dúinn coir dian t-srúill na séad,
 'Nar ṁian le fir Éirionn dul ann;
An tráṫ ṫriall ċúġainn an ġrian-ṁilis béiṫ,
 Go dian 's í 'n-éag-ċruiṫ go lom!
A ċiaḃ-ḟolt breáġa, niaṁrac, go féar,
 Ag fás léi-si roimpe 's na deaig;
"A Ḃhriain ḋil! cread é 'n dian-ġol so gníḋir,
 Do ċiap me go h-aeġiḃ ós mo ċionn!"

Ní sgaoilfead-sa prioṁ-rún mo sgéil,
 Go n-innsir cá taoḃ díom ar ġabair?
An tú Aoiḃill-ḃeag, ċaoin-ċleasaċ, ċlaon,
 Mar líonair go léir me do d' ġreann!
No 'n t-síṫ-ḃean ṫug buiḋin-truip na Trae,
 Gur líonadar Gréaguiġ 'na deaḃaig;
Nó 'n Ḃhriġdeaċ le'r ċlaoiḋeag lé gan réim,
 Clann Uisniċ na tréin-ḟir, gan ċaḃair!

"Ní díoḃ me, cia díṫ liom do sgéal,
 Aċt síġe-ḃean ó 'n d-tréan-lios úd tall;
Do ṡíor-ġoin do ṡíor-ġol a g-céin,
 'S as teinn liom tú traoċta ag neart Gall!
Glac inntin! Faig cloiḋeaṁ 'na m-beiḋ faoḃar,
 Ag rainnce air ċaoil-eaċ go seang;
Gaiḃ timċioll gaċ crioċ 'na ḃ-faġair Gaoiḋeil,
 Go n-innsir do sgéal dóiḃ gan ċam?"

D'éisdeas le binn-ġuṫ a béil,
 'S d'éirgios do léim ar mo ḃonn;
D'innsios gur teinn cúis mo sgéil,
 Le líng-goil naċ léigionn dam laḃairt!
Bíoḋgan mo ċroiḋe stig le léan,
 Agus silim fuil ṫréan as mo ċeann;
Mo ċaoin-roisg dá leaġaḋ 'nam mar ċaor,
 Ag síor-ṡile déara go trom!

As I gazed on the silvery stream,
So loved by the heroes of old,
There neared me, as though in a dream,
A maiden with tresses of gold.
I wept, but she smilingly said—
"Whence, Brian, my dearest, those tears?"
And the words of the gentle-souled maid
Seemed to pierce through my bosom like spears.

"O, rather," I cried, "lovely One,
Tell *me* who you are, and from whom!
Are you Aoibhill, and come here alone
To sadden my spirit with gloom?
Or she who brought legions to Troy,
When the Grecians crossed over the wave?
Or the dame that was doomed to destroy
The children of Uisnigh the brave?"

"I am none of all three," she replied,
"But a fairy from yonder green mound—
Who heard how you sorrowed and sighed
As you strayed o'er this elf-haunted ground.
And now gird around you your sword,
And spring on your swift-footed steed—
And call on the Gael, serf and lord,
And Eire's green land shall be freed!"

So spake she in musical tones,
And I started as wakened from sleep,
I told her the cause of my groans,
And the anguish that forced me to weep—
Why my eyes were thus blinded by tears,
And my bosom tormented with pains,
Why my heart had been breaking for years,
And the blood growing cold in my veins.

Ag an mín-t-sruiṫ nuair bím-si liom féin,
 Ar binn lisín aoraċ an Bhroġaḋ ;
Ag smaoineaṁ ar ġníoṁarṫaib an t-saoġail,
 An iosbairtsi ar Ghaoiḋil ag neart Gall,
Tá Fleet na d-trí ríġṫe go tréan,
 'S an Stiobhart san Séamus, 'na ċeann ;*
Laoisig dá líonaḋ faoi réim,
 Mile 's seaċt g-céad ann gaċ long.

CAIT NI NEILL.

Anois ó ṫárlaḋ, a b-príosún árd me, a n-géibeann ċruaiḋ,
'S go raċainn do stáir, mar a b-fuil mo ġráḋ geal, 's go b-pógfainn í ;
Do ḃrailfin mo láiṁ ḋeas air a bráġaid, nó faoi na coimín caoil,
As é 'dubhairt Cáit liom, "ġeabaḋ náire, mar a d-tóigfir díom !"

Ní ṫógfad díot, a stóir mo ċroiḋe, mar is tú ḃreoiġ me 'raoir,
Chuir saiġead am ċroiḋe, ná léigisfior díom, go bráṫ re m' rae !
Dá m-beiṫ an Chúirt na suiġe, 's mé le croċa triot, 's mo ċúis dá ṗléiḋ,
Le torad cloiḋiṁ, do ḃainfinn díob tú, a Cháit Ní Néill !

* *Ceann, head, chief, captain, leader,* James, the Chevalier de St. George.

She vanished on hearing my tale,
But at evening I often roam still
To lament the sad fate of the Gael,
And to weep upon Bruff's Fairy Hill.
O! may we soon see the three Kings,*
And JAMES, above all, in this land!
May the winds on their favoring wings
Waft swiftly their fleet to our strand!

KATE NI NEILL.

Now that, in prison, and all forsaken, my fate I rue,
Fain would I seek her, my only true-love, and wed her too,
Around her white waist I'd press my arm with a pleasure new,
But still she tells me—"O, leave me! leave me! you shame me, you!"

No, no, my darling, I'll never shame you; but all night long
You wound my bosom! I'm grown most feeble—I once so strong!
Come good or evil, come Death or Life, or come Right or Wrong,
Sweet Kate Ni Neill, love, I'd choose you only among the throng.

* The King of Ireland, England, and Scotland.

Is ínte ċíḋtear, an alaḋ úin, nár ċáineaḋ béal,
'Na ḃ-fuil gruaig a cinn, na lúba buiḋe léi, ag fás go féar;
Is geal a píb, is suiġte a cóm, 's a cnáṁa go léir,
A ḃ-fuil as súd síos, go bárr a tróiġe, níl cáim fae'n saoġal.

Tá tuile gníoṁarṫa, 'gam le n-insint ort, a ṡéiṁ-ḃean ṡuairc,
Is mear do sgríoḃṫá, bana caol, is léir 's as lsaiṫ;
Do ruiṫfá *Reel*, air fuid an tíġe, go mear, éadrom, buan,
'S le guṫ do ċinn, go g-cuirfeáḋa céad laoċ, ċum suain!

Gaċ béiṫ ḋeas dá d-tagaċ ċúġamsa, ní ḃeiḋinn sásda léi,
Tír na lóng a g-ceart 's a g-cúntas, 's a ḟágail le béib;
Pórt Ṁaṫġaṁna air fad gan ċúntas, an Spáinn 's an Ghréig,
Go m'ḟearr liomsa ḃeiṫ air leabaḋ ċlúiṁ leat a Cháit Ní Néill.

Ghlacainn ċúġam tú gan baḋ, gan púint, gan áireaṁ spréiḋ,
'S as leat do ṡiúbalfainn maidion drúċda, air ḃárr an ḟéir;
As é mo ċreaċ go dúḃaċ gan mé 'gus tú, a ḃláṫ na g-craoḃ!
A g-Caisioll Múṁan 's gan do leabaḋ fúinn, aċt Clár Bog Déil!

Your lovely features, O, glorious creature, attract all eyes!
Your golden tresses flow brightly downward in dazzling guise;
Your neck so snow-white, your waist so slender, your features fair,
Exalt you over all mortal maidens beyond compare!

O! beauteous damsel, the light and lustre of Eire's land,
Yours is the ready, the quick yet steady, the writer's hand!
Yours is the light foot, the bounding figure for saraband,
And yours the voice that nor king nor hero could e'er withstand.

To all the lasses I have met with my heart was steel,
No wealth, nor honour, could ever tempt me to them to kneel,
Not all Portumna, not Spain or Hellas, could make me feel
One moment faithless to you, my darling, sweet Kate Ni Neill!

O! were you landless, and owned not even one blade of grass,
All other damsels, the dead or living, you'd still surpass!
O, woe and sorrow! how sadly fare I! alas! alas!
Without my Kate, without friends or money, without a glass!

RÓIS GHEAL DUBH.*

Fonn:—Róis Gheal Dubh.

Is fada an réim do ṫug mé féin ó nae go 'niuġ,
An imioll sléiḃ 'muiċ, go h-imiollta, éadtrom, mar
b'eólaċ dam;
Loċ Eirne do léimear, cia gur mór an sruiṫ,
'S gan do ġile gréine am ḋéig-si, aċt mo Róis Gheal
Dubh!

* We present the reader with two different settings of this air, for from their extraordinary beauty we could not justly omit either. *Rois*

BLACK-HAIRED FAIR ROSE.

Fonn:—Róisín Dubh.

Since last night's star, afar, afar, Heaven saw my speed,
I seem'd to fly o'er mountains high, on magic steed,
I dashed through Erne:—the world may learn the cause
from *Love;*
For, light or sun shone on me none, but *Roisin Dubh!*

Gheal Dubh (Black-haired Fair Rose), sometimes written *Roisin Dubh* (Dark-haired little Rose), is supposed to be one of these names by which Ireland is known in the language of allegory.

Go d-tí an aonach má ṫéiġionn tu ag díol do stuic,
Má ṫéiġir, ná fan déanach san oiḋċe amuiċ?
Bíoċ bultaiḋ ar do ḋóirse 's mór-ġlais cip,
Nó as baoġal duit an cléiriċ ar an Róis Gheal Duḃ!

A Róisín ná bíoċ brón ort, ná cás anois,
Tá do ṗárdún o Ṗápa na Róṁa agad;
Tá na Bráiṫre teaċt tar sáile 's ag triall tar muir,
'S ní ċeilfior fíon Spáinneaċ ar mo Róis Gheal Duḃ!

Ta grád 'gam am lár duit le bliaġain a niuġ,
Grád cráiḋte! grád cásṁar! grád ciapaiḋṫe!
Grád d'ḟág mé gan sláinte! gan rian! gan ruiṫ!
'S go bráṫ, bráṫ, ní 'l aon ḟáġail agam ar mo Róis Gheal Duḃ!

Do ṡiúḃalfainn-si an Mhúṁain leat, 's ciúṁais na g-cnoc,
Mar ṡúil go b-faġainn rún ort, nó páirt le cion;
A ċráoḃ-ċúrṫa, tuigṫear dúinne, go b-fuil grád 'gad dam;
'S gur b'í plúr-sgoiṫ na m-ban múinte, mo Róis Gheal Duḃ!

Beiḋ an ḟairge na tuilte dearga, 's an spéir na fuil,
Beiḋ an saoġal na ċogaḋ ċroiḋearg ar ḋruim na g-cnoc,
Beiḋ gaċ gleann sléiḃe ar fuid Eirionn, 's móinte ar criṫ!
Lá éigin sul a n-éagfaiḋ mo Róis Gheal Duḃ!

My friends! my prayers for marts and fairs are these alone—
That buyers haste home ere evening come, and sun be gone;
For, doors, bolts, all, will yield and fall, where picklocks move—
And faith the Clerk may seize i' the dark, my *Roisin Dubh!*

O, Roisin mine! droop not nor pine, look not so dull!
The Pope from Rome hath sent thee home a pardon full!
The priests are near: O! never fear! from Heaven above
They come to thee—they come to free my *Roisin Dubh!*

Thee have I loved—for thee have roved o'er land and sea:
My heart was sore;—it evermore beat but for thee.
I could but weep—I could not sleep—I could not move;
For, night and day, I dreamt alway of *Roisin Dubh!*

Through Munster's lands, by shores and strands, far could I roam,
If I might get my loved one yet, and bring her home.
O, sweetest flower, that blooms in bower, or dell, or grove,
Thou lovest me, and I love thee, my *Roisin Dubh!*

The sea shall burn, the earth shall mourn—the skies rain blood—
The world shall rise in dread surprise and warful mood—
And hill and lake in Eire shake, and hawk turn dove—
Ere you shall pine, ere you decline, my *Roisin Dubh!*

ROISIN DUBH.*

Is mairg do 'n té úd d'ár b'éigion dul tar sáile soir!
'S nach boċt do 'n tréan-ċlann do ċaiṫfeaḋ éalóḋ gan spás tar muir!
Tá láṁ an tréatúir ag sgrios 'sa raobaḋ,—súd a ḃuaḋ a niuġ,—
Támaoid tréigṫe, fáṫ ár n-éalóḋ uait, a Róisín Duḃ!

Is buan smuainte mo ċroiḋe ort a stóir, a noċt,
Ad ḋíṫ-si is trom ċaoinim gan sgíṫ, gan toċt!
Or gan inneaḋ raṫ mo ṡaeġil leat, a ḃláṫ na sub',
Aċt faraoir! táim a n-daoirse uait, a Róisín Duḃ!

Ba ḋeas mo ḋóiṫ feaḋ do ḃíḋ me pósda le'm stóirín féin,
A d-túis m'óige ḃíḋ mé stróiġ lé gan easbaḋ aon níḋ;
Aċt mo ḋíṫ-ġuirt! ṫáinic aois dam, 's d'éaloiḋ mo ċruiṫ!
'S as éigion dam tú ṫréigion, a Róisín Duḃ!

Ba ḋeas do ċlóḋ ar gaċ aon ċor, a ċraoiḃ úr-ḃláṫ!
Ba ṁaiṫ do ċóisir ar bórdaiḃ glan, núaḋ, gaċ lá,—
Uċ! cuiṁniḋ a Róisín ar gaċ móide do ṫugais fein dam,
Giḋ' gur b'éigion dam do ṫréigion ar sáile a niuġ!

* This song was sent us as the composition of a Munster bard; but upon examination we found it deficient of that smooth and grace-

LITTLE BLACK-HAIRED ROSE.

O, bitter woe, that we must go, across the sea!
O, grief of griefs, that Lords and Chiefs, their homes must flee!
A tyrant-band o'erruns the land, this land so green,
And, though we grieve, we still must leave, our Dark *Roisin!*

My darling Dove, my Life, my Love, to me so dear,
Once torn apart from you, my heart will break, I fear,
O, golden Flower of Beauty's bower! O, radiant Queen!
I mourn in bonds; my soul desponds; my Dark *Roisin!*

In hope and joy, while yet a boy, I wooed my bride;
I sought not pelf; I sought herself, and nought beside,
But health is flown, 'tis old I'm grown; and, though I ween
My heart will break, I must forsake my Dark *Roisin!*

The fairest Fair you ever were; the peerless Maid;
For bards and priests your daily feasts were richly laid.
Amid my dole, on you my soul still loves to lean,
Though I must brave the stormy wave, my Dark *Roisin!*

ful flow peculiar to Munster poetry. The merit of the translation, however, entitles it to a place in the present collection.

The original song of *Roisin Dubh* is supposed to have been com-

Cuiṁniḋ fós air gaċ cóṁráḋ mín, cóir, gan ċlaoin,
Cuiṁniḋ a stóir gur leatsa a pósaḋ me a d-túis mo ḟaeġil!
Cuiṁniḋ a óigḃean an leabaḋ a córuiġeaḋ ḋuit féin 's daṁ,
Bláṫ na rós, 's sgoiṫ na món-ṁáġ, mo Róisín Duḃ!

Naċ ḃ-fuil mo ṗáirt leat a ċúil fáinneaċ na n-dual cas m-buiḋe!
Naċ tú mo ġráḋ-sa d'á ḃ-fuil do'n Aḋaṁ-ċlainn, a ċailín ċaoin!
Gonuig an lá 'niuġ a n-gníoṁ ná ráiḋtiḃ ní ḃ-fuair tú guiṫ,
'S naċ cruaiḋ an cás gur cuireaḋ gráin ort, a Róisín Duiḃ!

Ná biḋeaċ brón ort a Róisín! aċd bioḋ ad ṫoċt,
Tá do ċáirde ag teaċt tar sáile gan spás a noċt;
Tiocfaḋ a lán do ṫreiḃ na Sbáinne leó a noir,
'S beir a Róisín gan bron na ḋeoig sin, 's go deo faoi ċion!

Go d-tiġ' an tráṫ sin céad slán leat a stór mo ċuim,
Go d-tiocfaḋ an lá san míle slán leat, a ċroiḋe naċ tim!
Biḋ gáirdeaċ, táim ad t-fágḃáil a stóir, a niuġ!
Aċd fillfead le áṫus 's mór-ġárdas, ar mo Róisín Duḃ!

posed in the reign of Elizabeth for the celebrated *Aodh Ua Domhnaill*, Prince of *Tir Chonaill* (Tirconnell). The allegorical allusions

In years gone by, how you and I seemed glad and blest!
My wedded wife, you cheered my life, you warmed my breast!
The fairest one the living sun e'er decked with sheen,
The brightest rose that buds or blows, is Dark *Roisin!*

My guiding Star of Hope you are, all glow and grace,
My blooming Love, my Spouse above all Adam's race;
In deed or thought you cherish nought of low or mean;
The base alone can hate my own—my Dark *Roisin!*

O, never mourn as one forlorn, but bide your hour;
Your friends ere long, combined and strong, will prove their power.
From distant Spain will sail a train to change the scene
That makes you sad, for one more glad, my Dark *Roisin!*

Till then, adieu! my Fond and True! adieu, till then!
Though now you grieve, still, still believe we'll meet again;
I'll yet return, with hopes that burn, and broad-sword keen;
Fear not, nor think you e'er can sink, my Dark *Roisin!*

to Ireland under the name of *Roisin*, have long been forgotten, and it is now known by the peasantry merely as a love song.

EAMONN AN CHNOIC.

Fonn:—Eamonn An Chnoic.

Cia h-é sin amuiċ,
'Na b-fuil faobar ar a ġuiṫ,
Ag raobaḋ mo ḋoruis ḋúntaḋ?
Mise Eamonn an Chnoic,
'Tá báiḋte, fuar, fliuċ,
O ṡíor-ṡiúbal sléibte 's gleanntaḋ!
A laoġ ḋil 's a ċuid,
Cread ḋéanfainn-si ḋuit,
Mun a g-cuirfinn ort beinn da m' ġúnaḋ,
'S go b-fuil púġdar go tiuġ,
Dá ṡíor-ṡéide riot,
'S go m-beaḋmaois a raon múċta!

EDMUND OF THE HILL.

AIR:—"*Edmund of the Hill.*"

EDMUND O'RYAN, better known as *Eamonn an Chnoic* (Edmund, or Ned of the Hill), was born at Shanbohy, in the parish of Temple-beg, in the upper half barony of Kilnemanagh, in Tipperary, previous to the wars of 1691. His father, who possessed a considerable amount of property after the confiscations and plunders of 1641, was descended from the valiant and warlike race of the O'Ryans, of Kilnelongurty, many of whom lost their lives and properties in the obstinate, but ineffectual struggle for independence, by the Earl of Desmond, in the reign of Elizabeth. His mother was of the ancient family of the O'Dwyers, lords of Kilnemanagh. Edmund was intended for the priesthood; but by an affair in which he took a prominent part after his return from the Continent, where he had studied for the clerical profession, he had to relinquish that idea. After many strange vicissitudes in life, his body now lies interred on the lands of Curraheen, near Faill an Chluig, in the parish of Toem, in the upper half barony of Kilnemanagh, near the Hollyford copper mine, and the precise spot is marked on sheet 45 of the Ordnance Survey of Tipperary, as the grave of *Eamonn an Chnoic.*

We have received a long sketch of him from a distinguished literary member of the family, but are obliged to reserve it for another volume.

"You, with voice shrill and sharp,
Like the high tones of a harp,
Why knock you at my door like a warning?"
"I am Ned of the Hill,
I am wet, cold, and chill,
Toiling o'er hill and vale since morning!"—
"Ah, my love, is it you?
What on earth can I do?
My gown cannot yield you a corner.
Ah! they'll soon find you out—
They'll shoot you, never doubt,
And it's I that will then be a mourner!"

Is fada mise amuiġ,
Faoi ṡneaċta 'gus faoi ṡioc,
'S gan dánaċt agam ar aon neaċ;
Mo ṡeisreaċ gan sgur,
Mo ḃranar gan cur,
A's gan iad agam ar aon ċor!
Ní'l caraid agam,
Is dainid liom san,
Do ġlacfaċ mé moċ ná déanaċ,
'S go g-caiṫfeaḋ mé dul,
Tar fairrge soir,
Os ann náċ ḃ-fuil mo ġaoḋaltaḋ:

A ċúil álainn deas,
'Na ḃ-fáinniḋe cas,
Is breáġa 'gus as glas do ṡúile!
Go ḃ-fuil mo ċroiḋe dá ṡlad,
Mar do ṡníoṁṫaoi gad,
Le bliaġain ṁór fada ag tnúṫ leat.
Dá ḃ-faġainn-si le ceart,
Cead sine sios leat,
Is éadtrom 's as deas do ṡiúḃalfainn
Go ḃ-fuil mo smaointe a ḃean,
Air éalóġaḋ leat,
Faoi ċoillṫiḃ ag spealaḋ an drúċtaḋ!

A ċumainn 's a ṡearc,
Raċamaoid-ne seal,
Faoi ċoillṫiḃ ag spealaḋ an drúċtaḋ!
Mar a ḃ-faġmaoid an breac,
'S an lon air a nead,
An fiaḋ 'gus an poc a búiṫre;—
Na h-éininiḋe binne,
Air ġéiginiḋe seinneaḋ,
'S an ċuaiċín ar ḃáirr ar úr-ġlais,
Go bráṫ bráṫ ní ṫiocfaḋ
An bás air ár n-goireaḋ,
A lárr na coille cúḃarṫa.

"Long I'm wandering in woe,
In frost and in snow,
No house can I enter boldly;
My ploughs lie unyoked—
My fields weeds have choked—
And my friends they look on me coldly!
Forsaken of all,
My heart is in thrall:
All-withered lies my life's garland,
I must look afar
For a brighter star,
Must seek my home in a far land!

"O! thou of neck fair,
And curling hair,
With blue eyes flashing and sparkling!
For a year and more
Has my heart been sore,
And my soul for thee been darkling.
O, could we but both,—
You nothing loth,—
Escape to the wood and forest,
What Light and Calm,
What healing balm,
Should I have for my sorrows sorest!

"My fond one and dear,
The greenwood is near,
And the lake where the trout is springing—
You will see the doe,
The deer and the roe,
And will hear the sweet birds singing,
The blackbird and thrush
In the hawthorn bush,
And the lone cuckoo from his high nest,
And you never need fear,
That Death would be near,
In this bright scenery divinest!

Beir sgéalaḋ uaim soir,
Go h-aingir ċiuin an t-suilt,
Gur ċailleadar na neid a n-éanlaiṫ;
Gur a raoir do ṫuit
An sneaċta ar na cnoic*
Amaċ ar feaḋ na h-Eirionn!
Dá mairioċ liom ruiṫ,
Go seaċdṁuin ó 'niuġ,
Raċfainn-se ar mire ad t-féaċaint,
Is go m'fearr liom anois,
A beiṫ báiḋte san muir,
Ná ráḋ go m-beiḋfeá réiġ liom!

* From this and the preceding line it would appear that the song was composed in the year of the great frost, 1739.

Fonn:—An Sioda atá ad Bhalluiṫ a Bhuaċaill.

"O! could the sweet dove,
The maiden of my love,
But know how fettered is her lover!
The snows all the night
Fell in valley and on height,
Through our fated island over,
But ere the sun's rays
Glance over seven days,
She and I, as I hope, will renew love;
And rather would I be
Deep drowned in the sea,
Than be faithless to her, my true love!"

THE WALLET OF SILK.

The air which we give on the opposite page, and to which words by *Eoghan Ruadh O'Suilliobhain*, will be found at p. 64 of our "Reliques of Irish Jacobite Poetry," originated in the following anecdote.

One of those young men, better known among the community as "poor scholars," whom a thirst for education, in bygone days, sent from various parts of the kingdom to the south, was accosted in the following manner, by a young woman, perhaps the daughter of his host, in reference to the *wallet*, or *satchel* in which he carried his books.

"*An sioda ata ad wallet,*
An sioda ata ad wallet,
An sioda ata ad wallet a bhuachaill?
An sioda ata ad wallet,
An sioda ata ad wallet,
No abhla do bhlaiseach mna uaisle?"

To which he replied:—

"*Ni sioda ata am wallet,*
Ni sioda ata am wallet,
Ni sioda ata am wallet a stuaire!
Ni sioda ata am wallet,
Ni sioda ata am wallet,
Na abhla do bhlaiseach mna uaisle!"

"Is it silk that's in your wallet,
Is it silk that's in your wallet,
Is it silk that's in your wallet, my buachaill?
Is it silk that's in your wallet,
Is it silk that's in your wallet,
Or apples for ladies to eat of?"

"'Tis not silk I have in my wallet,
'Tis not silk I have in my wallet,
'Tis not silk I have in my wallet, my fair one!
'Tis not silk I have in my wallet,
'Tis not silk I have in my wallet,
Nor apples for ladies to eat of!"

A MHAIRE 'GUS A MHUIRNIN.

Fonn :—A Mháire agus a Mhúirnín.

A Mháire 'gus a ṁúirnín, 's a lúibín na g-craoḃ-
    ḟolt,
An cuiṁin leat mar do ṡiublamaois ar ḋrúiċtíníḋe
    an ḟéir ġlais ;
A ḃláṫ na n-aḃall g-cúḃarṫa, na g-cnó buiḋe, 's na
    ġ-caoraḋ,
Do ṗáirt-si níor ḋiúltaiġear, cé ḋúḃaċ taoim ad
    t-éiliom !

MY DARLING MARY.

This beautiful love-song is the composition of one of the humbler rank of the peasantry, and breathes, like all other poems of the same class, the most intense feeling of deep affection, and burning tenderness of expression.

To show with what fidelity our poet has adhered to the original, we need only refer our readers to the following literal translation of the first stanza:—

> O, my darling Mary—my fair one of the ringlets,
> Do you remember how we together trod the dew on the green grass;
> Blossom of the sweet-scented apple-tree—the golden nuts—and berries,
> Your affection never deserted me—tho' in sadness you have left me.

There are many compositions of this class current among the peasantry, which should be collected before they die away, and we earnestly hope our Munster friends will take care to preserve the many beautiful songs which, though long popular among the peasantry of the south, have never yet appeared in print.

O, ringletted young maiden! O, my own darling Mary!
We've trod the dew together in the fields green and airy,
O! blossom of the apple-tree! my heart's fount of gladness!
I always loved you fondly, though you've left me now in sadness.

A ġráḋ ḋil 's a rúinín, tar taoiḃ liom oiḋċe éigin?
Nuair luiġfeaḋ mo ṁuintir go m-beiḋeam ag caint
le na ċéile;
Mo láṁ ar do ċuimín, ag déiṁniúġaḋ mo sgéil
duit,
'S gur b'é do ġráḋ a ṁaiġdean, ḃuain raḋarc flaṫais
Dé ḋíom!

Dá m-beiṫ ḟios ag mo ḋearḃráṫair mo ġearán 's
mo ḃuairioṁ,
Dá m-beiṫ ḟios (dar Párán), ḃeiḋeaḋ fuarán ró-
ṁór air,
Mo ċéad-searc am ṫréigion, 's céile eile dá luaḋ
léi,
'S tar ṁná deasa Eirionn, is í mo ġráḋ geal ná
fuaṫ-fainn.

A ċailín breáġa uasail—uaigneas mo láir tú,
A ċúl buiḋe na g-cocán 's a ġrianán ban Eirionn;
Do rinn tú mo ḋíoġḃáil, 's farior ní'l léiġios air,
Cread do b'áil liom do t-iarraiḋ 's a ḋian-ġráḋ
ná faġainn tú.

Dá m-beiḋinn-si am iasgaire ṫiar a m-Beinn Eidir,
'S Máire na n-geal m-bráġad na bradán ar loċ
Eirne;
Is súgaċ 's as meaḋraċ do ra'ain-si dá h-éiliom,
'S do ġeaḃainn ann mo líontán "Grianán ban
Eirionn."

Dá m-beiḋinn-si am laċa 's fairsinge sléiḃe 'gam,
'S raḋarc ar na Flaiṫċis d'ḟonn m'anam do ṡaoraḋ;
Do ṫabarfainn an ainġir a baile dá b-féad-fainn,
'S léigfin dá h-aṫair a ḃeiṫ sealad dá h-éiliom!

My purest love, my true love, come some night to me
kindly,
We both will talk together of the love I gave you
blindly;
With my arm round your slender waist, I'll tell how
you won me,
And how 'twas you, my Mary, shut Heaven's gates
upon me.

O! if my brother knew but of my woe and my sorrow,
A bitter heart he'd have through many a day and
morrow;
O! none of Eire's maidens do I prize like to you,
love,
And yet you now forsake me, though I thought you
my true love!

O, loveliest of damsels, the sad truth must be spoken,
But, maid of golden tresses, my sore heart you have
broken;
My suffering is grievous, but I fain must endure it,
My wound it is a deep one, but you will not cure it.

O! were I in Beinn-Eidir, a fisher skilled and wary,
And you down in Lough Erin, a salmon, O my
Mary,
I'd rise up in the night-time, and haste to its waters,
And I'd catch you in my net, before all Eire's
daughters!

Or if I were a wild duck, and the heath hills before me,
And Heaven in its glory so blue shining o'er me,
I'd bring you home, my fair one, and this I tell you
plainly,
That if your father sought you, he should long seek
you vainly!

Dá m-beiḋinn-si a Lundain mar ċeann ar an n-gárda,
'S cead agam o'n b-Frannċaċ mo long do ċur tar sáile;
Ċhúig ṁíle púnta dá m'ḟiú sin gaċ lá me
Is í Máire mo roġa-sa, 's do ḃronn-fain mo stát di.

Eirġiḋ ad ḟuiġe a ḃuaċaill 's gluais ar do ġearrán?
Gaċ bealaċ dá m-buailir bíḋ' ar ṫuarais mo ḋian-ġráḋ,
Do ḃíḋ-si dá luaḋ liom o ḃíḋeas am leanḃ-bán,
'S ba ḃinne liom naoi nuaire í ná cuaċ 's ná orgáin.

Fonn:—An Smaċdaoin Crón.

O, were I in London, a naval commander,
And France gave me charters o'er ocean to wander,
Tis hundreds of thousands of guineas I'd squander
On Mary, my darling! no queen should be grander.

Up, boy! Mount your steed! 'Tis a bright eve and airy,
And each road you travel inquire for my Mary!
She loved me while yet but a child like a fairy—
That sweet one whose tones shame the thrush and canary!

THE BROWN LITTTE MALLET.

THE epithet *Smachdaoin Cron* (Brown Little Mallet) was applied to a stout description of tobacco, smuggled into Ireland about the middle of the last century, and in which an extensive traffick was carried on in Munster. There are many songs to this air current among the peasantry; but we believe the following is the first stanza of the earliest known specimen:—

"*Eirghidh ad shuighe a chailin!*
Cuir sios potataoi 's feoil!
Sud e nios an garraidhe,
Rabaire an Smachdaoin Chroin.

"*Oro, ro, mo Smachdaoin!*
Caradh mo chroidhe, mo Smachdaoin!
Oro, ro, mo Smachdaoin!
O, mo Smachdaoin Cron!"

"Arise! get up my girl!
Boil potatoes and meat!
Here comes up the garden
The lad with the *Smachteen Cron*.

"Oro, ro, my Smachteen!
Love of my soul, my Smachteen!
Oro, ro, my Smachteen!
O my Smachteen Cron!"

AN SEABHAC SIUBHAIL.

Muiris Ua Gríoḃṫa, ccc.

Fonn :—An Clár Bog Déil.

Is é measdar liom ar leagaḋ túr, 's áitrioḃ récs,
Ar easbaḋ siúḃail, ar ḟeasaṁ smúit neaṁ-ġnáṫ,
san spéir ;
Ar ċreaċaḋ triúċ, ar leagaḋ dúil, 's ar árd-
sgread béiṫ,
Go b-fuil malartúġaḋ le teaċt do'n ċúis, nó lá
ḃreaṫ' Dé !

THE WANDERING EXILE.

BY MAURICE GRIFFIN.

AIR:—"*Soft Deal Board.*"

WE have several songs to this air in our collection, but have selected this Jacobite effusion of Maurice Griffin, for the present occasion. The original words will be found in Hardiman's "Irish Minstrelsy," vol. i., p. 238, with a translation by Thomas Furlong; and as we have made it a rule never to *reprint* Irish songs while we have an abundant stock in MS., we hope our readers will feel pleased with that which we here lay before them.

The original version of "*Clar Bog Deal*" (Soft Deal Board) is better known under the title of "*Caisioll Mumhan*" (Cashel of Munster), and may with justice be attributed to the Rev. Wm. English, as we possess copies of it, and of several other songs ascribed to him, written early in the last century. As previously mentioned, the reverend writer, before his assumption of the Augustinian habit, was the author of many beautiful compositions; among which we may reckon the celebrated "*Cois na Brighide,*" "By the Bride's Silvery Waters," of which the following is the opening stanza:—

"Cois na Brighide seal do bhiosa go sugach samh,
Ag dearca sios air aingir chaoin an urladh bhlath;
Ba ghile a pib na sneachta air craoibh 's na drucht air ban,
'S ni coigcrioch me acht buachaill brioghmhar o Dhun na m-bad?"

"By the Brighid awhile I dwelt, merry and gay,
Glancing down on the mild maiden, of the beaming eye;
Whose neck is whiter than snow on trees, or dew on lea,
And I am not a stranger, but a brave youth, from Dun of the boats."

We cannot tell what place is meant by *Dun na m-bad*, which the writer states is his birthplace, unless it be Dungarvan, in the county of Waterford, a place celebrated for its fishing-boats.

Methinks Earth reels and rocks, and feels towns fall
and towers,
The gloomy sky looks heavy on high, and blackly
lowers.
The wailing of maids, the hourly raids that waste the
land,
Would seem to say that the Judgment Day is nigh at
hand.

Is é deir an cúinge caṫa cúil, 's an Spáinneaċ tréan,
'San bean-sa d'úṁ'laiḋ teaċt gan ċúinse, a b-páirt na laoċ;
Ná stadfaid siúd dá g-cleasaiḃ lúiṫ, 'na lann-ċaṫ n-géar,
Go g-caiṫfid cúmplaċt náṁaid ár n-dúiṫċe, air fán le faoḃar!

Is dearḃ ḋúinn a ċaraid ċlúṁuil, 's a ráib ḋil ġlé,
Go n-geallaid siúd go tapaiḋ cóngnaṁ bárc, 's laoċ;
Go fras do'n ṗrionnsa ċeannais ḋúṫċais ċáirde Chéin,
'Tá ag fada tnúiṫ le neart an triuir ċum teaċt a réim.

Is fear ó d'iompaiḋ an aingir lonnraiḋ, láidir, léir,
Go ceart le Laoiseaċ lasair ionnraic, a b-páirt gan ṗléiḋ;
Go b-fearfar dlúiṫ-ċeaṫ, treasaċ, trúpaċ, táin-teaċ, tréan,
Do ċaiṫfios Búir go Breatain ċionntaċ as áitrioḃ Gaoḋal.

Beiḋ ceallaḋ 's úird gan smaċt ann súd, gan sgáṫ, gan baoġal,
Beiḋ reaċt na d-triúċ mar leasa ar d-túis ag Pápa Dé;
Beiḋ ceart 's cúinse bleaċtṁar búaḋaċ, do ġnáṫ ag Gaoiḋeil,
'S ár "Seaḃac Siúḃail" gan ċead do'n m-brúid, go bráṫ a réim.

On the battle-plain blood runs like rain: the Spaniard brave
And she who comes to free our homes o'er Ocean's wave,
Have sworn they will fight for Truth and Right,—fight evermore
Till they drive afar the hounds of War from Banba's shore.

Be of cheer, my friend; we never will bend! Our barques and troops
Will muster in pride; and Woe betide the heart that droops!
Our swords we draw for our King and Law, nor we alone—
Three Princes he hath to clear his path, and rear his throne!

Since the Maiden bright, unmatched in might, joined Louis of France,
We have sworn to stand, a marshalled band, with gun and lance,
On the battle-ground, and fight till crowned with victory—
Yea, till we chase the Sassenach race across the sea!

From tyrannous men our temples then, all free shall rise—
And the Pope of God will bless our sod, and still our sighs.
And Right and Might rule day and night in Eire's isle—
And we shall sing to our exiled King glad hymns the while!

Ba seasgair súbaċ ag cantain ciuil an dáiṁ, le dréaċt,
A m-bailtiḃ Múṁan go maisioċ, muinte, gáirdeaċ, glé;
Gaċ dragan úr do ċlanna Lúġaiḋ, Chárrṫaiġ, 's Chéin,
Ag teaċt go h-úṁal gan stad a g-cúirt, le gráḋ do 'n sgléip.

AN BRANNDA.

Diarmuid mac Doṁnaill, ṁic Fingin Chaoil, ṁic Chárrṫaiḋ, cct.

A ḋalta ḋil dár ṫugasa mo ann-saċd dian,
Geallaim duit go raċainn-si, giḋ' fann mo rian;
Ad ḟaicsin-si le carṫannaċd an am gaċ blia-ġain,
Aċd ar eagla a ḃeiṫ treasgarṫa ag an m-Brannda ṡiar!

Ní seasgaireaċd fá n-dearna ḋam, ná clampar ṡiaċ,
Ná an'ṁuinn do ċraipinneaċ mo ċeann, giḋ' liaṫ!
Ná seaċain dul tar ġarb-ċnocaiḃ raṁaraḋ, liag,
Aċd eaglaḋ a ḃeiṫ treasgarṫa ag an m-Brannda ṡiar!

With music and song the bardic throng through Munster's towns
Shall chant their joy, and each minstrel boy win laurel crowns.
Each noble chief shall forget his grief, and Lughaidh's name
And Mac Cartha Mór * shine out as of yore with brighter fame.

WHISKEY ON THE WAY.

BY DERMOD MAC DOMHNALL MAC FELIX (THE SLENDER) MAC CARTHY.

My gay and brilliant friend, though my health is rather poor,
I wouldn't be so slow to cross your hospitable door—
Once a twelvemonth at the least would I give you up a day,
If I didn't fear the sly assaults of Whiskey on the Way!

'Tis not disturbance of mine ease, not bailiff's grasp I dread,
Nor noises that might rattle through and through my hoary head.
Nor even climbing over craggy hills and mountains grey—
I'm afraid of nothing earthly but of Whiskey on the Way!

* Mac Cartha Mor, Doncadh Earl of Clancarty.—*See note*, p. 268.

Eascarraid do'n anam—agus naṁaid do Dhia,
Do leagas cuirp dá ċalmaċt gaċ ball dá d-triall,
Glaise stoic 's airde stilleaḋ,—Brannda riaṁ,
Aṫair-neiṁe ba ṁinic ṫug mo ċeann gan ċiall!

Is cleaċtaḋ leis an leanḃ beag—gíḋ' gann a ċiall
Nuair ḟatalas ar aiṫinne ná air a ṡaṁuil do ṗiann;
Go seaċnan an lasair ann gaċ ball dá d-triall,
'S ní taise dam roiṁ ragairne an Bhrannda ṡiar!

Glac-sa sin óm' ṫeaċdaire, gíḋ gann liom iad,
Mo sgata bruingioll gan faice bruit, 'ná bean dá riar!
Tabair cuid do d' ḃanaltra is ceann-sa mian,
'S géaḃaid uile am ainim-si do ċlann ad rian!

An Ceangal.

A ṡuairc-ḟir ġroiḋe do gníḋ an greann 'sa sult,
Ní fuaṫ dod' ṁnaoi, ná dib, tug mall me a n-dul,
Ná fuaṫ do'n t-sliġe, cé ċím gur raṁar na cnoic,
Aċt fuaṫ mo ċroiḋe do ḃion do'n m-Brannda agam!

A traitor to the soul it is—to God and Man a foe—
It makes the veriest sage a fool—it lays the stoutest low—
The accursed swash, the still-house wash!—it lures but to betray—
A serpent oft around my neck was Whiskey on the Way!

The infant-child, though all untaught by mother, nurse, or sire,
If burned or scorched, in after years will fear and flee the fire.
And that's the case, alas! with me—I've been so oft its prey,
That now I dread like Hell itself all Whiskey on the Way!

But, though thus forced to stop at home—a thought that makes me sad—
My daughters—comely damsels they! though somewhat thinly clad,
Will gladly visit you, my friend, for well I ween that they
Don't run much risk of being o'ercome by Whiskey on the Way!

SUMMING-UP.

Believe me, then, O, sprightly friend! O, youth of cheerful mind!
'Tis no ill-will to you or yours that keeps me here confined—
'Tis no dislike to scale the hills or climb the mountains grey—
'Tis my sincere and wholesome fear of Whiskey on the Way!

AN DRAONAN DONN.

Fonn:—An Draonán Donn.

Silean céad fear gur leo féin me an uair d'ólaim
liún,
'S tiġean ḋá d-trian sios diom ag cuiṁne air a
g-coṁráḋ liom ;

THE BROWN SLOE-TREE.

AIR:—"*The Brown Sloe Tree.*"

THE *Draonan Donn*, *i.e.*, "The Brown Sloe-tree," or "Thorn," is the name of another of those beautiful love-songs peculiar to the Irish peasantry, and which, in almost every instance, have been adapted to our most admired airs. There is some similarity between the air of the *Draonan Donn* and that of the *Rois Gheal Dubh* (Black-haired, fair-skinned Rose), which we give at p. 210. Yet there is a slight difference—only perceptible to a refined ear.

The *Draonan Donn* tree is called "Draonan" from its sharp-pointed prickly thorns. It blossoms early in the month of August, and produces full ripe sloes in September. With respect to these, much depends on the quality of the soil where the tree grows: if it be fertile, the fruit is nearly as large as a plum; but if in barren soil, as small as the haws which grow on the common *Sgeach gheal*, or hawthorn bush.

The Connacht version of this popular song may be seen in Hardiman's *Irish Minstrelsy*, vol. i., p. 234.

When, amid my gay friends the brown-beaded ale I quaff,
I droop in deep sorrow, despite the song and laugh—

Sneaċta séiḋte 's é dá ḟíor-ċur ar Shliaḃ na m-Ban
Fionn, *
'S tá mo ġráḋ-sa, mar ḃláṫ an áirne, ar an Drao-
nan Donn!

Dá m-beiḋinn ann ḃádóir is dear do ṡnáṁfainn an
ḟairge a núnn,
'S do sgríḃfinn ċúġad líne le bárr mo ṗeann;
Faraoir ġéar! gan mé 's tú, a ċráḋaig mo ċroiḋe,
A n-gleanntán sléiḃe le h-éirgiḋ gréine 's an
drúċt na luiḋe!

Cuirim féin mo ṁíle slán leat a ḃaile na g-crann,
'S gaċ baile beag eile dá m-bíḋeaċ mo ṫriall ann;
Is iomḋa bealaċ, fliuċ, salaċ; agus bóiṫ'rín cam,
Tá 'dir mé gus an baile, 'na ḃ-fuil mo stóirín ann!

Léiġfinn-si leaḃar Gaoiḋeilge 'gus Laidin di ar
neoin,
Sgríḃfin-si síos é le bárr mo ṗeann;
Bheiḋinn ag éalóġaḋ ḟaoi na léine 's ag ḟásgaḋ a
com,
'S an lá ná féadfainn bean do ḃréagaḋ, ní'l an
báire liom!

* *Sliabh na m-Ban Fionn* (*i. e.*, The Mountain of the Fair-haired Women), forms a long range of hills lying about four miles north-east of the town of Clonmel, and known by the name of *Sliabh na m-ban*, but the origin of the appellation "*fionn*" (fair-haired) is rather mystical. This mountain is remarkable as the place of an en-campment of a small body of the Irish in 1798, who were dispersed by the king's troops, on the day after their appearance on the hill, on which occasion some rhymer produced a song, of which the following is part:—

"Is dubhach 's as lean liom bualadh an lae ud,
Do dhul air Ghaoidheil-bhoichd 's na ceadta shlad;
Gur 'mo fear eadrom 's crobhaire gleigiol
On am go cheile do gabhag le seal!
'Na bh-fuil corduighe caola ag buaint luith a n-geag diobh,

A thinking on my true-love, who is fairer than the sun,
And whiter than the white blossom of the Draonan Donn.

O! were I a mariner, 'tis I that would often write
Across the sea to my darling all the long stilly night:
My grief and my affliction it is that I cannot pass
The early morning hours with her, ere the dew gems the grass.

A thousand farewells of sorrow to the villages all
Where I spent my time so blithely from dawn to even-fall.
O many are the high mountains and dark winding dells
That sever me from the hamlet where my true-love dwells.

I would read for her in the noon from a Gaelic or Latin book;
I would write her pure thoughts down by some clear pebbly brook;
I would take her around the waist, and press her to my breast,
And the day that I couldn't please her, I'd lose my heart's rest!

A n-duinseoin dhaora go deo faoi ghlas,
Nior thainig ar *Major* a d-tuis an lae chugain,
'S ni rabhamair fein ann a g-coir na g-ceart,
Ach mar seolfaidhe aodhaire le bo chum sleibhe
Do bhi Gaoidheil-bhoicht air Shliabh na m-ban!"

"To me how woful was that day's battle
Gained over the Gael, of whom were hundreds slain;
And many youths of powerful arm,
Were then unjustly seized,
With slender ropes now their limbs are fettered
In foul dark dungeons 'neath bolts and locks.
Our Major was not with us early,
To lead us, as was his duty;
But like cattle driven by herdsmen,
Were the Gael that day on Sliabh na m-ban!"

Taḃair do ṁallaċt do t-aṫair 's do d' ṁáṫairín
 féin,
Nár ṫug beagán tuigsionna ḋuit mo láiṁ do léa-
 ġaiṁ;*
Is moċ ar maidin ċuirfinn ċúġad-sa bríġ mo sgéil,
Bioċ mo ḃeannaċt agad go g-casfar ort a n-uaig-
 neas mé.

A Ṁuirne ḋilis! cread do ḋéanfad má imṫiġean
 tú uaim,
Ní'l eolus ċum do ṫiġe 'gam, do ṫeaġlaig, ná do
 ċlúid;
Tá mo ṁáṫairín faoi leaṫ-trom, 's m'aṫair san
 uaiḋ,
Tá mo ṁuintir ar fad a ḃ-fearg liom, 's mo ġráḋ
 a ḃ-fad uaim!

Más ag imṫeaċt a táir uaim anois a ṁúirnín, go
 ḃ-filleaḋ tú slán!
Is dearḃṫa gur ṁairḃ tú mo ċroiḋe ann mo lár,
Ní'l coite 'gam do ċuirfin ad ḋiaig, ná bád;
Tá'n ḟairge na tuilte eadrainn, 's ní eól dam
 snáṁ!

* See the penal enactment against education at page 31.

On the subject of education in Ireland we have the following testimony from Mr. Christopher Anderson, an honest intelligent Scotchman: "I may assure the reader, that such has been the eagerness of the Irish to obtain education, that children have been known to acquire the first elements of reading, writing, and arithmetic, without a book—without a pen—without a slate! And indeed the place of meeting was no other than a graveyard! The long flat stones with their inscriptions were used instead of books, while a bit of chalk and the stones together served for all the rest! But then this eagerness for

A shame for her father and her mother it was indeed,
That they never taught my darling either to write or read,
'Twere a task so delightful to write to her o'er and o'er,
But my blessing be on her till we both meet once more!

O! holiest Virgin Mother, let me not lose my love!
Far away from her, alas! this dark day I rove;
My mother is in trouble; my father is dead and gone,
And I, I am left friendless,—friendless and all alone!

I entreat, O fairest maiden, that you and I may not part,
Though your smiles and your glances have broken my sad heart;
Alas! that the wide ocean should roll between us dark,
And I be left pining here, without a fisher's bark!

knowledge, though more generally felt, is not novel. Let any one inquire minutely into local circumstances during the last fifty or sixty years, and he will find it here and there as a strong feature of the Irish character. When we advert to the native Irish and education in their native tongue, we see what avidity can suggest. Then we can mention evening scholars, who have been endeavouring literally to go on by the help of moonlight, for want of a candle, and even men and women, particularly within these few years, acquiring an ability to read in so short a period, that, until the facts of the case are examined or witnessed, the statement might seem incredible."—*Sketches of the Native Irish*, p. 205. Third edition. 12mo. London: 1846.

AISLING EADBHAIRD DO NOGLAICH.

Fonn :—Osgail an Dorus go Ciuin O!

[The last two lines of each verse are to be repeated.]

Lá 'gus mé ag taisdiol ar maidin am aonar,
'S taiṫneaṁ na gréine ar an n-drúċt, O!
Do ṫárlaiḋ an ainnir na seasaṁ le m' ṫaoḃ-sa,
Go barraṁuil, béasaċ, gan ṗúir, O!

Ba áluinn a pearsa, ba ṫaiṫnioṁaċ, tréimreaċ,
Ba ċamarsaċ, péarlaċ a cúl, O!
Ba bláṫṁar a mala mar ġearra le caol-ṗinn,
Ba leaṫan a h-éadan gan smúit, O!

EDWARD NAGLE'S VISION.

AIR—" *Open the Door, O!*"

THIS song is the production of Edward Nagle, a native of Cork city and brother to the poet, James Nagle. The brothers lived about 1760, and we possess a large collection of their poetical compositions.

Edward Nagle was a tailor: he refers to his profession in the tenth stanza; and it is probable that his friends participated the feelings of "le pauvre et vieux grand père" of the greatest of modern song writers:—

" La vieux tailleur s'ecrie: 'Eh quoi! ma fille
Ne m' a donné qu' un faiseur de chansons!
Mieux jour et nuit vaudrait tenir l' aiguille
Que, faible écho, mourir en de vains sons.' "
Béranger. La Tailleur et la Feé.

To the air of "Open the Door," Moore has composed his beautiful song on Sarah Curran, "She is far from the land where her young Hero sleeps."

As I wandered abroad in the purple of dawn,
Ere the flowers yet woke to the air, O!
I met a young maiden who trod the green lawn,
So stately, so comely, so fair, O!

Her figure was queenly; her ringletted hair
Fell down in rich curls o'er her face, O!
Her white marble brow was beyond all compare
For beauty, and lustre, and grace, O!

Sgáil ġeal gan sgamal na raṁar-rosg péarlaċ,
Sneaċta 'gus caora 'na gnúis, O!
Ráiḋte gan asmuilt, aċt laḃarṫa béasaċ,
Blasda, 'gus bréiṫre ba ċiuin, O!

A bráġaid mar an sneaċta le taiṫnioṁ na gréine,
Seasaṁ mar ġeis ar an srúill, O!
Ba bláṫṁar a mama 's a leaḃair.ċroḃ aolda,
Ba ṫaiṫnioṁaċ, caol-deas, a cóm, O!

Le na breáġṫaċt do ṁeasas gur pearsa ban-déiṫe í;
Pallas, no *Venus*, no *Juno!*
Nó 'n sdáidbean le'r caillioġ gan aisioc na céadta,
A g-casmairt na Trae ṡoir go dúḃaċ, O!

No 'n ṁánla do ṫaisdiol tar calaiṫ a g-céin seal,
O Thailc ṁic Tréin na d-triúċ, O!
Nó 'n ḃáin-ċneis dár ḃ'ainim di Taise ba ṫaoḃ-geal
Leanḃ na Gréige 's a plúr, O!

Nó 'n árus an Fhir Ḋeacair ba ḋearḃ na sgéalta,
An ainġir do claonaḋ le Fionn, O!
Nó 'n sdáid-ḃruinġioll ċailce dár ḃ'ainim di Ḋéirdre,
Go h-Albain d'éalaig le triúr, O!

Ḋ'árdaiġeas go meanmnaċ m'aigne a néinḟeaċt,
Ḋo laḃaras léisi go ciuin, O!
A ġráḋ ġil na g-carraḋ 's a ṫaisge mo ċléiḃ-si,
Taḃair do ġéag ḋam go dlúiṫ, O!

“Sdráille fir magaiḋ ṫu” radas an ḃéiṫ liom,
Ṁeasaim gur léiṫis ad ċúl, O!
Ḋáilimsi faire leat! seacainn do ṗlae orm,
Ná sailig m'éadaċ sa ṗlúid, O!

Her blue eyes were stars that not Death could eclipse—
    On her cheek shone the lily and rose, O!
Like honey, sweet words ever dropped from her lips,
    As morning's dew-pearls upon snows, O!

O! 'twas bliss beyond all bliss to gaze on her breast,
    Milk-white as the swan's on the lake, O!
Her neck, and her hand, that no mortal e'er pressed—
    I felt I could die for her sake, O!

From her figure I deemed her a goddess at least,
    A Pallas, or Venus, or Juno—
Or that wonderful damsel renowned through the East
    For whose sake Troy was burned too soon, O!

Or her who, far voyaging over the sea,
    From Tailc obtained a release, O!
Or Taise, the fairest of damosels, she
    Who of old was the glory of Greece, O!

Or her who eloped with the Fionn of yore,
    As Seanachies tell in their tales, O!
Or Deirdre, whom Naois, out of love for her, bore
    To Alba of stormiest gales, O!

Awakening up, as it were, from a trance,
    Thus spake I the maiden so bland, O!
"My treasure, my brightest! O grant me one glance,
    And give me your lily-white hand, O!"

"False flattering man!" cried the maiden to me,
    "Why the hair on your head has grown grey, O!
Shame on you, old wretch, to think I could agree
    To wed one of your age and your way, O!"

Is ceárrda fir cealgaiḋ mearaim, cé d'aosais,
T-ainimsi, léig ḋam ar d-túis, O!
Is grána do leacaḋ 's as searḃ do ḃréiṫre,
Mealla na m-béiṫe ann do rúm, O!

Ná cáin-si mo leacaḋ, 's na h-abair-si bréag liom,
Taiṫníḋean mo ḃriaṫra 's mo *lute*, O!
Le stáid-ḃruingioll barr-ḟionn do ṁaiṫiḃ na h-Eireann,
M'ainim-si Eadḃard, a rúin, O!

Gráḋ liom do leaca, do ṁala, do léiṫ-rosg,
Radas an ḃéiṫ liom ann súd, O!
Gráḋ liom do ṗearsa, do ṡeasaiṁ, do ṫréiṫe,
Taiṫniom mo ċléiḃ-si do ṫiuin, O!

Fonn:—Toirḋealḃaċ Láidir.

Quoth I, "I'm a tailor." "A tailor, forsooth!"
She exclaimed. "You go on a bad plan, O!
You're an ugly old brute, and you don't speak the truth,
And I fear you're a very sad man, O!"

"Look at me more nearly," I said with a smile,
"For mine is a very wide fame, O!
I am loved by the daughters of Eire's green isle;
And Edward, 'tis true, is my name, O!"

"Ah! now," said the maiden, "I know who you are—
I love your high forehead so pale, O!
Your bearing bespeaks you as fashioned for war—
Yes! you are the Prince of the Gael, O!"

TURLOGH THE BRAVE.

Toirdhealbhach Laidir (*i.e.*, Turlogh the Brave, Valiant, Stout, or Mighty) flourished about the middle of the last century. His real name was Turlogh O'Brien, and he belonged to the family from whom *Leim Ui Bhrian* (Lemebrian), a townland in the county of Waterford, takes its name. He frequented all the fairs and patterns of Munster, particularly those of his own county; and, from his stalwart appearance, was an object of terror wherever he went. We remember the following stanzas of a doggrel rhyme attributed to him, when clearing a fair green, or pattern:—

"*Cumadh na beiridhean tu bainge dham?*
Cumadh na cuirean tu im air?
Cumadh na teighir go dti an maraga,
Ag ceanach luadh pinghine d'uibhe dham?"

"Why don't you boil up the milk for me?
Why don't you thicken it with butter?
Why don't you hasten to market,
To buy me a pen'orth of eggs there?"

"*Hurroo! ce bhuailfeach mo mhadra?*
Hurroo! ce shracfach mo chaba?
Hurroo! ce dhearfach nach gaige me?
'S gur b'ainim dam Toirdhealbhach Laidir!"

"Hurrah! who'd sneer at my little dog?
Hurrah! who'd tear my old cape off?
Hurrah! who'd say I am not a gentleman!
For my name is Turlogh the Mighty!"

AISLING PHADRUIG CUNDUN.

Fonn:—An Stáicín Eórnaḋ.

Maidion 's me am aonar cois taoḃ coille dṙille-
ġlaise,
Ag déanaṁ mo h-iomannaḋ ba ġnáṫac mé ann;
'S mire air luisne Phoebrs tré ġéagaiḃ le rṙṫne-
ġlaine;
A pléiriocṫ le criosdal-ṡiosmaḋ ḟaoḃrac na
d-tonn;—
Ealtaiomḋa éanlaiṫ air ċraoḃaiḃ go mioċair-ċlisde,
Ag séiseaḋ 's ag seinne-ḃinne air ġéaga gaċ crann,
Bruic 's Sionaig ċlaonaḋ roiṁ ḟaol-ċoin ar] mire-
ruiṫe,
'S laoċraḋ go h-inniollta dá d-traoċaḋ gaċ am!

PATRICK CONDON'S VISION.

AIR:—"*The Little Stack of Barley.*"

PATRICK CONDON, the author of this song, was a native of the barony of Imokilly, county of Cork, and resided about four miles from the town of Youghal. About thirty years ago he emigrated to North America, and located himself some distance from Quebec.

The Englishman who has ever, in the course of his travels, chanced to come into proximity with an Irish "hedge school," will be at no loss to conjecture the origin of the frequent allusions to heathen mythology in these songs. They are to be traced, we may say, exclusively to that intimate acquaintance with the classics which the Munster peasant never failed to acquire from the instructions of the road-side pedagogue. The Kerry rustic, it is known, speaks Latin like a citizen of old Rome, and has frequently, though ignorant of a syllable of English, conversed in the language of Cicero and Virgil with some of the most learned and intellectual of English tourists. Alas! that the acuteness of intellect for which the Irish peasant is remarkable should not have afforded a hint to our rulers, amid their many and fruitless attempts at what is called conciliation! Would it not be a policy equally worthy of their judgment, and deserving of praise in itself, to establish schools for the Irish in which they might be taught, at least, the elementary principles of education through the medium of their native tongue? This course, long advocated by the most enlightened of every class and creed, has been lately brought forward in an able manner by Mr. Christopher Anderson.—See his *Sketches of the Native Irish.*

The evening was waning: long, long I stood pondering
  Nigh a green wood on my desolate lot.
The setting sun's glory then set me a-wondering,
  And the deep tone of the stream in the grot.
The birds on the boughs were melodiously singing, too,
  Even though the night was advancing apace;
Voices of fox-hunters,—voices were ringing too,
  And deep-mouthed hounds followed up the long chase.

Iar g-caiṫeaṁ eiṫneaċ cnó ḋam ḃiḋ buacaċ ar bile
ag sile,
Luaḋail laċt gan time rinneaḋ faosaṁ do'n
ḃ-fann;
Sásaṁ biḋe gan ġrsaim ann, do fuaras, 's mile-
ḃlaise,
Stuaim agus ionnar-ċruiṫe glé-ṫuigse am ċeann;—
Gur casag tríd an m-buan-doire a nuas ċ'sġam ar
fuinnioṁ-ruiṫe,
Uaisleaċt na ḃ-finne-ḃan a sgéiṁ-ċruiṫ nár ġann;
Aingir aoiḃinn uamaċ, lán-ḃracaċ tar cinne-Scuiṫe,
Buaḋaċ, binn, milis, mioċair, séiṁ tar gaċ dream.

Do ḃ'ḟada, dlaoiṫeaċ, péarlaċ, a craoḃ-ḟolt a
titim-ḃrisde,
Dréimreaċ, cas, ionannda, a ḃ-fiġ néata ó na
ceann;
A dearca ḃiḋ mar réalta na spéire le rúiṫne-
ġlaine,
Géis-ḋaiṫ no gile an lile, niaṁ-ċriġnn a com;
Ba ḋeas, ba ċruinn a déada, le ċéile do crireag
siġte
A béal ḃi go friotal-ċlisde a m-bréiṫre lán lonn.
'S bláṫ an draoin tre ċaoraḋ na sgéiṁ 's na deirg-
luisne,
Niaṁ siġe friṫ-te oilte a réiġṁeas go bonn.

Do ṡeasaim si liom suas 's do ḃuan-aṁarc mise
isteaḋ,
A d-tuairim gur bruingioll innioll déiṫe ḃi ann,
Nó ceaċtar ḃi an spéir-ḃean le caoṁnas na doire-
geinte,
A téarnaḋ ċum feiṫiṁ inte tréiḃse gan ḃeann;
D'ḟiosraḋ mé do ḃréiṫre caoin, néata, ceart,
clisde-ṡniḋte,
"An tu *Calypso* no *Ceres*, no *Hecate* na rann,
Minerva nó *Thetis* do ṫréin-ḃriseaċ longa ar uisge,
Bateia ṫais, no *Hebe* ḋeas, ón spéirnim ṫig fann!

Nut-trees around me grew beauteous and flourishing—
Of the ripe fruit I partook without fear—
Sweet was their flavour,—sweet, healthful, and nourishing—
Honey I too found—the best of good cheer!
When, lo! I beheld a fair maiden draw near to me;
The noblest of maidens in figure and mind—
One who hath been, and will ever be dear to me—
Lovely and mild above all of her kind!

Long were her locks, hanging down in rich tresses all—
Golden and plaited, luxuriant and curled;
Her eyes shone like stars of that Heaven which blesses all:
Swan-white was her bosom, the pride of the world.
Her marvellous face like the rose and the lily shone;
Pearl-like her teeth were as ever were seen;
In her calm beauty she proudly, yet stilly shone—
Meek as a vestal, yet grand as a Queen.

Long-time I gazed on her, keenly and silently—
Who might she be, this young damsel sublime?
Had she been chased from a foreign land violently?
Had she come hither to wile away time?
Was she Calypso? I questioned her pleasantly—
Ceres, or Hecate the bright undefiled?
Thetis, who sank the stout vessels incessantly?
Bateia the tender, or Hebe the mild?

Ní ceaċdar díoḃ d'ár luadais ad ḋrantaiḃ ar
 ise, mise,
Aċt aingir ċlaoiḋte, ṫreasgárṫa, tre ionaċlann
 na n-Gall;
'S as gairid díḃ an uair 'na m-beaḋ mór-ḋaċt 's
 mire búr n-dliġṫe,
Sásaṁ cruinn bŕr n'aindeise beaḋ feasda 'guiḃ
 gan ṁeall:
Cur cúig a steaċ neaṁ-ġrrama, le fraimeint mar
 ṫrille, 's fiṫċe,
Le ais an níḋ búr b-faisdine ḃí tagarṫa leas tall
'S as dearḃ díḃ naċ buan ḃeiġ an ċuaill so sa b-finne
 sgriosda,
A laċt sa líon beaḋ sgarṫa líḃ, bíoċ m'anam leis
 a n-geall.

AISLING CHONNCHUBHAIR UI SHUILLIOBHAIN.

Fonn:—"Sean-ḃean Chríon an Drantáin."

Tré m' aisling a raoir 's me'm ṡuan táṁ,
Do ḋearcas ríoġuin na g-cuaċ m-bán;
Bhíḋ lasair trí litir, ag cearnaċ 's a coiṁeasgair,
Na h-aġṫa 's ní'l ḟios cia fuair bárr!

A carn-ḟolt trínseaċ is leaḃair d'ḟás,
Go camarsaċ, dlaoiṫeaċ, tiuġ, trom, 'tá;
'Na m-beartaiḃ a tíġeaċt ḟria, go baċallaċ, buiḋe-
 ċas,
O ḃaṫas a cinn ġil go bonn tráċt.

Ba ċailce a déid-ṁion, ba ró ḃláṫ,
A mbéal-tana b'éiseaċtaċ cóṁráḋ;
A ramar-roisg ċlaona, 's a mala ḋeas ṁaorda,
Mar ṫarrangfaċ caol-ṗinn a g-clóḋ, 'táid.

"None of all those whom you name"—she replied to
me:
One broken-hearted by strangers am I;
But the day draweth near when the rights now denied
to me
All shall flame forth like the stars in the sky.
Yet twenty-five years and you'll witness my glorious-
ness:
Doubt me not, friend, for in God is my trust;
And they who exult in their barren victoriousness
Suddenly, soon, shall go down to the dust!"

THE VISION OF CONOR O'SULLIVAN.

Air:—"*The Growling Old Woman.*"

Last night, amid dreams without number,
I beheld a bright vision in slumber:
A maiden with rose-red and lily-white features,
Disrobed of all earthly cumber.

Her hair o'er her shoulder was flowing
In clusters all golden and glowing,
Luxuriant and thick as in meads are the grass-blades
That the scythe of the mower is mowing.

With her brilliant eyes, glancing so keenly,
Her lips, smiling sweet and serenely,
Her pearly-white teeth and her high-archèd eyebrows,
She looked most commanding and queenly.

Ba ṡaṁuil a sgéiṁ-ḋreaċ, 's a leaḃair-ḃráġaid,
Fria sneaċta na h-aon-oiḋċe a n-gleann-táin;
'S a leaḃair-ċrob aolda, ba ċailce laġ-ṁéaraċ,
Do sṗreagaċ air ṫéad-ċruit gaċ streann-cán.

A nuair ṁeasas í ṫeaċt an ċóṁ-ḋáil,
Facaim go h-ísеall le mórḋáil;
Feasaim go caoin dísi a h-ainim, 's bríġ a tsruais,
Nó 'n baile 'na m-bíon sí gaċ cíonn-tráiṫ.

Do ḟreagair an ríogain go ró ṡáṁ,
'S ba ṫaiṫnioṁaċ binn-ġuiṫ a cóṁ-ráḋ;
Mise bean dílis na ḃ-flaṫa do díbríog,
A's Albain roiṁe seo, gíḋ beó 'táid!

A ċsmainn ná tréig mise a n-dó-lás,
Suiġ anso taoḃ ḟríom go fóill, má
Is tú 'n ḟinne-ḃean t-Séamuis,—buime na laoċraḋ,
Tabair cruinneas gaċ sgéil dam, nó ġeabaḋ bás!

Dearḃaid draoiṫe 'gus sean dáiṁ,
Tharrangair Naoiṁ 's gaċ dream Ḟáiġ;
Go d-taistiolfaċ mílte fá armaiḃ líoṁṫa,
Air Charolus Stíoḃard tar mall-tráig.

A ḋalta ná bíoḋ fearda ag ceann-rán,
Spreagaċ do ċroiḋe 'nois, ní h-ionn-tráṫ;
An am anfaḋ ċíḋfir an ċaḃair a n-gaoir ḋuit,
Biaḋ sgaipe air gaċ daoiste 'na raṁar-ṁás.

Déiniḋ gáir-ṁaoiḋte le lúṫġáir,
'S taosgaig tráiṫ fíonta ós cíonn cláir;
Déantar cnáiṁ-ṫeinnte, agus séid stoc na píbe,
Agus gléastar gaċ caoin-ċruit 's tiom-páin?

Her long taper fingers might dally
With the harp in some grove or green alley;
And her ivory neck and her beautiful bosom
Were white as the snows of the valley.

Bowing down, now, before her so lowly,
With words that came trembling and slowly,
I asked what her name was, and where I might worship
At the shrine of a being so holy!

"This nation is thy land and my land,"
She answered me with a sad smile, and
The sweetest of tones—"I, alas! am the spouse of
The long-banished chiefs of our island!"

"Ah! dimmed is that island's fair glory,
And through sorrow her children grow hoary;
Yet, seat thee beside me, O, Nurse of the Heroes,
And tell me thy tragical story!"

"The Druids and Sages unfold it—
The Prophets and Saints have foretold it,
That the Stuart would come o'er the sea with his legions,
And that all Eire's tribes should behold it!

"Away, then, with sighing and mourning,
The hearts in men's bosoms are burning
To free this green land—oh! be sure you will soon see
The days of her greatness returning!

"Up, heroes, ye valiant and peerless!
Up, raise the loud war-shout so fearless!
While bonfires shall blaze, and the bagpipe and trumpet
Make joyous a land now so cheerless!

Iar d-teaċtan ċum tíre go Cionn-t-Sáil,
Do'n laoċraḋ sin laoiseaċ na d-trúp láin;
Beiḋ Gaoiḋeil-boċt ag ċoiṁġlic,—déanaḋ éirlig
'ς díoġaltais,
Air ṁéirlioċa 'n ḟéill ḋuib dá g-cṙrsáil!

FREAGRADH DHONNCHADH UI SHUILLIO-BHAIN AIR CHONCHUBHAR.

Fonn:—"Sean-bean ċríon an drantáin."

An ġealṫan-ċruiṫ ċaoin-ċailce, seang ṁnáṁuil,
Do ḋearcais tré d' smaointe go leabar-bláṫ;
A pearsa 's a gníoṁa, 's a mama gíḋ' h-aoibinn,
Ní'l tairbe ḋíob ann aċt ion-tlás.

Is dearmad suigte 'gur feall tráiṫ,
Air Bhanba ċinn-gearrṫa ċóm-ċáig;
Ní ġlacaċ iona cuim tú, ná neaċ eile ḋod' sínnsear,
Go g-casaċ sruiṫ-líonta gaċ abaḋ lán.

Is taiṫniomaċ linn gan fóbat d'ḟáġail
Air banaltra ċíoċ-ġeal na d-tróm-ḋáiṁ;
Thug geallaṁuin dílis le searaṁ gaċ n-díreaċ,
Do ġarraḋ ġroiḋe-ċlisde an rann-gáis

Tar calaiṫ glas taoide no a n-gleann-m-báin,
Dá d-tagaḋ do laoiseaċ sria Fhrann-cáin;
Biaḋ aguinne taoisig ba ċalma a n-gníoṁ-goil,
Do leagfaḋ neart saoiṫe do ġam-ráin.

"For the troops of King Louis shall aid us;—
The chains that now gall and degrade us
Shall crumble to dust, and our bright swords shall slaughter
The wretches whose wiles have betrayed us!"

DONOGH O'SULLIVAN'S REPLY TO CONOR O'SULLIVAN.

AIR:—"*The Growling Old Woman.*"

That maiden so fair and so slender,
Whom you saw in your vision of splendor,
Can give you, alas! no hope and no fancy
That Time will not make you surrender.

'Tis a dream that was longtime departed
That of Banba, the generous-hearted,
Till the streams and the rivers roll back to their sources
The aims of her sons will be thwarted!

We love the Antique and the Olden,
We gladly glance back to the golden
And valorful times of our sages and heroes,
But those shall no more be beholden!

Were Louis to come with his legions
O'er ocean from France's proud regions,
There are hosts in the island to meet him in battle,
Who would scatter his soldiers like pigeons!

Ag Briatannaig líoṁṫa na n-aḃall m-bláṫ,
Ba ḟeargaċ líoṁṫa 'na lom-dáil;
Go maċaire an ċoiṁeasguir dá d-tagaiḋ, do ċíḋ-
fear
Do Charolus Stioḃard, 'na ṫoll-dád!*

Gé fada beiṫ iseall a ḃ-fonn fáġain,
Ag seasaṁ le daoirse gaċ tróm-ċáin;
Do'd ċeangal a n-geiḃlioċ ná sgarfaḋ leat ċoiḋċe,
Go d-tagaḋ do ṫaoisig go Cionn-t-Sáil!

An sgamal so líonta do ċróm cáċ,
An anḃruid Ṁuiṁnig, gan *power* tláṫ;
Ba ṁeasa ḋuit líne ḟlioċt Chairil a n-íoċtar,
Ná easbaḋ guiṫ píbe, 'gur tiom-pán?

AISLING AN ATHAR PADRAIC UI BHRIAIN.

Tógfaḋ sé atuirse 's brón díḃ,
An aisling do ċonarc air Ṁhóirín;
An ḃanaltra ḃréagaċ,
Do ṫáil ar gaċ aoin neaċ,
O d'imṫig a céile—mo ḃrón í!

A cnear mar an sneaċta ba ró ṁín,
A bas faoi na leacaḋ 's í deór-ġuil;
A mama-beag gléigeal,
Ag conairt an ḃéarlaḋ;
Dá slamaḋ gan traoċa—gan coṁnuiġe!

* *Toll-dad.* Topsy-turvy.

The armies of Britain wield ample
Resources to vanquish and trample.
Charles Stuart's o'erthrow, should he venture o'er hither,
Will be dreadful beyond all example!

Long you groan under sorrows unspoken—
But the slumberiug band hath not woken.
Till a nobler Kinsale* shall atone for the former,
Your fetters will never be broken!

The cloud hangeth dark o'er our nation;
Momonia drees black tribulation,
And worse than the want of your "bagpipes and timbrels"
Is, alas! Cashel's deep degradation!

THE REV. PATRICK O'BRIEN'S VISION.

The marvellous vision I've lately seen
Will banish, my friend, your sorrow and spleen,
'Twas her whom her spouse has, alas, forsaken.
The gay, the good, the kind Moirin!

Her fair smooth skin it shone like snow—
Her bosom heaved with many a throe,
That bosom the English wolves have mangled
And her head reclined on her white arm low.

* An allusion to the battle of Kinsale, A.D. 1601.

Is é dúḃairt an ṁuc-allaḋ do ġlór-ċaoin,
An ḃ-fuil tú ad ċodla a Mhóirín?
Éirġiḋ cois toinne,
'Gur dearc ar na daoine,
Tá teaċt ċúġainn tar taoide le mór-ḃuiḋin!

Ann-sin beiḋ agad-sa ad ċófruiġe
Airgiod go fairsing 's ór buiḋe,
Mar ċaḃair do na céadta,
Tá cneada 's a béice,
Da g-creaċa 's dá g-céasa le mór-ċíos!

Atá éanlaiṫ na coille go ró-ḃinn,
A n-éinḟeaċt a seinnim a nótaiḋe;
Go meanamnaċ, aoraċ,
Dá insint dá ċéile,
Ná beiḋ fearg ṁic Dé linn a g.cóṁnaiḋe!

Do ċualaḋ dá ṡeinnim an ċeól-píḃ,
Go ḃ-fuil Coileaċ 's Fiolar ag deóraiġeaċt;
Do ṗiocas na súile,
Ar an n-duine nár ḋúṫċas,
Bheiṫ aguinn a Lúndain 'na ċoṁnuiġe!

Beiḋ *Hector* 's *Cæsar* go beól-ḃinn,
Bowler 's *Ranger* a geónaiḋil;
'S gearrḟiaḋ 'ca ar saoṫar,
O Chaisioll go Béara,
Go d-ṫitiḋ a n-éinḟeaċt an órluiḋe!

Ann sin go foirneaċ pór-fuiġear,
An duine nár sileaḋ le Ṁóirín;
'S cruinneóċaḋ na céadta,
Do ṁaṫaiḃ na h-Eirionn,
Go mullaċ Chnoic Gréine le ceól-siṫ!

And thus methought I softly spake :—
Moirin, Moirin, dost thou sleep or wake?
  O! look forth seaward, and see what heroes
Are sailing hither for thy sweet sake!

O! soon again, shalt thou have, as of old,
Bright heaps of silver and yellow gold,
  And soon shall thine arm raise up the Fallen,
Now trampled by Tyranny uncontrolled.

The very birds of the forest sing
The prophecy of thy coming Spring—
  "Gone by," they warble, "for ever and ever
Is the anger of the Almighty King!"

I heard the bagpipes playing an air
Of an Eagle and Cock—a wondrous pair—
  Who will pick the eyes of a certain man out
Now throned in London's regal chair!

My Hector and Cæsar, they rage and fret,
And Bowler and Ranger howl and sweat;
  They are coursing from Cashel to broad Bere-
    haven,
And will rend the hare asunder yet!

And then in Wedlock's golden chains
Will the Hero clasp Moirin of the Plains—
  And Eire's nobles will all assemble
On green Cnoc Greine to fairy strains.

Tugṫar ċúġainn *Punch* agus beoir ġroiḋe,
'S bioḋtar dá d-tarraing a g-cóṁnuiḋe ?
Cuir an ainḋeise ar cáirde
Go maidion a máraċ ;
'S gan casaḋ go bráṫ ná go deó í !

Bé faid do ḃéiḋ sgilling am ṗóicín,
Ní sgarfainn le cuideaċta Mhóirín ;
Olfamaoid sláinte,
An ḟir atá n-dán di,
Chum cuidiúġaḋ go bráṫ lé, 's go deó 'rís !

Atá cluiṫċe le h-imirt ag Móirín,
Tuitfeaḋ an Curata 's ní brón linn ;
Atá aon-a-hart séiḋte,
'S an ríġ dul ar éigin,
'S an ḃan-ríoġuin 'na ḋéig sin a tóruiġeaċt !

Ann sin preabfaḋ an bórd síos,
An Cionáḋ is fada faoi ċeó-draoiġeaċt ;
Sguabfaiḋ a n-éinḟeaċt,
Na bearta le ċéile,
'S bainfeaḋ sgilling gan ḃaoḋaċas, 's c'róinn
díoḃ !

Beiḋ cnaipiḋe dá n-déanaḋ 'ge Seoirsín,
Faoi ṫuairm an éadaig nár córuiḋeag ;
Beiḋ hata maiṫ Béabair,
Ar Dhoṁnall na Gréine,
Dá ċaṫaṁ is na spéarṫa le mór-ċroiḋe !

Go m-baintear an briste dá ṫón síos,
An duine nár ṁian beiṫ ag ól diġe,
Faoi ṫuairm an sgéil sin,
'S tuille ná déarfad ;
Dá m-beiḋinn-si gan léine ! gan cóitín !

Bring hither punch and foaming ale !
We must not droop, we will not wail !
  Away with sorrow ! and may she never
Come back to us with her doleful tale !

As long as I have a shilling to spend
My fair Moirin I will ever defend !
  Here's now to the health of Him who will wed her,
And guard and guide her as her friend !

Moirin is about to hazard a game,
The Knave will be beaten with utter shame—
  And the King and Queen—whom nobody pities,
Will fly, and forfeit name and fame.

Then up shall spring on the table so proud
The Five, long under a darkling cloud—
  He will seize on the Crown, and grasp the shilling,
And win, with the game, the cheers of the Crowd !

Then Georgey will quake, and shake, and bow,
He is left in the lurch, he discovers now !
  But "Dan of the Sun" will fling high his beaver
With a joyous heart and a beaming brow.

Now here's to Moirin, and to her success !
And may he be stripped of breeches and dress
  Who would wrong her in aught,—whether priest or layman,
Or cause her a moment's pain or distress !

AN ABHAINN LAOI.

Eóġan (an Ṁéirín) Mhac Cárrṫaiġ, cct.

Fonn:—Air Eire ní 'neósainn cia h-í.

A ċumplaċt ġlan ċaoiṁ-ċroṫaċ ċaoin,
Ur-léigionta go líonṁar a n-dán ;
Bhúr n-dúṫraċt ag géar-ṁolaḋ Laoi,
(Ba ḟaoṫar a n-inntleaċt is fearr)
An lúb-ṡroṫaċ, glé-ċriostal, ṁín,
Is féile ar biṫ fíor-uisge cáil ;
Gur ṫúirling gaċ séan le na taoiḃ,
Do b'ḟéidir fá ríġeaċt neiṁe d'ḟáġail.

THE RIVER LEE.

BY EOGHAN MAC CARTHY (THE SMALL-FINGERED).

AIR:—"*For Eire (Ireland) I'd not tell her Name.*"

The original words to this beautiful air will be found at p. 132 of a volume of "Irish Popular Songs," edited by Mr. Edward Walsh, and published by Mr. James M'Glashan, from which we quote the first stanza:—

"A raoir 's me tearnamh air neoin,
Air an taobh thall don teora 'na m-bim;
Do thaobhnaig an speirbhean um choir,
D'fhag taomnach, breoidhte, lag, sinn.
Do gheilleas du meinn 's da clodh,
Da briathra 's da beol-tana, binn;
Do leimeas fa dhein dul na coir
'S air Eire ni 'neosfainn cia hi!"

"One evening as I happen'd to stray
By the lands that are bordering on mine,
A maiden came full on my way,
Who left me in anguish to pine—
The slave of the charms, and the mien,
And the silver-toned voice of the dame,
To meet her I sped o'er the green;
Yet for Ireland I'd tell not her name!"

"The pleasant waters of the river Laoi" (Lee) have their source in the romantic lake of Gougane Barra in West Muscraidhe (Muskerry). Spenser describes it as—

"The spreading Lee that, like an island fayre,
Encloseth Corke with his divided flood."

The length of the river from its source to the city of Cork has been computed to be twenty-six Irish miles.

Bright Host of the musical tongue,
Rich Branches of Knowledge's Tree,
O, why have you left so unsung
The praise of the blue-billowed Lee?
That river so shining, so smooth,
So famed for both waters and shore!
No pleasure were greater, in sooth,
Than to dwell on its banks evermore!

Is cúḃarṫa 's as craoḃ-ṫorrṫaċ ḃíḋean,
  Gaċ gaorṫa 'na tímċioll ag fás ;
Fá aḃ'laiḃ, fá ċaoraiḃ, fá ḟíon,
  Ag claonaḋ go h-ioċtar a tráġa !
Aball-ġoirt fá ġéagaḃ ag luiġe,
  Ar an ḃ-féar-glas an uair líonaid a m-bláṫ,
Mar luḃ-ġort *Hesperia* do ḃí,
  Dá ċaoṁnaḋ le draoiġeaċt ar feaḋ spás.

Ba ḟúgaċ flaiṫ féile air gaċ taoiḃ,
  Go féasdaċ, go fíonṁar do ġnáṫ ;
'S túirling na cléire d'ionsaiġe,
  Na saor-ḟear ; na tiġearaċa breaġa ;
Is dúḃaċ liom a réim 's a g-cíos,
  Na stéigiḃ dá sníoṁ idir ċách ;
'S an prionnsa an *Altona* 'na luiġe,
  Nár ṫréig creidioṁ Chríost ar a stát !

The "Church's true son" mentioned in the last stanza of this song was Donchadh Mac Carthaigh (Donogh Mac Carthy) Earl of Clancarty, who lost an estate of £60,000 per annum by his attachment to his unfortunate King James II. He died at Altona, 1734.

The family of Mac Carthy traced their immediate pedigree up to the commencement of the third century, from which period they were the lords of *Deas Mumhain*, or South Munster. The great antiquity of this family has been commemorated by a modern bard :—

"Montmorenci, Medina, unheard was your rank
By the dark-eyed Iberian and light-hearted Frank,
And your ancestors wandered, obscure and unknown
By the smooth Guadalquiver, and sunny Garonne—
Ere Venice had wedded the Sea, or enrolled
The name of a Doge in the proud Book of Gold ;

Around it the wild flowers blow,
  And the peaches and plums in the beams
Of the sun ripen redly, and grow
  Even down to the brink of the streams.
Each valley, and garden, and bower
  Shines brightly with apples of gold—
'Twould seem that some magical power
  Renewed here the marvels of old!

And yet, though the Nobles and Priests,
  And Gaels of both high and low ranks,
Tell tales, and indulge in gay feasts
  On its dark-green and flowery banks,
I mourn for the Great who are gone—
  And who met by the Lee long ago—
But most for the Church's true son,
  Who now in Altona lies low!

When her glory was all to come on like the morrow,
There were chieftains and Kings of the clan of Mac Cartha!

* * * * * *

Mac Cartha, the pride of thy house has gone by,
But its name cannot fade, and its fame cannot die,
Though the Arigideen, with its silver waves, shine
Around no green forests or castles of thine,
Though the shrines that you founded no incense doth hallow,
Nor hymns float in peace down the echoing Allo;
One treasure thou keepest, one hope for the morrow,
True hearts yet beat of the clan of Mac Cartha."

The "Clan of Mac Cartha," by D. F. MacCarthy.

A full and accurate account of the Mac Carthys may be seen in the "Green Book," by J. C. O'Callaghan, Esq. 8vo. Dub. p. 101. 1844.

SLAN CHUAM PADRAIC SAIRSEAL.*

A Phádraic Sáirséal slán go d-tí' tú!
O ċuaḋair do 'n Fhrainc 's do ċampaiḋe sgaoilte,
Ag déanaṁ do ġearáin leis na Ríġṫe,
'S d'ḟág tú Eire 'gus Gaoiḋeil-ḃoiċt claoiḋte!
Och! ochón!

A Phádraic Sáirséal is duine le Dia tú,
Is beannaiġṫe an talaṁ ar ṡiúḃail tú riaṁ air;
Go m-beannaiġe an Ghealaċ ġeal 's an Ghrian duit,†
O ṫug tú an lá o láṁa Ríġ Uilliam leat.
Och! ⁊c.

* Patrick Sarsfield was descended from an ancient family, consisting of several honorable branches, one of which possessed the title of Lord Kilmallock. Patrick inherited, from his elder brother, the family castle and estate of Lucan, County Dublin, with £2,000 a-year. He first served in France, as Ensign to Monmouth's regiment; then, as Lieutenant to the Guards in England; whence, in 1688, he followed James II. into France. In March, 1689, he accompanied James into Ireland, and was made Colonel of Horse, Brigadier, and Commander of the force appointed to protect Connacht from the Inniskilling or Northern rebels. This he did, till the effects of the unfortunate affair of Newton-Butler, July 31st, and the raising of the blockade of Derry, by the landing of Major-General Kirke's troops from England, compelled him to retire to Athlone. That autumn, however, he retook Sligo, and entirely expelled the enemy from Connacht. In July, 1690, he served as Major-General at the battle of the Boyne; and by his noble exhortations, and his memorable surprise of the English battering artillery, ammunition, &c., August 12th, only about seven miles from the besiegers' camp, he mainly contributed to the triumphant defence of Limerick. In December and January, 1690–91, he foiled the military efforts of the English, aided by treachery, to cross the Shannon into Connacht, and was, soon after, made a Lieutenant-General, and ennobled as Earl of Lucan, by James II. In June and July he was at the gallant defence of Athlone, and the fatal, though nobly-contested, battle of Aughrim. Soon after he detected, denounced, and arrested, for corresponding with the enemy, his intimate friend and neighbour Colonel Henry Luttrell, of Luttrellstown; though

A FAREWELL TO PATRICK SARSFIELD.

Farewell, O, Patrick Sarsfield! May luck be on your path!
Your camp is broken up—your work is marred for years;
But you go to kindle into flame the king of France's wrath,
Though you leave sick Eire in tears.
Och! ochone!

May the white sun and moon rain glory on your head,
All hero, as you are, and holy Man of God!
To you the Saxons owe a many an hour of dread,
In the land you have often trod.
Och! ochone!

that traitor was either too wary, or too powerful, to be condemned. After the Treaty of Limerick, in October, 1691, to which his Lordship was a chief contracting party, he used all his influence to make as many as possible of the Irish adhere to the cause of James, and accompanied the national army to France; thus sacrificing to his loyalty his fine estates, and the best prospects of advancement from William III. In 1692 he was appointed by James to the command of his Second Troop of Irish Horse-Guards—the King's son, the Duke of Berwick, having the First Troop. In the defeat at Steenkirk, in July, 1692, of the English and Allies, under William III., by the French, under the celebrated Marshal de Luxembourg, Lord Lucan was complimented by the Marshal, as having acted in a manner worthy of his military reputation in Ireland. In March, 1693, his Lordship was created Maréchal-de-Camp, by Louis XIV.; and at the great overthrow, in July, of the Allies under William III., by Luxembourg, at the battle of Landen, he received his death-wound. Lord Lucan's character may be comprehended in the words, simplicity, disinterestedness, honour, loyalty, and bravery. In person, he was a man of prodigious size. By his wife Honor de Burgo, second daughter to William, seventh Earl of Clanrickard, he left one son, who, after serving under his illustrious stepfather, the Marshal Duke of Berwick, died in Flanders, without issue.

† *Go m-beannaighe an Ghealach gheal 's an Ghrian duit*, i. e., May the bright Sun and Moon salute thee, a mode of salutation in use among our pagan ancestors.

A Pháḋraic 'Sáirséal guiḋe gaċ n-duine leat,
Mo ġuiḋe-si féin 's guiḋe mic Muire leat;
O ṫóig tú an t-Aṫ-Caol* ag gabail tre Bhiorra ḋuit,
'S gur ag Cuillinn O' g-Cuanaḋ† buaḋag leat Luimneaċ.
Och! 7c.

Geabaḋ-sa siar an sliaḃ-sa am aonar,
'S geabaḋ a niar a rír már féidir;
Is ann do ċonairc mé an campa gaoḋ'lach,
An dream boċt silte nár ċuir le na ċéile.
Och! 7c.

* *Ath Caol*, Narrow Ford, which must mean the river Narrow Water, in the county of Down.

† At Ballyneety (*Baile an Fhaoitig*, i.e., *the town of the Whites*), near Cullen, he surprised the great Williamite convoy, to the loss of which the raising of the siege of Limerick is mainly attributable. David Bruoder, a cotemporary poet, commemorates the event in a ballad of twenty-five stanzas, from which we extract the following:—

"*An tan do thiomsuig pearsa an Phrionnsa,*
Neart a thruip 's a airneise;
Timpchioll innill Inse Sionna,
'S Muimhnig uile fa mheala;
Nior fhag bumba, bad na uma,
Na ban bonn da b-pras-ghreithibh,
A m-Baile an Fhaoitig gan a sgaoile,
Mar ghal coinnle a n-dail speire.

"*Do shuil nach crionfadh clu na sgribe,*
Fuigfiod fillte a b-paipearaibh
Tuairm aithne air 'uair na faille'
Fuair an seabhac slan-easgadh
Se chead foghmhar, mile 's nochad,
Aois nach onna tath-eifiocht
Bliaghna an Choimhdhe, d'-fhiad san aoine,
Pian is ainnsin nach eidir."

The Son of Mary guard you and bless you to the
end!
'Tis altered is the time since your legions were astir,
When, at Cullen, you were hailed as the Conqueror and
Friend,
And you crossed Narrow-water, near Birr.*
Och! ochone!

I'll journey to the North, over mount, moor, and wave.
'Twas there I first beheld, drawn up in file and line,
The brilliant Irish hosts—they were bravest of the
Brave!
But, alas! they scorned to combine!
Och! ochone!

* Sarsfield was at Birr in the spring of 1689, when deputed by the Duke of Tyrconnell to inspect the national troops there; and also in September, 1690, when the Castle was attacked by the Duke of Berwick.

"All Momonia was stricken with sorrow,
When the Prince did, without restraint,
Muster his mighty troops and artillery
On the borders of Inishannon;
But Sarsfield left not a bomb, boat, or mortar,
Or a farthing's worth of their brass equipments,
Without scattering them in Ballyneety,
As the wind extinguishes the flame of a candle.

"That this event might not be forgotten,
I will leave recorded the time and place
Of the victory gained by our gallant hero.
Six hundred autumns, one thousand, and ninety
Have elapsed, since the Man-God suffered, on Friday,
A most dreadful pain and penalty."

Brise na Cruimminne* 's brise na Boinne,†
'S an tríṁúġaḋ brise ag Móta Ġhráinne óige‡;
An ceaṫraṁaḋ brise an Eaċ-Dhruim Dia-Doṁnaiġ,
'S buaileag buille ḋruim oruinn ag Tobar an Doṁ-
naiġ.
Och! 7c.

Mo ċúig céad slán ċúġaiḃ a hallaoi Luimniḋ,
'S ċum na buiḋin áluinn do ḃí 'nár g-cuideaċtaḋ;
Bhiḋeaċ teinte cnáṁa 'guinn, is cárdaiġe imearṫa,
'S briaṫra Dé ḋá léaġaṁ go minic ḋúinn.
Och! 7c.

A Lundain Doire§ bolgaċ ċúġad-sa
Air nós na sgáile air lasa le púġdar:
'S a liaċt farraire fada fionn-lúbaċ,
Gan sosg' ó 'n n-gaoiṫ, 'ná criaḋ dá g-cúṁdaċ!
Och! 7c.

* No details of this affair at *Cruimminne* have reached us. It was probably some local event of the Rapparee, or Guerilla warfare, between the campaigns of 1689 and 1690.

† The army of King James at the Boyne, was only from twenty to twenty-three thousand men, with six field-pieces. William's army contained between forty and fifty thousand men (vastly superior to their opponents in equipments and discipline), with from fifty to sixty heavy cannon, exclusive of field mortars. Yet James's army had none of their cannon captured, and but one pair of colours (if we may credit the hostile accounts, which *falsely* claim the capture of two more), and is admitted to have made an honorable retreat. On William's side, the battle was fought almost entirely by his Continental auxiliaries; his army being composed of men from ten European nations.

‡ The rout at the Moat of Graine Og, in the spring of 1691, was probably owing to the Irish there having been under such a commander as Clifford, who, in the following September, caused the fall of Limerick, by allowing the enemy to cross the Shannon.

§ For an account of the monstrous exaggerations to which the boasted defence of Derry has been indebted for so much unmerited celebrity, see *Green Book*, p. 78. 8vo. Dub. 1841.

I saw the royal Boyne, when its billows flashed with blood ;
I fought at Graine Og, where a thousand horsemen fell ;
On the dark, empurpled field of Aughrim,* too, I stood,
On the plain by Tubberdonny's Well.†
Och ! ochone !

To the heroes of Limerick, the City of the Fights,
Be my best blessing, borne on the wings of the air !
We had card-playing there, o'er our camp-fires at night,
And the Word of Life, too, and prayer.
Och ! ochone !

But, for you, Londonderry, may Plague smite and slay
Your people !—May Ruin desolate you, stone by stone !
Through you a many a gallant youth lies coffinless to-day,
With the winds for mourners alone !
Och ! ochone !

* The battle of Aughrim (*Cath Eachdhruim*), was fought on Sunday, 12th July, 1691. The Irish army, under Lieutenant-General St. Ruth, consisted of about 15,000 men, and its artillery of nine field-pieces. The Williamite army, under Baron de Ginkell, amounted to between twenty and thirty thousand men, with a vastly superior artillery. Up to the death of St. Ruth, about sunset, the engagement was so much in favor of the Irish, that it is generally considered that the loss of their General alone prevented them obtaining a complete victory.

In this action, as at the Boyne (*Boinn*), William's force was mostly composed of Continental troops. James's army, with the exception of a few French officers, was entirely Irish.

† *Tobar an Domhnaigh* (Tuberdonny), situated in the County of Louth, about two and a-half miles from the towns of Dunleer and Ardee respectively, and nine miles from Drogheda. We cannot explain the occurrence which the poet refers to ; but in other versions of this song, current in Munster, the line runs thus :—" *Do chailleamair an Francach an ceannphuirt ba mho 'guinn* "—" We have lost the Frenchman, our greatest bulwark"—which evidently refers to St. Ruth.

Do ḃí mé air sliaḃ lá breaġa gréine
Do ċonarc na Sagsannaiċ a ḃ-foċair a ċéile ;
An cór capall ba ḋeise ḃí n-Eire,
O' ! coiméad ḋam na bodaig go m-bainfead gé arda ?
Och ! 7c.

Is iomḋa saiġdiuir meaġraċ, meanam naċ,
Do ġaiḃ an t-sliġe-si le seaċt seaċtṁuine ;
Fae ġunaḋ, fae ṗiceaḋ, fae ċloiḋeaṁ cinn airgid,
Aċt tá siad sínte ḟíos an Eaċ-ḋruim !
Och ! 7c.

Cia súd tall air ċnoc Bheinn-Eidir ?*
Sáiġdiuir boċt mé le Riġ Séamus ;
Do ḃí mé a nurraig a n-arm 's a n-éadaċ,
Aċt'táim a m-bliaġannaḋ ag iarraiḋ déirce !
Och ! 7c.

Is é mo ċreaċ mar do ċailleamair Diarmuid,
Bhí ceann an sgaṫfaire air halbart iarruinn ;
Bhí a ċuid feóla dá sraca 's a ḃratac dá stiallaḋ,
'S gan fáġail ċarda 'ge dá ḃ-faġaċ sé Dia air !
Och ! 7c.

Is é mo ċreaċ-sa an t-sraiṫ dá tógḃan,
An dá ḟear ḋéag do ḃí ós cionn Feórach ;
Mo ḋias dearḃráṫar as iad is gleó liom,
Aċt mo ċúig céad díoṫ-ċuir Diarmuid an t-óig-ḟear !
Och ! 7c.

* *Beinn Eidir*, now the Hill of Howth.

I clomb the high hill on a fair summer noon,
  And saw the Saxon Muster, clad in armour, blinding
    bright.
Oh, rage withheld my hand, or gunsman and dragoon
    Should have supped with Satan that night!
      Och! ochone!

How many a noble soldier, how many a cavalier,
  Careered along this road, seven fleeting weeks ago,
With silver-hilted sword, with matchlock, and with spear,
    Who now, *mo bhron*,* lieth low!
      Och! ochone!

All hail to thee, Beinn Eadair! But, ah! on thy brow
  I see a limping soldier, who battled, and who bled
Last year in the cause of the Stuart, though now
    The worthy is begging his bread!
      Och! ochone!

And *Diarmuid!* oh, *Diarmuid!* he perished in the strife;†
  His head it was spiked on a halbert high;
His colours they were trampled; he had no chance of life,
    If the Lord God himself stood by!
      Och! ochone!

But most, oh, my woe! I lament, and lament
  For the ten valiant heroes who dwelt nigh the Nore;
And my three blessed brothers! They left me, and they
    went
  To the wars, and returned no more!
      Och! ochone!

* *Mo bhron*, pronounced *mo vrone*, literally, my sorrow.

† It is probable that *Diarmuid* was a Rapparee, or Irish Guerilla; two pounds being given by the Williamite government for the head of any Rapparee.

Do cuireaḋ an ċéad ḃrise orrainn ag droiċead na
Boinne,
An dara brise ag droiċead na Sláinge*
An tríṁiúġaḋ brise an Eaċ-ḋruim Ui Cheallaiġ
'S Eire ċúḃarṫa mo ċúig céad slán leat!
Och! 7c.

An uair las an teaċ ḃí an deataċ dár múċaḋ,
'S clann Bhil ḃradaiġ† dár n-greada le púġdar;
Ni'l aon *Volley-shot* dá sgaoilidir fúinne,
Ná fiafraiḋeaċ *Colonel Mitchel*‡ ar leagaḋ *Lord
Lucan*?
Och! 7c.

Tá leasúġaḋ ag O'Ceallaiġ§ naċ gainiṁ ná fuiġleaċ,
Aċt saiġdiuiriḋe tapa ḋéanfaḋ gairge le píceaḋ;
A ḟágfaḋ iad a n-Eaċ-ḋruim na sraṫannaḋ sínte,
Mar ḃeiḋeáċ feoil ċapaill ag madraiḋe dá sraoile!
Och! 7c.

Ann súd atá siad bárr uaisle Eirionn
Diuiciḋe, Búrcaig,‖ 's mac Riġ Séamus;
Captaoin Talbóid croiḋe na féile,
'S Pádraic Sáirséal! graḋ ban Eirionn.
Och! ochón!

* There is no account of any fighting at the Slaney, during the War of the Revolution in Ireland; perhaps the allusion is but an interpolation, as we had to take our copy of the poem from the mouths of the peasantry, never having met a manuscript copy of it.

† The poet here calls the Williamite soldiers "*The Sons of Billy the Thief*."

‡ Colonel John Michelburne, Governor of Derry, who commanded a regiment of foot in William's service in Ireland.

§ Colonel Charles O'Kelly, author of the "*Macariæ Excidium*," or, perhaps, his son Captain Denis O'Kelly, who commanded a troop in Lord Galmoy's regiment of horse at Aughrim, and had a horse shot under him at that battle.

‖ Of the De Burgos, or Burkes, of Norman, or French origin, five noblemen fought for King James, viz., Lords Clanrickard, Castlecon-

On the Bridge of the Boyne was our first overthrow ;
By Slaney, the next, for we battled without rest!
The third was at Aughrim. Oh, Eire! thy woe
Is a sword in my bleeding breast!
Och! ochone!

O! the roof above our heads it was barbarously fired,
While the black Orange guns blazed and bellowed around!
And as volley followed volley, Colonel Mitchel inquired
Whether Lucan still stood his ground,
Och! ochone!

But O'Kelly still remains, to defy and to toil;
He has memories that Hell won't permit him to forget,
And a sword that will make the blue blood flow like oil
Upon many an Aughrim yet!
Och! ochone!

And I never shall believe that my Fatherland can fall,
With the Burkes, and the Dukes, and the son of
Royal James ;
And Talbot the Captain, and SARSFIELD, above all,
The beloved of damsels and dames.
Och! ochone!

nell, Brittas, Bophin, and Galmoy. The son of royal James alluded to, is, the famous James Fitz James, Duke of Berwick, and subsequently Marshal, Duke, and Peer of France.

The following stanza, which should come in as the sixteenth in the song, was not versified by Mr. Mangan. We subjoin it here, with our own literal translation :—

"*Cia sud tall ag dorus na ceardchan?*
Na ceil air Righ Uilliam e, mise Brian laidir,
Fan ad sheasamh a bhodaig go g-caithfiod gran leat,
A ghiolla na praisge ni bh-facfad go brath leat.

"Who is that halting at the forge door?
Conceal it not from King William—I am Brian the Stalwart;
Stand, you churl, till I have a shot at you;
But, you stirabout-pot licker, I'll not mind you."

BRUACH NA CARRAIGE BAINE.

Fonn:—Bruac na Carraige Báine.

Shiar cois aḃan gan ḃréig, gan doḃat,
Atá'n aingir ċiuin-tais, ṁánlaḋ;
'Nar gile a com 'ná Alaḋ air an d-tonn,
O ḃaṫas go bonn a bróige!
Is í an sṫáid-ḃean í do ċráḋaiġ mo ċroiḋe,
'S d' ḟág m' inntinn brónaċ,
Leiġios le fáġail, ní'l agam go bráṫ,
O ḋiúltaiḋ mo ġráḋ geal daṁsa!

THE BRAES OF CARRICK-BANN.

TRANSLATED BY COLONEL BLACKER.

Bruach na Carraige Baine.—Bruach and Carrick are the names of two townlands lying contiguous to each other on the river Bann, and forming a part of the demense of Carrick Blacker, an ancient seat of the Blacker family, near Portadown, in the county of Armagh.

As the family residence was changed to this particular locality from another part of the property, on the marriage of William Blacker, Esq., with Elizabeth, daughter of the Hon. Colonel Robert Stewart, of the Irry, county Tyrone, and granddaughter of the first Lord Castlestewart, about, or shortly previous to, the year 1666, and as the subjoined poem coincides in its general structure and style with that period (being at least a century older than the succeeding effusion), there can be little difficulty in affixing very nearly a date to its composition as an *Epithalamium*, or "welcome home" song, and the party in whose honour it was composed.

To their successor in the fifth generation, Colonel Blacker, the present proprietor of Carrick Blacker, we owe the following very graceful, as well as close translation.

By yonder stream a maiden dwells,
Who every other maid excels ;
Less fair the swan, in snowy pride,
That graceful stems sweet Banna's tide.
The leech in vain would seek to cure
The pangs of soul that I endure,
Since of each joy and hope bereft,
That stately fair my sight has left.

Do b'ḟearr liom féin 'ná Eire ṁór,
'S ná saiḋbrios Ríġ na Sbáinne!
Go m-beiḋinn-si 's tusa a lúb na finne,
A g-coillte a ḃḟad ó ár g-cáirde;
Tusa 'gus mise a beiṫ pósda, a ġráḋ,
Le aon-toil aṫar 's máṫar,
A ṁaiġdion óg 's mílse póg,
Grian na Cairge Báine!

Is léanṁar mo ṫurus le tréiṁise gan sucart,
Is baoġalaċ go g-cuirfear ċum fáġain me!
Le géar-ḟearc do'n ḃruingioll is néata san ċruinne,
Do ċuir céadta air uirearsbaḋ sláinte!
Do ḃí a h-éadan mar luisne na gréine tre ċriosdal,
Téid éanlaiṫ ċum sucairt le gráḋ ḋi;
Tagan tréin-ḟir 's ríġṫe tar tréan-ṁuir da h-aṁarc,
Is í Grian na Cairge Báine!

Do b'í *Helen* an ainnir ċuir an Trae ṡoir na lasair,
Ba néata mar labaraid fáiġe!
Cuir *Ajax* 's *Achill*, 's na tréin-ḟir ċum caṫa,
Mo léan, is lé cailleaḋ na sáir-ḟir!
Do rug an spéirḃean lé an bárr a m-béasa 's a b-pearsa,
'S dob' éigion dóiḃ casa tar sáile,
A géile do 'n ainnir a g-clár na Banba,
Air Bhruaċ na Cairge Báine!*

Do raċainn le m' ḃuiḋean tar fairge a loing,
'S do ċuirfinn mo smuainte a d-táċt di;
Dá fásgaḋ le m' ċroiḋe air árd-leabaḋ ṁín,
'S ní sgarfainn le m' ṫaoġal ar stát lé!

* Bruach and Carrick are the names of two townlands on the river Bann, near Portadown, county Armagh, forming a part of the demesne of Carrick-Blacker.

Dear is my native isle, but she
That maid is dearer far to me;
To me her favour greater gain
Than all the boasted wealth of Spain.
Fair-hair'd object of my love,
I would that in some happy grove
'Twere mine to hail thee as my bride,
Of Carrick-braes the virgin pride.

But, oh! forbidden for a while
To revel in that sunny smile,
I seek some distant forest gloom,
To mourn in heaviness my doom,
And hear the wild birds warbling sing;
While o'er the seas come Prince and King,
In hopes to bask beneath the rays
Of her, the Sun of Carrick Braes.

The lovely Queen, whose fatal charms
Call'd Greece's bravest sons to arms
(Historic bards record their names
Who wrapp'd the stately Troy in flames),
Less worthy than this maid by far,
To bid those heroes rush to war;
The heart more willing homage pays
To Banna's maid, on Carrick Braes.

With her I'd roam o'er ocean's wave,
And ne'er to part each danger brave;
And as I pressed her to my heart,
My soul's most inward thoughts impart.

Raċaḋ gan ṁoill an arm an Riġ,
  Tá ceannas dá druim le fáġail dam,
Fillfead arís fá ċoimirc na naoṁ
  Go Bruaċ na Cairge Báine !

A ḃruingioll gan téiṁiol do ḃuaḋaig taiṫnioṁ mo
    ċroiḋe,
  'Nar ḃinne do laoiḋe 'ná 'n ċláirsioċ ;
'Nar ġile do ġnaoi ná sneaċta ar an g-craoiḃ,
  Le d' ṁall-rosg ġrinn do ċráḋais me !
Fill orm a rís le taiṫnioṁ gan ṁóill,
  'S taḃarfad cruinn ḋuit sásaṁ.
Caiṫfiom ár saoiġeal a ḃ-foċar ár n-gaoiḋeal,
  Air Bhruaċ na Cairge Báine !

Is méinn liom sgaraḋ ó gaċ saoġaltaċt air talaṁ,
  Le géar-ṡearc do d' ṗearsainn a stáid-ḃean ;
Níor ḃaoġal duit mairg le d' ṡaoġal dá mairfin,
  Ní ṫréigfin air a ḃ-feacaḋ de ṁnáiḃ tu !
Triall leam tar caise má 's léir leat mo ṗearsa,
  Tá reim 's ceannas a n-dán dam,
Go h-Eire ní ċasam—má ṫréigir do ċarait,
  Air Bhruaċ na Cairge Báine !

A stuaire an ċinn ċailce már dual go m-beiḋir agam,
  Beiḋ cóir ort do ṫaiṫneoċaḋ le d' ċáirde ;
Idir ṡíoda 's hata o ḃonn go baṫas,
  'S gaċ níḋ ann sa ċaṫair dá áilleaċt ;
Beiḋ do ḃó-laċt dá g-casaḋ gaċ nóin ċum baile,
  'S ceol binn ag ad ḃeaċaiḃ air bánta ;
Beiḋ ór air do ġlacaiḃ 's cóisde ad ṫarruint,
  Go Bruaċ na Cairge Báine !

But now I'll seek to win a name—
A soldier—on the field of fame,
In hopes, returning crowned with praise,
To win the gem of Carrick Braes.

Oh, peerless maid, without a stain,
Whose song transcends the harper's strain ;
Whose radiant eyes their glances throw
From features like the driven snow ;
Return, return, without delay,
While I atoning homage pay,
And let us spend our blissful days
'Mid those we love on Carrick Braes.

Oh were each earthly treasure mine,
For thee I would it all resign ;
Each fond regret my ardent love
Shall place my dear one far above.
Come, maiden, where, beyond the sea,
Both health and riches wait on thee ;
Repress each lingering thought that stays
On home, and friends, and Carrick Braes.

Lov'd charmer of the flaxen hair,
I'll deck thee forth with anxious care ;
All dress'd in silken sheen so fine,
The costliest in the land to shine ;
Unnumber'd herds shall low for thee,
Her honey store prepare, the bee ;
While rings of gold adorn thy hands,
And menials wait on thy commands ;
And friends behold, in fond amaze,
Thy splendour upon Carrick Braes.

A RAIBH TU AG AN G-CARRAIG?

Fonn:—A raiḃ tú ag an g-Carraig.

A raiḃ tú ag an g-Carraig 's a b-feacaḋ tú féin mo
  ġráḋ?
A b-feacaḋ tú gile, 'gur finne, 'gur sgéiṁ na mná?
A b-feacaḋ tú 'n t-aball ba ċúbraḋ 's ba ṁilse bláṫ?
A b-feacaḋ tú mo *Valentine*, no a b-fuil sí dá
  claoiḋ' mar 'táim?

HAVE YOU BEEN AT CARRICK?

Mr. M'Glashan, with his usual kindness, has permitted us to copy this song and translation from his recently-published volume of "Irish Popular Songs."

It is the *chef-d'œuvre* of Dominic O'Mongan, or Mungan, and was composed early in the last century, for a celebrated beauty of her day, Eliza Blacker, of Carrick, County of Armagh, who became afterwards Lady Dunkin, of Upper Clogher Court, Bushmills, County of Antrim, now called Dunderave Castle, and still held by her grandson, Sir Edmund Workman MacNaghten, Bart., M.P. for that County.

Miss Blacker was the eldest daughter of William Blacker, Esq., of Carrick, by his wife Letitia, sister and co-heiress of the Right Honorable Edward Cary, of Dungiven Castle, M.P. for the County of Londonderry, and the great-grand-daughter of the parties mentioned in the introduction to the preceding poem. The present house of Carrick (or Carrick Blacker) beautifully situated on the river Bann, is the ancient seat of the Blacker family. The building, commenced previous to the Revolution of 1688-9, was not finished until 1692. It is about a mile and a-half from Portadown, and now the residence of Lieut.-Col. William Blacker, D.L., the present head and representative of this family.

Dominic O'Mongan was a gentleman Bard, who was blind from his birth, and a native of the County of Tyrone. Bunting notices him at p. 78 of his *Ancient Music of Ireland*, to which we refer the reader.

Have you been at Carrick, and saw you my true-love there?
And saw you her features, all beautiful, bright, and fair?
Saw you the most fragrant, flow'ring, sweet apple-tree?—
O! saw you my lov'd one, and pines she in grief, like me?

Do ḃíos ag an g-Carraig, 's do ċonairc mé ann
do ġráḋ;
Do ċonairc mé gile, 'gus finne, 'gus sgéim na mná;
Do ċonairc mé 'n t-aḃall ba ċúḃraḋ 's ba ṁílse bláṫ,
Do ċonairc mé do *Valentine*, 's ní'l sí dá claoiḋ' mar
'táir!

Is fiú dá ġiníḋe gaċ ruibe dá gruaig mar ór,
Is fiú an oiread eile a cuideaċda uair do ló;
A cúilín trom truipiollaċ a tuitim lé síos go feór,
'S a ċuaiċín na finne, ar ṁirde do ṡláinte ḋ'ól!

Nuair ḃím-si am ċodla bion osnaḋ gan ḃréig am ċliaḃ,
'S mé 'm luiġe idir ċnocaiḃ go d-tigeaḋ an ġréin a
niar,
A rúin ḋil 's a ċogair, ní'l fortaċt mo ċúis aċt Dia,
'S go n-dearnaḋ loċ ḟola do ṡolus mo ṡúl ad ḋiaiġ!

Nó go d-tigiḋ an ċáisg air lár an ḟóġṁair buiḋe
'S lá ḟeile Pátraic lá nó ḋó'na ḋiaiġ;
Go ḃ-fásaḋ an bláṫ bán tre lár mo ċóṁraḋ ċaoil,
Páirt dod ġráḋ go bráṫ ni taḃarfad do ṁnaoi!

Siúd í síos an Ríoġ-ḃean álainn óg,
A ḃ-fuil a gruaig sgaoilte síos go béal a bróg;
Is í 'n eala í mar litir do ṡiolraiḋ ó 'n t-sár-ḟuil
ṁóir,
A ċaraḋ geal mo ċroiḋe stig, céad míle fáilte
róṁat!

I have been at Carrick, and saw thy own true love
there;
And saw, too, her features, all beautiful, bright, and
fair;
And saw the most fragrant, flowering, sweet apple-tree—
I saw thy lov'd one—she pines not in grief, like thee!

Five guineas would price every tress of her golden
hair—
Then think what a treasure her pillow at night to
share,
These tresses thick-clustering and curling around her
brow—
O, Ringlet of Fairness! I'll drink to thy beauty now!

When seeking to slumber, my bosom is rent with sighs—
I toss on my pillow till morning's blest beams arise;
No aid, bright Beloved! can reach me save God above,
For a blood-lake is form'd of the light of my eyes with
love!

Until yellow Autumn shall usher the Paschal day,
And Patrick's gay festival come in its train alway—
Until through my coffin the blossoming boughs shall
grow,
My love on another I'll never in life bestow!

Lo! yonder the maiden illustrious, queen-like, high,
With long-flowing tresses, adown to her sandal-tie;
Swan, fair as the lily, descended of high degree,
A myriad of welcomes, dear maid of my heart, to thee!

Fonn :—Bruaċ na Carraige Báine.

As our little volume has now drawn to a close, we cannot allow this page to remain blank, and therefore present our readers with another setting of that beautiful air *Bruach na Carraige Baine* (the Braes of Carrick-Bann), at p. 280; and with it we take leave of our kind patrons for the present.

THE END.

Dublin: Printed by EDWARD BULL, 6, Bachelor's-walk.

www.ingramcontent.com/pod-product-compliance
Lightning Source LLC
Chambersburg PA
CBHW022106230426
43672CB00008B/1298
* 9 7 8 3 7 4 4 7 3 8 0 5 7 *